RICHARD COBDEN

THE INTERNATIONAL MAN

WITH AN EXCERPT FROM
Ten Englishmen of the Nineteenth Century
BY JAMES RICHARD JOY

By

J. A. HOBSON

First published in 1919

This edition published by Read Books Ltd.
Copyright © 2019 Read Books Ltd.
This book is copyright and may not be
reproduced or copied in any way without
the express permission of the publisher in writing

British Library Cataloguing-in-Publication Data
A catalogue record for this book is available
from the British Library

CONTENTS

The Repeal of the Corn Laws 3

Richard Cobden 5

PREFACE 9

I. COBDEN'S PREPARATION FOR POLITICS 15

II. COBDEN AS PAMPHLETEER 26

III. THE TOUR IN EUROPE, 1846-7 40

IV. THE POLICY OF NON-INTERVENTION, 1850-2 . . . 54

V. PALMERSTONIAN FOREIGN POLICY 73

VI. THE CRIMEAN WAR 106

VII. PEACE AND RECOVERY 135

VIII. THE CHINA WAR AND
THE INDIAN MUTINY 192

IX. AN INTERLUDE OF PEACE 233

X. THE FRENCH TREATY 242

XI. CORRESPONDENCE 278

XII. THE CIVIL WAR AND THE
SUMMER LETTERS 331

XIII. COBDEN AND MODERN
INTERNATIONALISM 387

APPENDIX 410

SOME DATES IN THE CAREER OF
RICHARD COBDEN 413

INDEX 415

THE REPEAL OF THE CORN LAWS

AN EXCERPT FROM
Ten Englishmen of the Nineteenth Century
BY JAMES RICHARD JOY

The names of Sir Robert Peel and Richard Cobden are indissolubly connected with the legislation which repealed the "Corn Laws" and placed English commerce upon the basis of free trade—Cobden as the theorist and untiring agitator, whose splendid talents were unsparingly devoted to preparing public opinion for the economic revolution, and Peel as the protectionist Prime Minister, who was open-minded enough to become convinced of his error in persisting in the policy in which he had been trained. The necessity for a change of commercial policy grew out of the altered conditions in the nation. The agricultural England of the eighteenth century had in a generation been transformed into a hive of manufacturing industry. The rapid adoption of steam power and improved machinery in England on the one hand, and the paralysis of industry on the Continent during the Napoleonic wars, had wrought the change, while the commercial marine, guarded by her powerful navy, had brought the carrying trade of the world under her flag. The weakest point in the English system was the protective tariff, which lay heaviest on imports of grain—or "corn," to use the insular term. The Corn Laws were a body of legislation enacted from time to time by Parliaments which were controlled by the great land-owning interests. The land-owner, whose income was derived chiefly from rents upon agricultural lands, consistently favored a scale of tariffs which would maintain the price of cereal grains at the highest figure. At the close of the great war (1815) the nation was confronted with business disaster. "War prices" for grain fell rapidly, the markets were stocked with more manufactured goods than impoverished Europe could absorb, while the English labor market was glutted by the influx of several hundred thousand able-bodied soldiers and sailors in quest of industrial employment. As early as 1821 Mr. Huskisson, a cabinet colleague of Mr. Canning, had endeavored to lighten the burden of British manufactures by reducing the import duties upon the raw material used by the English looms. He was for getting at the root of the matter and disposing of the Corn Laws, so as to provide "free food" as well as "free raw materials," but his Tory companions believed that such legislation would vote the bread out of their own mouths. In 1838 an Anti-Corn Law Association was formed at Manchester. Under the direction of Richard Cobden, a young and successful manufacturer, who had become the most ardent of free traders, a league of similar clubs was organized throughout the country, and through it an agitation unsurpassed in the history of politics was prosecuted until its object was attained. In Parliament he became one of the most effective orators, and the chief target of his argument was Peel, the leader of the protectionists. In 1845-46 a more powerful argument than Cobden's was thrown into the scale. The failure of the Irish potato crop, the sole food supply of that unhappy island, "forced Peel's hand." In the face of two-thirds of his own party, in opposition to his own life-long political creed, he gave notice as Prime Minister that he should introduce a bill for the immediate reduction and ultimate repeal of the laws which were responsible for the high price of food. He had become a convert to free trade, and was ready to carry it into practice. The young Disraeli as the representative of the Protectionist element of his party, lashed the premier in the speech which first gave him a following in the Parliament that he was soon to control. But enough Peelites followed their leader into the camp of the free traders to carry the bill. The Corn Laws disappeared from the statute-book.

RICHARD COBDEN

[During the parliamentary session of 1846 when the bill for the repeal of the Corn Law was passing through its parliamentary stages, Mr. Cobden's letters from London to personal friends and to his wife afford frequent glimpses of his interest, his suspense, and his final exultation.]

"London, February 19th. To T. H. Ashworth: Your letter has followed me here. Peel's declaration in the House that he will adopt immediate repeal if it is voted by the Commons, seems to me to remove all difficulty from Villiers's path; he can now propose his old motion without the risk of doing any harm even if he should not succeed. As respects the future course of the league, the less that is said now about it publicly the better. If Peel's measure should become law, then the Council will be compelled to face the question, 'What shall the League do during the three years?' It has struck me that under such circumstances we might absolve the large subscribers from all further calls, put the staff of the League on a peace footing, and merely keep alive a nominal organization to prevent any attempt to undo the good work we have effected. Not that I fear any reaction. On the contrary, I believe the popularity of free-trade principles is only in its infancy, and that it will every year take firmer hold of the head and heart of the community. But there is perhaps something due to our repeated pledges that we will not dissolve until the Corn Laws are entirely abolished. In any case the work will be effectually finished during this year, provided the League preserve its firm and united position; and it is to prevent the slightest appearance of disunion that I would avoid now talking in public about the future course of the League. It is the League, and it only, that frightens the peers. It is the League alone which enables Peel to repeal the law. But for the League the aristocracy would have hunted Peel to a premature grave, or consigned him like Lord Melbourne to a private station at the bare mention of total repeal. We must hold the same rod over the Lords until the measure is safe; after that I agree with you in thinking that it matters little whether the League dies with honors, or lingers out a few years of inglorious existence."

"May 16th. To F. W. Cobden: I last night had the glorious privilege of giving a vote in the majority for the third reading of the bill for the total repeal of the Corn Law. The bill is now out of the House, and will go up to the Lords on Monday. I trust we shall never hear the name of 'Corn' again in the Commons. There was a good deal of cheering and waving of hats when the Speaker had put the question, that this bill do now pass.' Lord Morpeth, Macaulay, and others came and shook hands with me, and congratulated me on the triumph of our cause. I did not speak, simply for the reason that I was afraid that I should give more life to the debate, and afford an excuse for another adjournment; otherwise I could have made a telling and conciliatory appeal. Villiers tried to speak at three o'clock this morning, but I did not think he took the right tone. He was fierce against the protectionists, and only irritated them, and they wouldn't hear him. The reports about the doings in the Lords are still not satisfactory or conclusive. Many people fear still that they will alter the measure with a view to a compromise. But I hope we shall escape any further trouble upon the question.….I feel little doubt that I shall be able to pay a visit to your father at midsummer. At least nothing but the Lords throwing back the bill upon the country could prevent my going into Wales at the time, for I shall confidently expect them to decide one way or another by the 15th of June. I shall certainly vote and speak against the Factory Bill next Friday."

"May 18th. To Mrs. Cobden: We are so beset by contradictory rumors, that I know not what to say about our prospects in the Lords. Our good, conceited friend told me on Wednesday that he knew the peers would not pass the measure, and on Saturday he assured me that they would. And this is a fair specimen of the way in which rumors vary from day to day. This morning Lord Monteagle called on me, and was strongly of the opinion that they would 'move on, and not stand in people's way.' A few weeks will now decide the matter one way or another. I think I told you that I dined at Moffat's last Wednesday. As usual he gave us a first- rate dinner. After leaving Moffat's at eleven o'clock, I went to a squeeze at Mrs. —. It was as usual hardly possible to get inside the drawing-room doors. I only remained a quarter of an hour, and then went home. On Saturday I dined at Lord and Lady John's, and met a select party, whose names I see in to-day's papers.....I am afraid if I associate much with the aristocracy, they will spoil me. I am already half-seduced by the fascinating ease of their parties."

"May 19th. To F. W. Cobden: I received your letters with the enclosures. We are still on the tenter-hooks respecting the conduct of the Lords. There is, however, one cheering point: the majority on the second reading is improving in the stock-books of the whippers-in. It is now expected that there will be forty to fifty majority at the second reading. This will of course give us a better margin for the committee. The government and Lord John (who is very anxious to get the measure through) are doing all they can to insure success. The ministers from Lisbon, Florence, and other continental cities (where they are peers) are coming home to vote in committee. Last night was a propitious beginning in the Lords. The Duke of Richmond was in a passion, and his tone and manner did not look like a winner."

"June 10th. To F. W. Cobden: There is another fit of apprehension about the Corn Bill, owing to the uncertainty of Peel's position. I can't understand his motive for constantly poking his coercive bill in our faces at these critical moments. The Lords will take courage at anything that seems to weaken the government morally. They are like a fellow going to be hanged who looks out for a reprieve, and is always hoping for a lucky escape until the drop falls."

"June 18th. To Mrs. Cobden: The Lords will not read the Corn Bill the third time before Tuesday next, and I shall be detained in town to vote on the Coercion Bill on Thursday, after which I shall leave for Manchester. I send you a 'Spectator' paper, by which you will see that I am a 'likeable' person, I hope you will appreciate this."

"June 23d. To Mrs. Cobden: I have been plagued for several days with sitting to Herbert for the picture of the Council of the League, and it completely upsets my afternoons. Besides my mind has been more than ever upon the worry about that affair which is to come off after the Corn Bill is settled, and about which I hear all sorts of reports. You must therefore excuse me if I could not sit down to write a letter of news.....I thought the Corn Bill would certainly be read the third time on Tuesday (to-morrow), but I now begin to think it will be put off till Thursday. There is literally no end to this suspense. But there are reports of Peel being out of office on Friday next, and the peers may yet ride restive."

"June 26th. To Mrs. Cobden: My Dearest Kate-Hurrah! Hurrah! the Corn Bill is law, and now my work is done. I shall come down to- morrow morning by the six o'clock train in order to be present at a Council meeting at three, and shall hope to be home in time for a late tea."

PREFACE

THE close attachment of the name of Richard Cobden to the overthrow of the protective system and the establishment of Free Trade in our fiscal arrangements has tended to obscure the wider policy of international relations which this great achievement was designed to serve. Even if we add to the six strenuous years of his Anti Corn-Law agitation, crowned by the Act of repeal, the later negotiation of the French Commercial Treaty, we cover but a single section of his ever-widening activity for the realization of sound principles of foreign policy. Cobden was first and always what his French comrade, Emile de Girardin, called him, " an international man." His foreign policy was couched in the single term " non-intervention."

Protective tariffs and other trade impediments were condemned, not merely or mainly because they made food dear and otherwise impaired the production of national wealth, but because they interfered with the free and friendly intercourse of different nations, bred hostility of interests, stimulated hostile preparations, and swallowed up those energies and resources of each nation that were needed for the cultivation of the arts of peaceful progress.

Non-intervention may appear to some a cold and negative and a wholly insufficient conception of internationalism. To Cobden, however, it was the only safe and sure condition for the play of the positive forces of human sympathy and solidarity between the members of different political communities. Let Governments cease to interfere and then peoples will discover and maintain friendly

Preface

intercourse, first in the mutual interchange of goods and services for the satisfaction of their common needs, then in growing co-operation for all the higher purposes of life. Foreign statecraft, as he saw it throughout history and in his own time and country, was little else than a mischievous interference with the natural harmony of peoples. The keystone of our foreign policy was a balance of Powers conceived as essentially hostile to one another; the conduct of that policy was in the hands of an aristocratic caste governed by dynastic traditions and working by secret diplomatic methods wholly divorced from popular influence and interests. Cobden saw how easy it was for an ambitious or bellicose statesman to appeal to the fighting spirit of our people by the pursuit of a spirited policy directed, now against the aggressive intentions imputed to our traditional enemy France, now against the rising menace of Russia, and again for the punishment of some injury or insult imputed to some weaker State—Turkey, Greece, China or Japan. His parliamentary career virtually coincided with the Palmerstonian era, in which began to sprout the seeds of the modern imperialism, distinguished from the earlier processes of territorial aggrandizement by the plainer and more conscious action of commercial and financial interests handling the levers of State policy.

More widely travelled than any other British statesman of his time, Cobden had concerned himself far more closely with the material and industrial conditions of the different countries which he rightly regarded as the chief considerations in the art of good government, and viewed with intense suspicion and contempt the dangerous superficialities of the Foreign Offices of Europe. His writings, speeches and letters, furnish the fullest and most enlightened commentary upon our foreign and imperial policy during the long period of Victorian

Preface

history which comprised such critical events as the Crimean War and the Indian Mutiny in our own affairs, the establishment of the Kingdom of Italy, the American Civil War and the early stages in the development of the supremacy of Prussia in Germany.

This volume does not pretend to give this commentary in its completeness. It was designed, in the first instance, to rescue the memory of Cobden from the narrow misinterpretations to which it has of late been subjected, by giving stronger emphasis to his international work. For this purpose it is proposed to publish collections from his correspondence which either had not been printed before, or which had not been made accessible to the general public. The most important of the new material consists in the close correspondence between Cobden and the Rev. Henry Richard, for many years Secretary of the Peace Society, an active editorial writer in the *Morning Star*, and, after Cobden's death, Member of Parliament for Merthyr for twenty years. Cobden's letters to Mr. Richard date from 1849 to 1865, and, with certain gaps, form a pretty continuous and searching commentary upon every aspect of our foreign and imperial policy during that period, with a comprehensive survey of the damaging backstrokes which the Palmerstonian policy dealt to British Liberalism and the cause of peace, retrenchment and reform with which it had been associated. His early labours for the reduction of competing armaments, the new cause of international arbitration and the abolition of the right of "capture at sea" of mercantile vessels and cargoes, and other "pacific" causes to which his voice and pen were constantly addicted, are discussed in these letters with a freedom and enthusiasm which throw fresh light upon his public career as well as upon the inner history of these movements. Not less profitable are the numerous

Preface

passing criticisms upon the new power of the popular Press and the abuses to which it was exposed, and the failure of Lancashire and Yorkshire Radicalism, after the Free Trade success, to respond to the new demands of democratic progress. The dangers which lay in the refusal of our people to realize that the enlargement of communications and trade intercourse with the outside world meant that the key to every cause of internal reform lay in the control of Foreign Policy, were continually in the forefront of Cobden's mind. No man of his time realized so clearly how a tacit conspiracy of the leaders of the two great parties operated to support militarism, the Balance of Power and a spirited foreign policy, so as to absorb the money, men and interest needed for home development.

Though these letters, for the use of which I am indebted to the courtesy of Miss Evans, a niece of Mr. Richard, form the staple of many of these chapters, I have made large use of other material, partly speeches and published essays, partly letters, most of which have been published already either in the standard "Life" by Lord Morley or in less-known and less-accessible works, such as the "Reminiscences of Richard Cobden" by Mrs. Salis Schwabe, the Anti Corn-Law Circulars, and the *American Historical Review*. From this last source are recovered several long and valuable letters written to the American statesman Charles Sumner, and which, with others lying in the collection in the Harvard Library and hitherto unpublished, furnish an important commentary upon the international aspects of the American Civil War, and in particular upon the opinions and sympathies of the various sections of the British people in that critical time. For the arrangements for transcribing these letters we are indebted to the courtesy of the late Professor Charles Eliot Norton.

Preface

Though Cobden was no friend to formal political alliances, he may be said to be the first English statesman who fully realized the importance of our people cultivating the closest friendship with the peoples of the United States upon the one hand, and of France upon the other. More clearly and much earlier than others, he foresaw the rapid rise of the commercial and political status of the great Western Republic and the part she was destined to play in the spheres of world commerce and world politics, and he realized the importance of cultivating good relations with this powerful blood-relation and neighbour. But even more significant was the persistence of his efforts to bring our Government and people into friendly relations with those of France, and to dissipate those clouds of suspicion which ignorance, pugnacity and mistaken interests were constantly generating. Cobden was perhaps the first English statesman who expressed a desire for an *entente cordiale* between our people and the French, and the Commercial Treaty which he negotiated was the first valid act in bringing about that permanent improvement of relations which, with one or two brief relapses, has lasted for more than half a century.

While Cobden's international doctrines and activities are chiefly set forth in letters, speeches and extracts from his pamphlets, arranged with brief introductory notes, I have thought it worth while in an introductory and a concluding chapter to attempt some appraisal and interpretation of his internationalism in the light of subsequent events and the changes of policy to which these events and reflection upon them have brought most of those who to-day regard themselves as internationalists.

RICHARD COBDEN
THE INTERNATIONAL MAN

CHAPTER I

COBDEN'S PREPARATION FOR POLITICS

THE process of "settlement" to which the reputation of a great public man is subjected after he has passed away is almost inevitably attended by grave misrepresentations. The commonest form of that misrepresentation consists in dramatizing some single episode, or aspect, of his career and in assigning it to him as his sole and exclusive property. The career of Richard Cobden lent itself with peculiar facility to this popular falsification. For though his public life was one of numerous and varied activities, his direct contribution to positive and concrete statecraft lay almost entirely within the special field of commercial liberty with which his name is commonly associated. Few great public men in any age or country have by their own personal effort contributed so largely to the complete achievement of any great national policy as Cobden contributed to Free Trade. For though he had powerful coadjutors, two at least of whom figured with equal prominence in the eye of contemporaries, John Bright on the platform and in the House of Commons, Peel as the executant minister of the reform, popular opinion decided that Cobden was the determinant personal influence, and posterity has recorded this judgment

Richard Cobden : The International Man

by fastening upon the Free Trade movement the title "Cobdenism." This has secured imperishable fame for Cobden, but at a heavy expense to the true greatness of the man and of the wider statecraft which he sought to make prevail.

The misrepresentation has been twofold and conflicting. On the one hand, he has been charged with a narrow and grovelling commercialism; on the other, with a vague cosmopolitan idealism. The prolonged revival of fiscal controversy during the last fifteen years has familiarized our generation with these inconsistent presentations of Cobden and the Free Trade doctrines and policy of which he was the most successful exponent. The first view shows us Cobden and his Manchester School reducing the whole of politics, including the honour and the vital interests of his country, to terms of trade and money-making, conducted under the single principle of buying in the cheapest and selling in the dearest market. Government was simply to stand aside and keep a ring within which this sordid struggle of the material interests of individuals, classes and nations was to take place, on the assumption that its outcome would be the maximum of wealth and material prosperity. Nor was it really, these critics commonly contended, an equal regard for the material interests of all classes of the people that underlay the policy. It was the interests of the manufacturers as against the "landed interests," and the interests of Capital as against Labour in the manufactures. Even cheap food, the prime motive for the repeal of the Corn Laws, was chiefly valued as the necessary means of keeping money-wages and costs of production in the new manufacturing districts so low as to enable our cotton and other exported goods to hold and to extend their world-markets. Even those who are aware that Cobden personally neglected a thriving business of his own and incurred heavy pecuniary sacrifices in following a political career, have often stigmatized him as dominated by the commercial interests and aspirations of the new ambitious business class, the product of the industrial revolution, which sought to displace the aristocracy and to impose upon their country a definitely "business government." Others, or often the same men in a different mood, fastening upon his enthusiasm for free commerce as the great pacific and harmonizing influence in international relations, the intrinsic logic and morality of which was destined at no distant time to banish the fear of war and to liberate the forces of human brotherhood, derided him as a dangerous visionary who ignored the lessons of history, and believed in the rapid establishment of a millennium of peace and prosperity for all the peoples of the world.

Now each of these opposing views is a travesty of the truth, though taken together they tend towards a recognition of the truth. Cobden did strongly believe that the prosperous middle-class business men were the chief present instruments of political and social progress, and that the more power they had the better. Their prosperity was certain, by the operation of laws as moral as they were economic, to redound to the advantage of their fellow-men, both their own employees, the nation of whom they were a part, and, through the operation of free commerce and communications, to humanity at large. Capital had no separate interest from Labour, the accumulation of savings for profitable employment increased the wage-fund and improved the condition of labour. If the political and economic power and privileges of landlordism could be curbed, by removing food taxes and making land more accessible to those who could use it, if all legal or other obstructions to the free movement, sale and employment

Richard Cobden : The International Man

of capital and labour could be removed, the enlightened self-interest, primarily of the manufacturers and commercial men, would tend to a production and a distribution of wealth among the various classes of the community which would, by giving a solid basis of industry and material prosperity, afford a new leverage to all the forces of civilization.

In mind, as in the concrete conditions of his policy, Cobden was necessarily to a large extent the creature of his age. That age was pre-eminently and somewhat hardly utilitarian and rationalistic in its thought and endeavours. The new power of machinery as the instrument of wealth and social changes, coinciding with the rapid extension of scientific conceptions to human character and history, brought in the early nineteenth century among the educated classes an immense and excessive confidence in the pace and thoroughness with which great political and social transformations could be accomplished. The revolutionary rationalism, of Godwin, Shelley and the youthful Coleridge, still survived in the more austere and complex political philosophy of Bentham and his school of philosophic Radicals, while the widespread enthusiasm with which the amazingly audacious proposals of Robert Owen for a New Moral World was greeted, not by ignorant mobs but by persons of responsibility and learning, testifies to an extraordinary fervour of rationalistic idealism. In this confidence in enlightened self-interest, operating first on the material plane, there was nothing really base, or selfish in the bad sense, or fundamentally materialistic, for below all immediate appeals to individual self-interest there lay a law of social harmony. It was to this general body of thought, contained in definite principles, that Richard Cobden from his youth steadily adhered, and the consistency and energy of his public work were

Cobden's Preparation for Politics

attributable mainly to the powerful and vivid apprehension of these principles. Most politicians are primarily opportunists, and, even if they sincerely entertain general principles, discover that they are seldom able to apply them with any measure of severity. Cobden was not in this sense an opportunist. He insisted upon a degree of intellectual and moral consistency in the application of principles which, while precluding him from office and the direct exercise of governmental power, made him a powerfully invigorating and educative influence in his age, and in one important sphere of policy enabled him to achieve remarkable results.

An enthusiast for principles is almost of necessity an optimist, not only as regards the ultimate fate of humanity, but as regards the pace at which ideas can be realized. In a concluding chapter I shall discuss more fully the causes which have obstructed the successful advance of Cobden's principles. It is here sufficient to recognize how untrue is the suggestion that Cobden was an ordinary middle-class politician whose success consisted in the stubborn pursuit of a commercial policy accommodated to the ideas of his time and the interests of his class, or that he was a wild dreamer who led his country into dangerous dependence upon foreigners in pursuit of a vague vision of cosmopolitanism. It is true, as Lord Morley recognizes, that Cobden was an optimist temperamentally, as well as by intellectual conviction. " In his intrepid faith in the perfectibility of man and of Society, Cobden is the only eminent practical statesman that this country has ever possessed, who constantly breathes the fine spirit of that French School in which the name of Turgot is the most illustrious."[1]

[1] "Life of Cobden," i. p. 94 (Jubilee Edition).

Richard Cobden : The International Man

If man will only believe and apply the doctrine of mutual aid, his perfectability and that of Society are evidently attainable. And so the central principle of Cobden is that of the harmony of men, irrespective of political, racial, or linguistic barriers, by means of organized mutual aid. "He believed that the interests of the individual, the interests of the nation, and the interests of all nations are identical: and that these several interests are all in entire and necessary concordance with the highest interests of morality. With this belief, an economic truth acquired with him the dignity and vitality of a moral law, and instead of remaining a barren doctrine of the intellect, became a living force to move the hearts and consciences of men."[1]

It is impossible to understand the character and political career of Cobden, or the part which his Free Trade activities play in his policy, without a firm grasp of this guiding and ruling principle. Cobden was not, as he is sometimes represented, a commercial gentleman who came to elevate to the dignity of an international principle a policy of free exchange which he valued in the first instance as good for his country, and then by implication and extension good for the world at large. It is quite true that early in his public career he came to the conviction that free importation was essential to the trade and human prosperity of his country, and that it was the chief key to a sound foreign policy. But this policy was always conceived as belonging to a wider philosophy of human relations which for our immediate purpose may be summarized as non-intervention. That term, however, though useful for some purposes as involving a fixed and consistent protest against governmental and other interference with human beings in the peaceful pursuit of their own material and moral interests, does

[1] "Cobden's Work and Opinions," by Lord Welby, p. 18.

Cobden's Preparation for Politics

not convey the full meaning of the positive body of thought which Cobden had absorbed from such thinkers as Adam Smith and his own personal friend Combe. The conception of a reign of law, which, on the one hand, related the physical and moral structure of man to his history and environment, on the other, built up an ordered scheme of human society, operating by free social intercourse, and dependent upon the co-operation of diverse tastes and capacities in different material surroundings, came as a captivating revelation to thoughtful men of the early nineteenth century. This free human co-operation, transcending the limits of nationality and race, was the positive force, intellectual and emotional, of which non-intervention was the negative condition. The reason why the latter term and the meaning it conveyed came to have so much importance was the impulsion which the new social thought gave to the political and economic campaign of liberation. Remove the fetters and obstructions which governments, laws, and customs have placed upon the free play of the harmonious forces which bind man to man, let their real community of interest have full sway to express itself in economic, intellectual and moral intercourse, the false antagonisms which now divide nations, classes and individuals, will disappear and a positive harmony of mankind be established. So the removal of barriers upon human intercourse came to have the value of an actually constructive policy, liberating as it did the forces of social harmony to weave their own pattern of human co-operation. Wealth, security, happiness and every form of progress were to be won in this war of liberation.

To modern men and women it may seem strange that this policy should be conceived so exclusively or primarily in terms of governmental non-intervention. There are so many other modes of human oppression and

Richard Cobden : The International Man

inequality, especially within the national areas. It seems difficult to us to realize how acute and public-spirited statesmen like Cobden, Bright and Gladstone, should have lived a long public life without recognizing in the distribution of the ownership of land and capital, the control and motivation of industry and the visible class cleavages thus created, social diseases even deeper seated than those which engaged their reforming energies. But we must remember that the intellectual atmosphere of early nineteenth-century politics was filled with the spirit of revolt against what were considered artificial restrictions upon individual liberty imposed by class governments, and with a profound conviction that enlightened self-interest operating through free contract or free competition was the true instrument of individual progress and of social harmony.

It is true that there were various sorts of bondage to be broken, that which a State Church set upon the religious spirit of man, the bondage of ignorance and vice in a country where education was a monopoly of the well-to-do, the political and social tyranny exercised by the aristocracy as landowners, legislators and dispensers of justice. The Liberalism into which Cobden grew was by no means blind to these great needs, and all through his public life his sympathies responded powerfully to these reforming notes. But while, as Lord Morley says, " he never ceased to be the preacher of a philosophy of civilization," his personal experience, his demand for practical achievement, and his sense of order in progress, early determined his personal contribution to the great cause. That contribution was not Free Trade, but internationalism. Free Trade, though driven home to him by his early experiences of life as a great national need, soon took its proper place in his thought and heart as the instrument and vehicle of internation-

Cobden's Preparation for Politics

alism. Sometimes this policy has been described as cosmopolitan. But if this signifies that Cobden was indifferent to the sentiment of national patriotism, or thought that one country was just as good as another, the appellation is singularly ill-applied. Widely travelled as he was, and appreciative of the qualities of many foreign nations, Cobden always remained in personal tastes and sympathies profoundly English. Moreover, his internationalism was intellectually, as well as emotionally, an application of the principles of national self-interest, and of the human obligation under which a nation more enlightened and more advanced in the arts of government and commerce lay to extend by pacific means to other peoples its own advantages. To stigmatize the doctrine of non-intervention, on the other hand, as a selfish nationalism, is equally mistaken.

Cobden's early travels upon the Continent of Europe and in America, in which definitely business objects were combined with wider political and social studies, contributed to give substance to what otherwise might have remained merely general opinions and aspirations. Alike as a Free Trader and an International Man, he enjoyed great advantages over other statesmen by reason of the wider and closer knowledge of the condition of the people in his own and other countries which he gained in the formative period of his life. The cotton trade, which he entered as a clerk when fifteen years old, was doubly rooted in internationalism, drawing its materials entirely from foreign soil, and dependent, as it soon became, for its prosperity and profits upon the expansion of its world markets. When with two friends he first entered business on his own account as a commission agent for calico-printers, soon afterwards to undertake the work of calico-printing itself, he was filled with the

Richard Cobden : The International Man

enthusiasm which greeted everywhere the miraculous rise of Lancashire as the great exporting area.

His early years, as commercial traveller, had given him an intimate knowledge of his own country, including Scotland and Ireland, and, as soon as circumstances permitted, he took to foreign travel, partly for business, partly for relaxation, but largely for social and political information. Though a certain amount of foreign travel for pleasure, perhaps a grand tour, formed part of the equipment of a good many active young members of the governing classes, it may be safely asserted that no man of his time entered the House of Commons with so sound a knowledge of the world at large as Cobden brought when he entered Parliament at the age of thirty-seven. He had not merely passed along the ordinary paths of continental travel in France, Germany and Switzerland, but had visited Spain, Turkey, Egypt and Greece, and had formed from close contact with many places and many men first-hand views of the determinant factors of that Eastern Question which was destined to obtrude itself so often and in such impressive ways upon the foreign policy of his time. The close interdependence of economic and political conditions was a persistent underlying object of study, and vitalized the conceptions of international politics which formed the matter of his earliest political essays. His early European travels were reinforced by a tour in the United States, then almost a *terra incognita* to our educated classes, save for the casual caricatures of a few literary tourists like Dickens and Mrs. Trollope. Mere extent of travel is, of course, in itself no index of an international mind. But Cobden's diaries, selections from which are printed in some chapters of Lord Morley's "Life," show what care he took, not only to gather and record information, but to digest it into general judgments. He got on well with

Cobden's Preparation for Politics

foreigners, because they found in him none of the ill-concealed contempt or censorious superiority which galled them in the ordinary British visitor. Americans particularly of that period were properly resentful of what Lowell a generation later termed "a certain condescension in foreigners," and they were especially sensitive to such treatment from Englishmen. Cobden had sympathy and admiration for the spirit of hustle which he found in their country. "Great as was my previous esteem for the qualities of this people, I find myself in love with their intelligence, their sincerity, and the decorous self-respect that actuates all classes. The very genius of activity seems to have found its fit abode in the souls of this restless and energetic race. They have not, 'tis true, the force of Englishmen in personal weight or strength, but they have compensated for that deficiency by quickening the momentum of their enterprise."[1] This was his characteristic attitude of mind, to pay chief attention to the natural or human qualities, powers and opportunities, which distinguished the several nations and countries that he visited. For it was these differences of soil, situation, climate, and of the human nature and activities which they educated and evoked, that formed the true basis of that international co-operation which he sought to promote. It was this simple lesson Cobden never tired of teaching as the essence of sound international policy.

[1] Morley's "Life," i. p. 39.

CHAPTER II

COBDEN AS PAMPHLETEER

IT is important to recognize that very early in his public life Cobden had grasped the full connection between the negative and the positive aspects of the policy of non-intervention; how, on the one hand, by feeding international intercourse it brought increase of wealth, security, knowledge and goodwill, while, on the other, it cut out the roots of class monopolies, political corruption, and imperialistic ambition with their attendant dangers and extravagances in home policy. His first literary production, the pamphlet entitled "England, Ireland, and America," published in 1835 by "A Manchester Manufacturer," is valuable evidence that this broad current of political thought upon the connections between home and foreign policy possessed his mind long before he had devoted himself to the specific agitation for Free Trade.

It was the imminent and constantly recurring peril of a policy of diplomatic and forcible interference with the conduct of other countries, partly in obedience to a false and dangerous doctrine of Balance of Power, partly in pursuit of territorial aggrandizement, that called forth this early draft of Cobdenism. The immediate object of the pamphlet was to refute a pamphlet written by Mr. Urquhart, formerly Secretary of the English Embassy at Constantinople, containing an argued as well as an impassioned appeal to our Government to intervene for the

Cobden as Pamphleteer

protection of Turkey against the alleged aggressive designs of Russia. This was part of a prolonged, and in the end successful, attempt to embroil this country and France with Russia as claimant to the heritage of the Turk and to the future hegemony of Asia. Cobden, after a scathing indictment of the misrule of the Sultan, driven home by careful illustrations of the waste and destruction to which many of the most productive countries of the East were committed, asks what interest we can have to interfere for the protection of the Turk against a nation whose economic and commercial policy is at least far more enlightened than that of the Sultan, and whose trade and goodwill are of far greater value to us. He then grapples directly with the fallacy which assumes that territorial annexations are normal and natural additions of strength which would make Russia a more formidable neighbour. The argument he uses is as relevant to-day as then, and the illustrations as apt.

"Supposing Russia or Austria to be in possession of the Turkish dominions, would she not find her attention and resources far too abundantly occupied in *retaining* the sovereignty over fifteen millions of fierce and turbulent subjects, animated with warlike hatred to their conqueror, and goaded into rebellion by the all-powerful impulse of a haughty and intolerant religion, to contemplate adding still further to her embarrassments by declaring war on England and giving the word of march to Hindostan? Who does not perceive that it could not, for ages at least, add to the external power of either of these States, if she were to get possession of Turkey by force of arms? Is Russia stronger abroad by her recent perfidious incorporation of Poland? Would Holland increase her power if she were to reconquer the Belgian provinces to-morrow? Or, to come to our own door, for example, was Great Britain more powerful whilst, for

Richard Cobden : The International Man

centuries, she held Ireland in disaffected subjection to her rule, or was she not rather weakened by offering, in the sister island, a vulnerable point of attack to her continental enemies ?"[1] He then proceeds to open out the double-headed folly of pursuing this dangerous "spirited policy" in Europe to the neglect of the two great tasks which should rightly claim our immediate attention—the pacification and development of Ireland and the cultivation of sound commercial relations with the rising power of the United States. On both these matters he draws upon a rich fund of practical knowledge and a large imaginative statecraft. The crippling of Irish trade, the imposition of a costly alien Church, the servile land system, the degrading Poor Law, the lack of capital for railway and manufacturing development, all the vices of a neglected dependency, he lays bare with unsparing truth, ending with this searching question : "Does not the question of Ireland, in every point of view, offer the strongest possible argument against the national policy of this country, for the time during which we have wasted our energies and squandered our wealth upon all the nations of the Continent, whilst a part of our own Empire, which, more than all the rest of Europe, has needed our attention, remains to this hour an appalling monument of our neglect and misgovernment ?"[2]

The concluding section of the pamphlet is devoted to an exposition of the growing economic strength of the United States, and the importance of pursuing a more enlightened policy, alike in foreign and domestic affairs, if we are to cope successfully with her ascendancy.

Here Cobden appeals to national pride as well as to the pocket. In his desire to prove that we had better occupy our minds with what is happening on the other side of the Atlantic, instead of meddling on the Continent,

[1] "Political Writings," i. p. 20.   [2] Ibid. i. p. 74.

Cobden as Pamphleteer

he commits himself to a theory of trade rivalry which is not, it will be recognized, in accord with the fuller principle of commercial internationalism which he developed later on. Contrasting the rapid development of their national resources and their business policy in manufacture and in transport, their attention to education, the growth of their press, with the slow and reluctant steps taken in these directions by our Government and ruling classes, and dwelling on their lighter taxation and their immunity from militarism and the crushing burden of war debts, he appeals to the policy of non-intervention as the only one which will enable us to hold our own in the coming commercial struggle with this new power which sees its greatness not in terms of forcible conquest and territorial aggression, but in economic domination. "It is to the industry, the economy, and peaceful policy of America, and not to the growth of Russia, that our statesmen and politicians, of whatever creed, ought to direct their anxious study; for it is by these, and not by the efforts of barbarian force, that the power and greatness of England are in danger of being superseded; yes, by the successful rivalry of America, shall we, in all probability, be placed second in the rank of nations." [1]

An even more striking testimony to the breadth, independence and maturity of Cobden's thought, before he quitted business for politics, is found in the extended argument of his pamphlet on "Russia," published in 1836. It was evoked by the alarm of a Russian invasion which prevailed that year, and was made the occasion of an increase in our navy of five thousand men and of a carefully fomented demand for military preparations. Its method of appeal is the best illustration of the working of Cobden's mind in politics, his insistence upon applying to the ideas and catchwords

[1] Op. cit. p. 78.

Richard Cobden : The International Man

by which interested politicians sway the popular mind the test of facts and the interpretation of common sense. While he displays considerable subtlety and learning in unravelling and exposing the sophistry of the statecraft, the positive principles and policy he seeks to substitute are few, simple and obvious. Though suggested by a passing stroke of peril and primarily fitted to the occasion, it is intended to arouse deeper and more permanent reflections, and stands as his ablest and fullest formal exposition of the foreign policy of non-intervention.

The opening chapter directly challenges the Russophobe on the interest of England in the Eastern Question. By a comparison of the political and economic institutions of Russia and Turkey, Cobden confutes the arguments of those who pretend that our commerce, our colonies and our national existence, are imperilled by the encroachments of Russia upon the Turkish Empire in Europe or in Asia. After various citations from accepted authorities to show what Turkish government has actually meant for the countries which have fallen under its sway, and what are the present conditions and the prospects of Russia as a country rapidly emerging from barbarism and equipped with the physical and spiritual potentialities of Western civilization, he poses in a brilliant passage the salient question "Whether it is really a danger and a detriment to England that Russia should displace the Ottoman Powers?" He refuses to decide whether Russia is herself justified in undertaking this career of aggrandizement, narrowing the issue to that of British policy in intervention. The consequences of Russian conquest would, he contends, be favourable to humanity and civilization. "Can any one doubt that, if the Government of St. Petersburg were transferred to the shores of the Bosphorus, a splendid and substantial European city would, in less than twenty years, spring up in the place of those huts which now constitute the capital of Turkey? that noble public buildings would arise, learned societies flourish and the arts prosper? that, from its natural beauties and advantages, Constantinople would become an attractive resort for educated Europeans? that the Christian religion, operating instantly upon the laws and institutions of the country, would ameliorate the conditions of its people? that the slave market, which is now polluting the Ottoman capital centuries after the odious traffic has been banished from the soil of Christian Europe, would be abolished? that the demoralizing and unnatural laws of polygamy, under which the fairest portion of the creation becomes an object of brutal lust and an article of daily traffic, would be discontinued? and that the plague, no longer fostered by the filth and indolence of the people, would cease to ravage countries placed in the healthiest latitudes and blessed with the finest climate in the world?"

"Would such beneficent changes be detrimental to this country? Although Russia is a relatively backward country in commercial policy, it is far more advanced than Turkey, and we might reasonably expect a substantial development both of the raw materials of Turkey and of her markets for foreign produce. The great gains of such material development Russia could not keep to herself. Even supposing, however, that Russia, by apathy or misgovernment, failed to develop and civilize her growing territories, that failure would bring no menace to such a country as England, whose power, as compared with that of Russia, would be continually advancing by virtue of the fact that trade and wealth are the sinews of political and even military power."

"If that people were to attempt to exclude all foreign

Richard Cobden : The International Man

traffic, they would enter at once upon the high road to barbarism, for which career there is no danger threatened to rich and civilized nations ; if, on the other hand, that State continued to pursue a system favourable to foreign trade, then England will be found at Constantinople, as she has already been at St. Petersburg, reaping the greatest harvest of riches and power, from the augmentation of Russian imports." In the latter part of this chapter Cobden deals with the charge of aggrandizement brought by us against Russia, by bringing home the humorous effrontery of such a charge made by a nation which "during the last hundred years has, for every square league of territory annexed by Russia by force, violence, or fraud, appropriated to herself three." If we find our justification in the claim to have imposed order and material improvements with some measure of justice upon our enlarged empire, Russia may reasonably make a similar claim for the provinces in Europe and Asia which she has annexed.

This contention Cobden presses home by a comprehensive examination of the case of Poland, to which he devotes the second chapter of his treatise. Here he traverses the accepted stories of the wrongs and injuries inflicted upon that country by its dismemberment. The annals of republican Poland, for a century prior to its dismemberment, were, he contends, a history of anarchy, due to the intestine strife of the despotic gangs of nobles who owned and ruled the country, to the religious discords which rent the people, and to the recurrence of plague and famine, the natural train of incessant warfare. Poland, as a nation, never had its independence, and so could not lose it. Its dismemberment " has been followed by an increase in the amount of peace, wealth, liberty, civilization and happiness, enjoyed by the great mass of the people. Slavery no longer exists

Cobden as Pamphleteer

in Poland, the peasant is for the first time safe in life and limb, with liberty to plough his soil for his own advantage. Roads, bridges and other improvements have been introduced by Russia, and the Polish people, though far from prosperous, have enjoyed many benefits by their change of Government." The insurrection of 1830, commonly adduced to prove the oppression of Russia, is assigned by Cobden as the result of the instigation of the Polish aristocracy who, for their own selfish benefit, plunged their nation into the horrors of civil war by playing upon the sentiments of patriotism and nationality.[1]

Having thus disposed of the perils from Russia by a candid appeal to facts, and being unable "to discover one single ground upon which to find a pretence, consistent with reason, common sense, or justice, for going to war with Russia," Cobden then embarks upon a broader examination of the foundations of our international policy, as couched under the vague and fallacious phrase "Balance of Power." He shows, first, that international jurists and statesmen have never agreed as to the meaning of the term, applied to any Union or disposition of European Powers, and that no state of things corresponding to the meaning anywhere assigned to it has ever existed. He then shows that there is no agreed, or indeed possible, definition or measure of the "power" according to which the several state-claims shall be estimated, and finally that any such "balance," were it established, would be inoperative,

---

[1] Here Cobden gives naïve expression to his surprise that common people should prefer a bad government by members of their own race to a better government by foreigners. "Patriotism," as he remarks, "or nationality, is an instinctive virtue, that sometimes burns the brightest in the rudest and least reasoning minds; and its manifestation bears no proportion to the value of possessions defended, and the object to be gained" ("Political Writings," i. p. 178).

Richard Cobden : The International Man

because no provision could be made against "the peaceful aggrandizements which spring from improvement and labour." Next, he exposes the inconsistency of invoking such a theory in the case of Russian encroachment upon Turkey, as if Turkey were a part of the balance, while the United States and Brazil, whose wealth, position and striking power are far greater, were excluded from the "balance." The utter irrationality of alarms based upon balance of power is thus exposed. "Russia, in possession of Constantinople, say the alarmists, would possess a port open at all seasons; the materials for constructing ships; vast tracts of fertile land, capable of producing cotton, silk, wool, etc.; and she would be placed in a situation of easy access to our shores—all of which would tend to destroy the Balance of Power, and put in danger the interests of British commerce in particular. But New York, a port far more commodious than Constantinople, is open at all seasons; the United States possess materials without end for shipbuilding; their boundless territory of fertile land is adapted for the growth of cotton, silk, wool, etc., and New York is next door to Liverpool; for —thanks to Providence!—there is no land intervening between the American continent and the shores of this United Kingdom. Yet we have never heard that the North American Continent forms any part of the Balance of Power!"[1]

To America he appeals as the great witness for his gospel of non-intervention, and for the true internationalism which is its natural consequence, summarizing his lesson in the pregnant apothegm: "As little intercourse as possible between the *Governments*; as much connection as possible between the nations of the world." The final chapter of his pamphlet sets forth the right conditions of such international connection by peaceful and free inter-

[1] P. 210.

Cobden as Pamphleteer

change of goods and services. To what are we indebted for the recent growth of our commerce? Is it to territorial aggrandizement and the protection of a powerful navy? Not at all. The costs and risks of a colonial mercantilism sustained by force of arms have been sufficiently exposed by history. "Men-of-war to conquer colonies, to yield us a monopoly of their trade, must now be dismissed, like many other equally glittering but false adages of our forefathers, and in its place we must substitute the more homely but enduring maxim *Cheapness*, which will command commerce; and whatever else is needful will follow in its train."[1]

This reliance upon cheapness and quality of goods, as the mainstay of sound relations between peoples, means that every increase of trade, instead of requiring an increase of warlike armaments in its defence, itself furnishes an improved safeguard against the dangers of war. So we come to recognize the positive pacific virtues of free commerce. "The standing armies and navies—whilst they cannot possibly protect our commerce, while they add by the increase of taxation to the cost of our manufactures, and thus augment the difficulty of achieving the victory of 'cheapness'—tend to deter rather than attract customers. The feeling is natural; it is understood in the individual concerns of life. Does the shopkeeper, when he invites buyers to his counter, place there as a guard to protect his stock or defend his salesmen from violence a gang of stout fellows armed with pistols and cutlasses?" Liberate commerce, cheapen its production, extend its flow, you place international relations upon a safe, reasonable and advantageous footing, and relieve nations from the perils and wastes of those strifes which come from governmental conduct dictated by obsolete and false conceptions of the antagonism of States.

[1] Op. cit. p. 221.

Richard Cobden : The International Man

Wanted a foreign policy in which the common sense of statesmen expresses the general interests of peoples. "And how long will it be before the policy of this manufacturing and commercial nation shall be determined by at least as much calculation and regard for self-interest as are necessary to the prosperity of a private business? Not until such time as Englishmen apply the same rules of common sense to the affairs of the State as they do to their individual undertakings."

. . . . .

Thus we perceive that, before the establishment of the Anti Corn-Law League in 1838, and several years before his entry into Parliament, Cobden had by travel and reflection acquired the principles and policy of that internationalism which throughout his long public life directed and dominated his conduct. That internationalism had two aspects. The first was governmental non-intervention, applied alike to foreign and to colonial policy, "as little intercourse as possible between Governments." The second was the growth and encouragement of intimate and friendly intercourse between the members of different nations, international as distinguished from inter-governmental relations. Of this international intercourse free interchange of economic goods and services on terms of obvious mutual advantage was the most important channel and the best security.

Although the concentration of his efforts during the period from 1838 to 1846 upon the repeal campaign necessarily involved some neglect of the wider propaganda, he never lost sight of the larger human meaning of a policy which, in order to become effectual, must first be founded on an appeal to national expediency. In particular, the organic connection between the Free Trade and the Peace Movements was firmly established in his mind in 1842, when he proposed to Mr. Ashworth the

Cobden as Pamphleteer

offering of a Prize Essay on "Free Trade as the Best Human Means for securing Universal and Permanent Peace," adding that "It has often struck me that it would be well to try to engraft our Free Trade agitation upon the Peace movement. They are one and the same cause. It has often been to me a matter of surprise that the Friends have not taken up the question of Free Trade as the means—and I believe the only human means—of effecting universal and permanent peace. The efforts of the Peace Societies, however laudable, can never be successful so long as the nations maintain their present system of isolation." [1]

Though the main stress of the Anti Corn-Law argument both in Parliament and in the country was upon the urgency of repeal as a remedy for the poverty and insecurity of livelihood in which the general mass of the labouring population were living, while at the same time securing full employment and profitable trade for the capital and labour engaged in our manufactures, the orators of the League seldom failed to rally the intelligence and moral sense of their audience to the broader issues of peace, disarmament and amity of nations. Bright, Cobden and Fox never ignored the value of these larger and less distinctively material considerations to the success of their immediate cause. It was not merely an appeal to the stomach of the workers and the bank account of the manufacturers. Beneath this material economic struggle lay a clear sense of "the international." As Bright said in his great oration at Covent Garden Theatre in September 1843: "They wanted to have the question settled for the world as well as for England. They were tired of what was called the natural divisions of empires. They wanted not that the Channel should separate this country from France—they hoped and wished that Frenchmen

[1] Quoted in Morley's "Life," i. p. 230.

Richard Cobden : The International Man

and Englishmen should no longer consider each other as naturally hostile nations."[1]

The peroration of Cobden's speech at the same gathering gives a definition of Free Trade which shows that in his mind the larger vision never suffered an eclipse. "Free Trade—what is it? Why, breaking down the barriers that separate nations; those barriers behind which nestle the feelings of pride, revenge, hatred and jealousy, which every now and then break their bonds and deluge whole countries with blood; those feelings which nourish the poison of war and conquest, which assert that without conquest we can have no trade, which foster that lust for conquest and dominion which send forth your warrior chiefs to sanction devastation through other lands, and then calls them back that they may be enthroned securely in your passions, but only to harass and oppress you at home."[2]

This large spirit breathed through all his utterances in this great and triumphant campaign. Cobden never confined it to the single expression, liberty of commerce. He saw in it the spirit of human solidarity asserting itself above and beyond the limits of national patriotism. The destruction of the protectionist system of this country was but the liberation of the spiritual forces of humanity pervading men of diverse lands, races, colours, creeds and languages, scattered over the earth. In the peroration of his speech at the final meeting of the League Council (July 2, 1846), when, its work done, the dissolution of the League was decided, Cobden spoke the following words :

"It is in our moral nature necessary that when an organized body has fulfilled its functions it must pass into a new state of existence and become differently organized. We are dispersing our elements to be ready

[1] "Cobden and the League," p. 167.   [2] "Speeches," p. 40.

Cobden as Pamphleteer

for any other good work, and it is nothing but good works which will be attempted by good leaguers. Our body will, so to speak, perish, but our spirit is abroad and will pervade all the nations of the earth. It will pervade all the nations of the earth, because it is the spirit of truth and justice and because it is the spirit of peace and goodwill among men."

CHAPTER III

THE TOUR IN EUROPE, 1846-7

BUT though the fuller gospel of economic and political internationalism underlay the Anti Corn-Law propaganda, tactical considerations hampered its free expression even in this country. The notion or feeling that the trading interests of other nations are opposed to our own cannot easily be rooted out of the political economy of the average sensual man, and, if the repeal movement had had to wait for this conversion, its success would have been slow and precarious. Free Trade must be hammered in as a plain national advantage long before the full policy of mutuality upon which it rests is consciously grasped by most minds. Therefore it was that Cobden plainly recognized that the triumph of the League in 1846, though sounding the death-knell of food taxation, was no final security for the wider policy. As it had been expedient to dwell mainly upon the national gain accompanying Free Trade for this country, so it became important to disabuse the mind of other nations of the view that Free Trade was an exclusively British interest. The League during their propaganda expressly refrained from appealing to any foreign sentiment in favour of the cause. For they rightly judged that such appeals were certain to be misrepresented by the interests which stood behind protective tariffs and would play into the hands of their enemies. Cobden, some years later, reviewing the League policy puts this

The Tour in Europe, 1846-7

very clearly. " We came to the conclusion that the less we attempted to persuade foreigners to adopt our trade principles, the better; for we discovered so much suspicion of the motives of England, that it was lending an argument to the protectionists abroad to incite the popular feeling against the free-traders, by enabling them to say, 'See what these men are wanting to do; they are partisans of England and they are seeking to prostitute our industries at the feet of that perfidious nation. . . .' To take away this pretence, we avowed our total indifference whether other nations became free-traders or not; but we should abolish Protection for our own selves, and leave other countries to take whatever course they liked best." [1] Even Bastiat's early approaches with a view to a popular agitation in France were felt at first to be somewhat embarrassing. It was not until the overthrow of the Corn Law was actually achieved that Cobden felt free to engage upon any direct attempt to fortify the Free Trade policy of this country by foreign support. He recognized that, though the downfall of protective tariffs had to be the work of national agitation and statecraft within each country, it was possible to make the example of Great Britain an example and encouragement to the national reformers in foreign countries. Cobden believed in the force of this example, holding that he could succeed " in making now a stronger case for the prohibition nations of Europe to compel them to adopt a freer system, than I had here to overturn our protective policy." [2]

It was the growing urgency of this need which induced him to plan his comprehensive tour through Europe in 1846. " I will," he writes, " be an ambassador from the

[1] Cobden to Mr. Van der Maeren, 1856 (quoted, Morley, i. p. 310).
[2] Letter to Mr. Paulton, July 4, 1846 (quoted, Morley, i. p. 408).

Richard Cobden : The International Man

free-traders of England to the Governments of the great nations of the Continent."[1] No man was better qualified for such a rôle. The fame of his achievement preceded him. He had wrought a really revolutionary transformation of the business policy of the greatest commercial country in the world. Though primarily addressed to the national needs and interests of his own people, the policy carried with it manifest advantages to the producers and commercial classes of other countries. The adoption by other Governments and peoples of the same policy of the open door would multiply these benefits. The enthusiasm for what was at once a great economic discovery and a moral ideal spread among the liberal thinkers and the enlightened business men in every European country. For though most continental Governments were committed to Protection, partly by traditional mercantile doctrine, partly by fiscal needs, neither of these supports was unassailable. If it could be shown that the opening of ports to the free current of international commerce would at once stimulate the national powers of production, raise up new profitable manufactures and furnish them with great and growing foreign markets, antiquated notions of colonization and of taxation might easily be swept away in a general era of prosperity. Manufacturers in one country had not begun seriously to realize the perils of invasion in their "home" markets by the manufacturers of another nation, and so the prospect of free markets abroad filled them with enthusiasm. Nor had the Free Trade propaganda upon the Continent to meet the uncompromising active opposition of the agricultural interests. For every large continental country was virtually self-sufficing in the supplies of essential foods. While this fact weakened the pressure of the popular appeal for the cheap loaf which had

[1] Letter to Mr. Schwabe, "Reminiscences," p. 2.

The Tour in Europe, 1846-7

underlain the agitation in Great Britain, it averted the opposition of the landowners to the manufacturers and merchants who were favourably inclined to the new Free Trade doctrine, and to the internationalism which it carried.

He was well aware of the risk of misunderstanding in France, should he, a foreigner, above all an Englishman, appear as the instigator of a change of fiscal policy. The following letter, written in September 1846, to his French friend M. Arles Dufour,[1] is a sufficient commentary upon the tactics of French agitation.

"PAU, *September* 9, 1846.

"Before I left Bordeaux for this beautiful spot, I sent you a paper containing a report of our public dinner which I hope you received. Now let me offer a word or two for your own private ear. I must not be seen in *public*, in France, interfering with your politics, or stimulating Frenchmen to agitate for Free Trade, but I dare talk to *you* without reserve. Your commercial legislation is a disgrace to you. I had not the least idea, until I looked over your tariff with M. Anisson-Dupéron in Paris, that you were so lamentably behind other countries. Your tariff is far more illiberal *now* than ours in England was a quarter of a century ago, before Huskisson began his reforms. You have upwards of sixty articles of importance actually prohibited; many others on which the high duties are equal to a prohibition, and most of the raw materials required for your industry are absurdly taxed! With the exception of Spain, I do not know another country (unless it be Austria) where the commercial legislation is so barbarous and benighted as in France. If I were a Frenchman, and a merchant or manufacturer, my face would redden with shame at the

[1] A wealthy silk manufacturer of Lyons and an ardent Free Trader.

spectacle. You are far behind Germany, Italy and even Russia. Well, what must be done? *Why, help yourselves and God will help you.* You must AGITATE. The Government can do nothing unless aided by the Press and the public. The Press is busy about the marriage of a poor little girl in Spain, or Mr. Pritchard in Tahity, or anything else that is sufficiently foolish and contemptible to amuse the coteries of Paris. As for the public, its voice is never heard in France unless it be in the street for 'three days' behind barricades, and this is after all a very clumsy way of settling questions of political economy. The Government is ready to march forward if supported by the people. You must aid it. There are three great staple interests in France that ought to unite against the Protectionists—I mean the wine-growers, the silk manufacturers, and the Parisian industry. It seems to me as if your legislation was framed for the purpose of depressing these great *natural* branches of your trade to prop up some others which have not strength to stand without crutches, and yet these latter have the impudence to call themselves *par excellence* the National industry!

"Lyons ought to take the lead in this crusade against monopoly and selfishness, and *you* ought to marshal its forces. Now, my dear friend, set about the good work with all your native vigour—you have no time to lose. If you leave England to get a few years' start of you in Free Trade, your children—the next generation of Lyons —will have reason to curse the apathy and want of public spirit of their fathers. France must go back in the scale of nations unless she advances in the path of reform and improvement. You can no more continue in the old system of restriction, while England throws open her ports to all the world, than you could go on with diligence and roads, and let England possess the exclusive advan-

The Tour in Europe, 1846-7

tages of locomotives and railways. Do you agree with me in all this? Then I throw my mantle of an agitator over your shoulders, and bid you to commence the good work. Do not mix up any other question with it. Urge boldly forward the principle of Free Trade—denounce the very idea of Protection. It is a fraud and a *swindle*, and you must not compromise with it a moment. Make arrangements for a public meeting and let your voices be heard protesting against the *principle* of levying a tax to provide a 'civil list' for certain privileged classes. Tell them 'we are willing to be taxed for the public revenue—take all we possess if it is necessary for the good of the State—burn our houses over our heads if that be required for the interests of France. But not one sou will we pay for the benefit of particular men, or classes of men.' That is the tone to take to rouse public feeling and sympathy. Take no lower tone. Follow it up with energetic action, and you will succeed, as surely as we succeeded in England, against ten times the power which is arrayed against you in France. There! I told you I dared to speak plainly to *you*, and have not I done it? Yes; because I think I know you, and believe you know me, and that we shall not misunderstand each other. My wife and I are taking our ease amongst the lovely scenery of the Pyrénées. We shall remain in this neighbourhood for a short time, and then go to Italy for the winter. If you should find time to write me a few lines soon, after the receipt of this, it will find me *poste restante* at Pau. My wife joins me in remembrance to you.

" Believe me, dear sir,
" Faithfully yours,
"RICHARD COBDEN."

It is not surprising that Cobden in his tour through Spain, Italy, Germany and Russia, during the fourteen

Richard Cobden : The International Man

months from August 1846 to October 1847, met with great attention wherever he went. The story of his triumphant progress is told by himself in his diary, in letters to his wife, and in the volume of "Reminiscences" published in 1895 by Mrs. Salis Schwabe,[1] who, with her husband, had accompanied Cobden during the greater part of the tour and kept a careful account of his doings and of the public interest he aroused. The story is the more remarkable inasmuch as no plan of propaganda and no preconcerted arrangements were made by Cobden for his tour.

Mr. and Mrs. Cobden did not spend much time in France but pushed on to the Pyrénées frontier, where they were joined by their travelling companions Mr. and Mrs. Schwabe. "Mr. Cobden," the latter notes, "is much courted here in France, strangers of the first rank call on him and Mrs. Cobden and invite them. To-day the local paper (Pau) contained a poetic panegyric on Mr. Cobden."[2] Declining formal gatherings at Pau and Bayonne, Cobden pushed on to Spain, where he spent some eleven weeks in sightseeing, in conversations with political and business men and in rousing an intelligent appreciation of commercial internationalism in an inert and backward people. It is, however, noteworthy that Cobden's fame had so far preceded him that in Madrid, Seville, Cadiz and Malaga, Free Trade banquets were improvised in his honour. It could hardly be said that there was a Free Trade movement in Spain. But the repeal of British import duties on foods and raw materials had naturally appealed strongly to the interests of a nation largely exporting these supplies and possessing few powerful organized manufactures. Cobden, however, never played upon the note of selfish interest alone.

[1] "Reminiscences of Richard Cobden" (Fisher Unwin), compiled by Mrs. Salis Schwabe.   [2] "Reminiscences," p. 5.

The Tour in Europe, 1846-7

He always founded his appeal upon the broader base of international solidarity. Like every skilled preacher, he sought at once to touch the emotions of his audience and convince their understanding by presenting a clear image of an ideal. The following passage from his speech at the Free Trade banquet at Madrid well illustrates this practice.

"I know that there are individuals to be found in every country who say, 'We will produce everything we require within our own boundaries; we will be independent of foreigners.' If Nature had intended that there should be such a national isolation, she would have formed the earth upon a very different plan, and given to each country every advantage of soil and climate. My country, for example, would have possessed the wines, oils, fruits and silks, which have been denied to it, and other countries would have been endowed with the abundance of coal and iron with which we are compensated for the want of a warmer soil. No, Providence has wisely given to each latitude its peculiar products, in order that different nations may supply each other with the conveniences and comforts of life, and that thus they may be united together in the bonds of peace and brotherhood. Gentlemen, I doubt not that ere long the public opinion of this great nation may emancipate its commerce from those restrictions which recently fettered the industry of my country. I remember that more than three centuries ago a great man sailed from your shores to discover a new hemisphere. Let me not be accused of underrating the glory of that great achievement if I say, that the statesman who gives to Spain the blessings of commercial freedom will, in my opinion, confer greater and more durable advantages upon his country than it derived from the discovery of America. The genius of Columbus gave to your ancestors an uncultivated

Richard Cobden : The International Man

continent, thinly peopled by a barbarous race, but Free Trade will throw open a civilized world to your enterprise, and every nation will hasten to bring you the varied products of their ingenuity and industry to be offered in exchange for the superabundant produce of your favoured and beautiful country."

From Spain, Cobden passed to Italy, a country where the new industries were already more firmly rooted than in Spain, and where the principal Northern cities were already touched with the Free Trade spirit. In Genoa, Rome, Florence, Turin and Venice, public banquets with speeches were given, and were attended by influential men both of the nobility and the business classes. Nor less important were the many private interviews with personages of political and official importance. In Rome, Cobden was received by the Pope, who "avowed himself a partisan of my views, and said all that lay within his power, and adding modestly that it was but *little*, he would do to promote Free Trade principles."[1] It is characteristic of Cobden's courage that he should have seized the opportunity to represent to His Holiness the disgust he had experienced in Spain with the degrading spectacle of the bull-fights held " in honour of the Virgin and the Saints on their fête days," and that he should have urged the Pope to bring pressure on the clergy to discountenance such abominations.

In his address at Florence Cobden naturally adopted a gratulatory tone. For Tuscany alone of all the countries in Southern Europe had put in practice the Free Trade faith. " To Tuscany is undoubtedly due the glory of having preceded by half a century the rest of the world in the application of the theories of commercial science to its legislation." Then after a eulogium

[1] Letter to Mrs. Schwabe, " Reminiscences," p. 57.

The Tour in Europe, 1846-7

upon the founder of that policy, he proceeds to pass this striking commentary upon its results.

"During the last eight months I have been travelling in nearly all the countries of Southern Europe, and I am bound to state, without wishing to disparage other nations, that I find the conditions of the people of Tuscany superior to that of any people I have visited. The surface of the country resembles that of a well-cultivated garden; the people are everywhere well dressed; I have seen no beggars, except a few lame or blind; and in this season of general scarcity there is less of suffering from want of food here, with a perfect freedom of export and import of corn, than in probably any other country in Europe."[1]

At Naples he saw the King and "conversed for a short time with him on Free Trade, about which he did not appear to be altogether ignorant or without some favourable sympathies. He questioned me about the future status of the Irish difficulty, a question which seemed to be uppermost in the minds of all statesmen and public men on the Continent"—this in 1847, the famine year.

In May 1847 Cobden had an interview with King Charles Albert, "a very tall and dignified figure, with a sombre, but not unamiable expression of countenance; received me frankly; talked of railroads, machinery, agriculture and other practical questions. Said he hoped I was contented with what his Government had done in the application of my principles, and informed me that his Ministry had resolved upon a further reduction of duties upon iron, cotton, etc." "In the evening Count Revel, Minister of Finance, came in, with whom I had a long discussion upon Free Trade; a sensible man. Speaking to Signor Cibrario upon the subject of the commerce of the Middle Ages in Italy, he said that the

[1] Schwabe, 64.

Richard Cobden : The International Man

principle of Protection, or Colbertism, was unknown; that, however, there were innumerable impediments to industry and internal commerce, owing to the corporations of trades and the custom-houses, which surrounded every little State and almost every little city."[1]

As Cobden passed from Italy into Austrian territory the political atmosphere, of course, was chillier. In Vienna no public demonstration of free-traders was held, and the most interesting occurrence was some personal intercourse with Prince Metternich, whose conversation was found to be "more subtle than profound." "He is probably the last of those State physicians who, looking only to the symptoms of a nation, content themselves with superficial remedies from day to day, and never attempt to probe beneath the surface to discover the source of the evils which afflict the social system. This order of statesmen will pass away with him, because too much light has been shed upon the laboratory of Governments, to allow them to impose upon mankind with the old formulas."[2] In Milan, however, then under Austrian rule, and in Trieste, friends of Free Trade were permitted to give Cobden banquets which were numerously attended.

In a rapid tour through Germany he had two interviews with the King of Prussia, dining with him at Sans Souci, and met several of the high officials and other persons of eminence, among them Baron von Humboldt. Though the political atmosphere was cooler than in Italy or Spain—for the German manufacturers were beginning to press for higher protective tariffs—Cobden received a good deal of attention, not only in Berlin but in Hamburg, Stettin and Danzig, where dinners were improvised in his honour. The following is his account of the Berlin meeting: "In the evening attended a public dinner given to me by about 180 free-traders of Berlin, the mayor of

[1] Diary, quoted "Life," i. pp. 436-7.   [2] Ibid. i. p. 448.

The Tour in Europe, 1846-7

the city in the chair; he commenced the speaking at the second course, and it was kept up throughout the dinner, which was prolonged for nearly three hours. Two-thirds of the meeting appeared to understand my English speech, which was afterwards translated into German by Dr. Ashe. The speeches were rather long and the auditory phlegmatic when compared with an Italian dinner-party. Mr. Warren, the United States Consul at Trieste, made the best speech, in German. Alluding to my tour in France, Spain, Italy and Germany, he said that no English politician of former times, no Chatham, Burke or Fox, could have obtained those proofs of public sympathy in foreign countries which had been offered to me; in their days the politics of one State were considered hostile to others; not only each nation was opposed to its neighbour, but city against city, town against country, class was arrayed against class, and corporations were in hostility to individual rights: he adduced the fact of my favourable reception in foreign countries as a proof of the existence of a broader and more generous view of the interests of mankind." [1]

Not the least interesting part of Cobden's tour was the stretch of six weeks from mid-August to the close of September spent in Russia, chiefly in St. Petersburg, Moscow and Nijni Novgorod. Here again he met the chief financial and commercial authorities, official and other, and discovered the beginnings of foreign business penetration in the shape of English mill managers and German officials. He collected much economic information and some valuable judgments upon Russian conditions which he put to good use in later years. Here is an interesting generalization which sheds much light upon the place of Russia in the economy of Europe.

"Baron Alexander Meyendorff called, chief of a kind of Board of Trade of Moscow, an active-minded and

[1] Diary, quoted "Life," i. p. 448.

Richard Cobden : The International Man

intelligent German, possessing much statistical knowledge about Russian trade and manufactures. . . . He thinks the geographical and climatical features of Russia will always prevent it being anything but a great village, as he termed it, it being a vast, unbroken plain ; there are no varieties of climate or occupation, and, as the weather is intensely cold for half the year, every person wants double the quantity of land which would suffice to maintain him in more genial climates ; as there is no coal, the pine forests are as necessary as his rye fields. Wherever the winter endures for upwards of half the year, the population must as a general rule be thin." [1]

Cobden returned to England on October 11, 1847, having performed a work of a twofold educational value, expounding among influential men in many European countries the gospel of Free Trade and Internationalism, while at the same time filling and fortifying his own mind with a large stock of first-hand knowledge and impressions on which to draw for his great task of teaching a sane foreign policy to his own countrymen. Hardly any other English statesman has taken so much trouble to equip himself for the wider art of statecraft. Cobden knew ten times as much about Europe as did his great antagonist Lord Palmerston, and was fully justified in claiming the authority to which such industry entitled him. There is no note of arrogance in the claim he made in a letter addressed three years later [2] to his West Riding constituents : " Without egotism, I may perhaps say that few Englishmen have had better opportunities of learning the effect of our foreign policy upon other countries than myself. I travelled throughout Europe under the rare circumstances of having free access, at the same time, to the Courts and Ministers and to the popular leaders of the continental States. I came back convinced that the

[1] Diary, quoted "Life," i. p. 454.   [2] July 17, 1850.

The Tour in Europe, 1846-7

interference of our Foreign Office in the domestic affairs of other countries worked injuriously for the interests of those towards whom all my sympathies were attracted—I mean the people—by exciting exaggerated hopes, encouraging premature efforts and teaching reliance upon extraneous aid, when they ought to be impressed with the necessity of self-dependence. I found, too, that the principle of intervention, which we sanctioned by our example, was carried by other Governments in opposition to ours without scruple, and with at least equal success to ourselves." [1]

[1] Schwabe, p. 113.

CHAPTER IV

THE POLICY OF NON-INTERVENTION, 1850-2

COBDEN's return to England from his continental mission closely coincided with the advent of Lord Palmerston to the Foreign Office and the initiation of the active intervention of Great Britain in all parts of the world which marked the Palmerstonian era. A strenuous foreign policy, increased armaments, high expenditure and high taxation, such was the political chain every link of which was to Cobden a separate object of detestation. The long direction of our foreign policy by Lord Palmerston called forth all his powers of criticism and active opposition. Lord Morley summarizes the position by observing that "his political history, from this time down to the year when they both died, is one long antagonism to the ideas which were concentrated in Lord Palmerston."[1]

The early fruits of the policy were our mischievous intervention in the affair of the Spanish Marriage, the dispatch of a British fleet to the Tagus in pursuance of our claim to dictate a form of constitutional government to Portugal, an opposition to the Algerian policy of France, the dispatch of Lord Minto on a roving mission to Italy, and a series of pushful acts in Nicaragua which threatened serious trouble with the United States. The outbreak of revolutionary movements in France, Austria and Germany, the terrible famine and discontent in

[1] "Life," ii. p. 6.

The Policy of Non-Intervention, 1850-2

Ireland, and the Chartist demonstrations in this country under Fergus O'Connor, conspired to give an unusually menacing atmosphere to politics. Cobden's concern with Ireland was deep and intimate, and he early grasped the essential importance of a radical land policy which should place the peasants in effective control of their land and in enjoyment of the fruits it bore.

But his larger thought busied itself with the undermining of the politics which kept the fear of war always alive in Europe and absorbed so large a share of the results of economic progress in armed preparations. In 1849 this thought found political expression in a motion in the House of Commons in favour of international arbitration. "My plan," he writes to George Combe, "does not embrace the scheme of a congress of nations, or imply the belief in the millennium, or demand your homage to the principles of non-resistance. I simply propose that England should offer to enter into an agreement with other countries—France, for instance—binding them to refer any dispute that may arise to arbitration. I do not mean to refer the matter to another sovereign's powers, but that each party should appoint plenipotentiaries in the form of commissioners, with a proviso for calling in arbitrators in case they cannot agree."[1] The House of Commons was not yet educated up to grasping the importance or the practicability of such a proposal. Cobden was not, however, disheartened by a chill reception, and wrote: "Next session I will repeat my proposals, and I will also bring the House to a division upon another and a kindred motion, for negotiating with foreign countries, for stopping any further increase of

[1] Quoted "Life," ii. p. 44. This is an anticipation of what is virtually the policy adopted by the United States Government in 1914 in the conclusion of a series of arbitration treaties with Great Britain, France and other countries.

Richard Cobden : The International Man

armaments and, if possible, for agreeing to a gradual disarmament." [1]

"In fact, I merely wish to bind them to do that before a war which nations always virtually do after it. As for the argument that nations will not fulfil their treaties, that would apply to all international engagements. We have many precedents in favour of my plan. One advantage about it is that it could do no harm; for the worst that could happen would be a resort to the means which has hitherto been the only mode of settling national quarrels. Will you think again upon the subject, and tell me whether there is anything impracticable about it ?"

In August 1849 Cobden attended the Peace Congress at Paris over which Victor Hugo presided, a very successful gathering, which brought him once more into personal touch with his friend Bastiat. The following account of the gathering and its proceedings was given by Charles Sumner, the Chairman of the American delegation at the Congress :—

"The month of August last witnessed at Paris a Congress or Convention of persons from various countries, to consider what could be done to promote the sacred cause of Universal Peace. France, Germany, Belgium, England and the United States were represented by large numbers of men eminent in business, politics, literature, religion and philanthropy. The Catholic Archbishop of Paris and the eloquent Protestant preacher, M. Athanase Coquerel ; Michel Chevalier, Horace Say and Frédéric Bastiat, distinguished political economists ; Émile de Girardin, the most important political editor of France ; Victor Hugo, illustrious in literature ; Lamartine, whose glory it is to have turned the recent French Revolution, at its beginning, into the

[1] Quoted "Life," ii. p. 48.

The Policy of Non-Intervention, 1850-2

path of peace ; and Richard Cobden, the world-renowned British statesman, the unapproachable model of an earnest, humane and practical reformer—all these gave to this august assembly the sanction of their presence or approbation. Victor Hugo, on taking the chair as President, in an address of persuasive eloquence, shed upon the occasion the illumination of his genius ; while Mr. Cobden, participating in all the proceedings, impressed upon them his characteristic common sense.

" The Congress adopted, with entire unanimity, a series of resolutions, asserting the duty of Governments to submit all differences between them to arbitration, and to respect the decisions of arbitrators ; also asserting the necessity of a general and simultaneous disarming, not only as a means of reducing the expenditure absorbed by armies and navies, but also of removing a permanent cause of disquietude and irritation. The Congress condemned all loans and taxes for wars of ambition or conquest. It earnestly recommended the friends of peace to prepare public opinion, in their respective countries, for the formation of a Congress of Nations, to revise the existing International Law and to constitute a High Tribunal for the decision of controversies among nations. In support of these objects, the Congress solemnly invoked the representatives of the Press, so potent to diffuse truth, and also all ministers of religion, whose holy office it is to encourage goodwill among men."

No little part of the success of the arrangements was due to the recently appointed secretary of the Peace Society, the Rev. Henry Richard, to whose name and person a considerable importance attaches. For during the remainder of his public life Mr. Richard was Cobden's most energetic colleague and the recipient of his closest confidence in matters of foreign policy and internationalism. As editor of the *Herald of Peace*, the organ of the

Richard Cobden : The International Man

Society, and, later on, in 1855, one of the editorial writers in the *Morning* and *Evening Star*, he did immense service to the cause of an enlightened policy. In his later years, after Cobden's death, he sat in Parliament, entering it in 1868 as Member for the Merthyr Boroughs, and held his seat for nearly twenty years. His greatest parliamentary achievement consisted in carrying, in 1873, a motion in favour of international arbitration similar to that which Cobden brought forward in 1849. In 1880 he also introduced into the House a motion in favour of gradual disarmament by mutual arrangement, which was accepted in a modified form by the Government.

With Mr. Richard from 1849 onwards until his death Cobden conducted a voluminous correspondence, the greater part of which has been preserved and forms an intimate revelation of the unceasing thought and energy which Cobden brought to bear upon all matters of an international bearing. I propose to draw largely upon this source, hitherto with certain rare exceptions unpublished, taking the matter year by year, and incorporating, by way of enlargement and explanation, other letters and material which have not been made public or which, if published, have not been made accessible to general use.

There is no better illustration of the close outlook which Cobden kept upon the wide and various scope of our world relations than is afforded by his strictures upon the Borneo affair in 1849, and his endeavours to drag into the light of public day a remote piece of wrongdoing which seemed likely to be hushed up.

To Mr. Richard he writes (date November 26th) as follows :—

"Something should be done about that horrid and cowardly butchery on the coast of Borneo. See the

The Policy of Non-Intervention, 1850-2

Daily News of to-day for a letter of mine on the subject, signed 'A Watchful Looker-on.' You might insert it in the *Herald of Peace* or write an article. You will find in the *Illustrated News* a fortnight or three weeks back, a full account of the massacre with pictures of head-roasting by Rajah Brooke's allies. If such cruel and cowardly atrocities as these go unnoticed, we shall sink, as a nation, to the level of the Spaniards of the sixteenth century."

An undated letter of this period adds the following piece of criticism :—

"It seems little short of madness, with India in a blaze, to be embarking in fresh conquests of territory in Borneo. But to that it will come unless Lord Derby be encouraged to resist the cliques and jobbers who will now beset him. There are debts and mortgages and pecuniary interests of all sorts impelling certain parties to incessant activity to get the Government to take to Sarawak."

"Those who are opposed to such a foolish policy, those who wish to avoid a repetition of the wars and crimes of the Cape and of India, all free-traders who really know what their principles mean, will sign the Memorial to Derby."

He follows up (December 10th) by urging Mr. Richard to summon a meeting of the Peace Society to take action.

"I have a letter from Mr. Hume, who is in Norfolk, enclosing a communication for the *Daily News*, which will appear to-morrow upon the Bornean massacre. If he should be in town, I think he would take the chair at your public meeting. It is no longer a matter of choice whether the Peace Society should have a meeting.

Richard Cobden : The International Man

You have been so often called upon that, unless you raise your public protest, your moral power will be injured in other directions."

A duplicate of the longest and most interesting of these letters, addressed to John Bright,[1] appears in Morley's "Life." The agitation on the Borneo affair occupied a good deal of Cobden's attention in the early weeks of 1850, though, as the letter of January 5th shows, other issues of wider import began to open out. There is no more convincing proof of Cobden's penetrating grasp of the directing forces in foreign and imperial policy than his constant exposure of the loan-mongering and debt-collecting operations in which our Government engaged either as principal or agent. The allusion to an attempted Russian loan in a following letter is the discovery of scent which grew very hot a little later on.

His early correspondence with Mr. Richard was largely given to these questions of the pressure of finance in moulding foreign policy.

"*December 6th.*

"You must get Captain Mundy's edition of 'Brooke's Diary.' It was published originally by Captain Keppel, and some horrid passages were omitted by the discretion of his friends; but a new edition by Captain Mundy was published, whilst Brooke was afterwards at home, and those parts were restored—see the first volume, pp. 311, etc., and p. 325—there are details of bloodshed and executions, which, if they had appeared in the first volume, would have checked the sentimental mania which gave Brooke all his powers for evil.

"The above is information which I have from a friend

---

[1] Cobden frequently wrote the same letter on public affairs to two or three correspondents.

The Policy of Non-Intervention, 1850-2

who knows all about the affair from the beginning, and it may be relied on. I have not the book—I fear Gurney will be an obstacle to anything being done. I sometimes doubt whether his obstruction at every step does not more than counteract any advantage derived by this Society from the influence of his name. I don't understand *men of the world*, when they tell us we must rely upon the influence of Christian principles, and boggle at every proposal to enforce them in the current proceedings of Governments and societies. If a monk held such language in his cell, and invited us to rely upon fasts and flagellations, I could see some consistency in it, but when such sentiments come from a millionaire in Lombard Street, they pass my comprehension! If I wished to *do* as little as possible, I should wish to be able to convince myself that I was in this path of duty when I folded my arms, and exhorted people to pray for the triumph of Christian principles. St. Paul *did* something more than that, and so *did* George Fox. See the *Manchester Examiner* of Saturday next for an article which I have sent upon this Borneo affair. The paper will be forwarded to you. I shall be at Leeds and Sheffield the week after next, and will allude to the subject if I can. It shocks me to think what fiendish atrocities may be committed by English arms, without rousing any conscientious resistance at home, provided they be only far enough off, and the victims too feeble to trouble us with their remonstrances or groans. We, as a nation, have an awful retribution in store for us, if Heaven strike a just reckoning, as I believe it does, for wicked deeds, even in this world. There must be a public and solemn protest against this wholesale massacre. The Peace Society and the Aborigines Society are *shams*, if such deeds go unrebuked. We cannot go before the world with clean hands on any other question if we are silent spectators of such atrocities. I will think over and talk over with you the form of my motion."

. . .

"*January* 5, 1850.

"The House meets, I believe, on the 31st, therefore the 30th would be a good day for your Bornean meeting. Gurney's decision is precisely what I should have expected from the first—Lombard Street associations and his family connections have so smothered his natural instincts, and paralysed his individual action, that you must never expect to see him in the public arena upon any question which does not pass current with *The Times* and its readers, or have the sanction of the Prince, or a Bishop. It is a sad pity that so much native goodness should be neutralized by the smiles of fortune. The old Churchmen who penned the Liturgy were wise in making us Episcopalians pray for deliverance 'in the time of our wealth.' The Friends ought to adopt the prayer.

"I have heard that there are agents in London negotiating for a loan for the Russian Government; I am trying to satisfy myself of the correctness of the information. If such a project be publicly launched, you must call a public meeting, and I can make such an appeal as will shame anybody from taking a part in the transaction who may not be lost to all sense of humanity, justice or patriotism."

"*April* 18, 1850.

"Look in the 'money articles' of *The Times* to-day. The creditors of the Spanish Government are talking of petitioning Parliament to collect their debts. We must watch with jealousy the first attempt of this kind, and be prepared to agitate against it. Did you see the report in the paper of the Admiral on the South American

The Policy of Non-Intervention, 1850-2

Station having demanded paying of the debts due to English creditors by the Government of Venezuela? I am anxious to know whether the Stock Exchange Loans are included in the claim. Do you know anybody in the City who would inform us?

"Have you ever thought of collecting some facts showing the demoralizing influence of the barracks in our large towns—the depreciation of the value of property or rather the check to the increase in its value as compared with other parts of the town, their interference with the convenience of the towns by preventing females of respectability and families from taking promenade exercise in the direction of the barracks—the number of beer-shops and brothels in their neighbourhood, the number of cases in which young women are debauched and become charged to the parish with illegitimate children, etc.?

"You might, through your own friends and members of the Society, collect some startling information upon these points."

"*April* 20, 1850.

"Since I wrote, I learn that at the Spanish-Bonds Meeting to which I referred, Baron Rothschild, M.P., spoke against any appeal to our Government for aid, and he told his hearers that if a motion were made in Parliament for aid to force payment from the Spanish Government he should vote against it. This was spoken for the hustings, and is a proof that our anti-loan meetings have told. I am obliged to you for your tract about Indian wars. But in my opinion you ought to bring the cases of Lord Gough and Major Edwards specifically before the public, so as to turn the current which is flowing in their favour."

. . . . .

But the year 1850 was illuminated by a bigger and a graver issue of the same nature in which the character

Richard Cobden : The International Man

of Palmerstonian policy was dramatized, the celebrated Don Pacifico incident. This person was an obscure Levantine Jew whose financial operations had made him so unpopular in Athens that a mob had sacked his house. A naturalized British subject, he called upon our Government to exact compensation. Lord Palmerston willingly espoused his cause and, failing by diplomatic means to bring the Greek Government to reason, directed Admiral Parker to blockade the coast and to seize Greek merchant vessels. Thus Greece was forced to yield. Incidentally the episode caused strained relations with France and the withdrawal of her Ambassador, by reason of the unceremonious treatment accorded to his proposal of "good offices." Palmerston was strongly attacked in Parliament, and a hostile resolution in the Lords, proposed by Lord Stanley, was carried by a majority of twenty-seven. A great historic debate took place in the House of Commons in which Palmerston, enunciating the famous "Civis Romanus" doctrine, won a temporary triumph, and, far more important, established the novel precedent upon which so much of our later financial imperialism has been sustained.

Cobden was quick to realize the profound significance of "the Greek affair," and we find him as early as April 23rd, in a letter to Mr. Richard, urging the suitability of the Don Pacifico case for international arbitration.

"It seems that there is, if we may judge by the article in to-day's *Times*, a prospect of still further delay about the Greek affair. Would it not be well to draw up a memorial to the Prime Minister or else a petition to Parliament upon the subject? The object, of course, should be to show the propriety of submitting the whole affair to the arbitration of disinterested parties. It is just the case for arbitration. And the memorial should speak

The Policy of Non-Intervention, 1850-2

in terms of strong condemnation of a system of international policy which leaves the possibility of two nations being brought to such a state of hostility upon questions of such insignificant importance. Here is a dispute about a few thousand pounds, or of personal insult, matters which might be equitably adjusted by two or three impartial individuals of average intelligence and character, for the settlement of which a fleet of line-of-battle ships has been put in requisition, and the entire commerce of a friendly nation largely engaged in trade with our own people has been for months subjected to interruption. It should be stated that apart from the outrage which such proceedings are calculated to inflict upon the feelings of humanity and justice, they must tend to bring diplomacy into disrepute. Without offering any opinion on the merits of the question, you should pray that our Government should agree at once to submit the whole matter to the absolute decision of arbitrators mutually appointed, and it might be added that this case affords a strong argument for entering upon a general system of arbitration treaties, by which such great inconveniences and dangers springing from such trivial causes may be averted for the future.

"It seems to me that this is an occasion on which you might frame a very *practical* memorial, and thus put the present system in the wrong in the eyes of even those men of business and politicians who do not go with you on principle."

Apart from his unceasing attempts in Parliament to secure a revision and reduction of military and naval expenditure as an integral part of a pacific foreign policy, two other matters of international import occupied Cobden during this year. One was the preparation for the Great Exposition, of which towards the close of this year he was appointed one of the Commissioners. The following extract from a letter from Mrs. Cobden to Mrs. Schwabe, dated December 27th, relates to this appointment :

"Do you take much interest in the Exposition of Arts and Manufactures which is to take place in 1850 in London? We are likely to be pretty much in the thick of it, for Mr. Cobden is appointed one of the Commissioners of twenty, and the Duke of Richmond is one of his colleagues ! ! ! I am told that several lists of names were presented to the Prince and that Mr. Cobden's name appeared in them all." [1]

In this Exposition Cobden saw a mighty instrument of international goodwill and took up his duties with great enthusiasm. How the Greek affair rankled is, however, seen in the earliest of the letters which show him launched upon his new interest :

"If you present a memorial about Greece, it must now be of a retrospective character, as I suppose the affair is finished, disgracefully I think to ourselves.

"With reference to the memorial about warlike instruments in the Exposition, I would advise you to send it to the Prince in the usual way, but would not press him for an interview. I know that he is sorely perplexed by the disaffection of a portion of the aristocracy towards his (for them) too generous and philanthropic scheme. We of the Peace Party ought to give him every possible support and seek to avoid cause of embarrassment to him. Therefore, I would advise you not to call for an interview but to content yourselves by recording in a memorial to him your opinion against exhibiting weapons of human destruction. At the same time I hope you will be not

[1] "Reminiscences," p. 150.

The Policy of Non-Intervention, 1850-2

sparing in your expressions of approval of his truly magnificent project. . . .

"I intend to move for a return of the ships, men, guns, etc., employed in collecting this miserable £10,000 from the Government of Greece. What a satire upon our modern system of diplomacy!"

In the latter months of this year a good many letters to Mr. Richard are concerned with the proposed visit to London of the great French thinker, writer and statesman, M. Lamartine. At first some hopes were entertained that he would appear and speak at an Exeter Hall demonstration of a definitely "peace" nature. But the bird was shy, as the following letters show:

"*September* 13, 1850.

"Lamartine is in an uneasy position, personally and politically. He is a disappointed man, if not a ruined one; and his visit to London will probably have for its object to try to retrieve his embarrassed fortunes, and regain some of his political prestige. The Peace Party does not, at present, offer him a sufficiently firm or lofty pedestal from which to harangue the world. At least this is probably his opinion. He is not a man of fixed principles, and is incapable of continuous logical action. There is quite as much danger as security in such allies. In fact, I am losing all confidence in men of impulsive temperament, and cannot inspire myself with faith, hope or charity towards the mere *phraseurs*."

"*September* 14, 1850.

"As soon as I received your note apprising me of the decision of M. Lamartine not to accept an invitation to meet the Peace Party at Exeter Hall, I made some arrangements which preclude my visiting London or appearing in public for some weeks to come. I am

Richard Cobden : The International Man

sorry, therefore, that I cannot meet M. Lamartine at the London Tavern on Wednesday. It does not appear very clearly from your note what is the immediate object of the demonstration. If it be a national one, it must fail, from want of time to make the preparations. I do not see how it can be private, since his speech is to be published; and besides many of those who will attend may, like myself, be personally unacquainted with him. But what *public* object do you hope to gain by so ill-defined if not equivocal a demonstration. It does not identify him with the Peace Congress movement. May not it possibly identify those who assist at it with something else ? I am puzzled, I confess. Nor has any letter come from Mr. Gilpin to enlighten my ignorance."

"*September* 18, 1850.

"If you can elicit from Lamartine a letter expressive of sympathy for the Peace Movement, you will do well. His utterances, whether by voice or pen, like the trumpet of an Archangel, are heard and felt by all the nations of the civilized world. Nor will you run any risk in identifying yourselves with his *past* conduct. He behaved in the truest spirit of Christian heroism during the terrible ordeal of the Paris revolution, and for the stand he then made in the cause of peace and humanity, he is entitled to our lasting gratitude. But for the *future* I tremble at identifying ourselves with any one whose impulses are constantly taking the bit of reason between their teeth and running away with them beyond the region of logic."

An undated fragment of a letter sheds a curious light upon Lamartine's " business " object in his visit :

"When at Frankfort, I heard something about Lamartine's intention to come to England to try to

The Policy of Non-Intervention, 1850-2

interest people here in a project for colonizing his domain (lately given to him by the Sultan) in Asia Minor. The attempt, if made, must fail, and if openly launched would not, I think, increase his moral influence. If the land were under any Christian government it might be worth consideration. I mention this privately for your own information, and that you may let any others into the secret whom you think proper. I fear his affairs are involved to an extent not even suspected by his friends, and although he is making a glorious fight for independence, I fear he will be beaten. Anything that can be legitimately done to help him by our friends in England it is desirable to do, but no feelings of enthusiasm for the man, or gratitude for his exertions in the cause of peace, ought to tempt any of our influential friends to give their *names* to a project which will pretty certainly end in disappointment to all who are tempted to join it."

How close an eye Cobden kept on the continental situation is illustrated from the following letter dealing " faithfully " with the opportunism of the daily Press. The German situation had grown critical. For Austria, having now overcome the revolts of 1848 in Hungary and other territories, summoned the Diet of the Germanic Confederation over which she presided, in order to organize resistance against the Prussian claims for hegemony. Two rival organizations formed themselves, and for a short time the danger of war was real, until finally Prussia gave way and the former Constitution of 1815 was restored and accepted by all parties. Other letters of this year show the deep concern which Cobden always manifested lest his stress on principles should lead him to be regarded as a " mere idealist " or a " sentimentalist."

Richard Cobden : The International Man

"*December* 2, 1850.

"There is an article in Saturday's *Daily News* which made me rub my eyes and look again at the heading of the page to see if it could really be that paper which was saying directly the opposite of what it said exactly a fortnight before, when commenting upon the Wrexham meeting. *Then* we were doing great service, *now* we ought to discontinue the agitation ! What has altered the case ? The state of Europe was the same precisely on the 16th as the 30th. The danger of war in Germany was more imminent on the former than the latter date. This paper has more power to injure us than has *The Times*, because it is supposed to be honestly with us. It must be repudiated and exposed by the Peace Party. I wish you would get the two articles, that of the 16th or 17th, and that of Saturday—compare them—make extracts of the contradictory passages, and let them be published somehow or somewhere. The editor ought to be made to swallow the leek himself, and probably the best way would be if you were to write a letter to him containing a couple of short extracts from the rival articles, and ask which is to be understood as expressive of the real opinion of the *Daily News*, and ask what are the public circumstances which have wrought such a sudden change—that it cannot have been the warlike demonstration in Germany, for they were more imminent and threatening on the 16th than the 30th. We are bound in self-defence to expose this shocking apostasy. For my own part I consider the *Daily News* henceforth utterly untrustworthy. You may substitute *The Times* for it in your office again with my full consent whenever you please. I shall write privately to Smith, the proprietor, if I can get his address. It is Palmerston influence which is at work, and which I have seen for

The Policy of Non-Intervention, 1850-2

some time. Will the time ever come when an *honest* daily paper will pay ?

"By the way, if there be truth in the report of an intended loan to Prussia in the City, we are bound to oppose it at a public meeting, otherwise we shall be open to remark. Besides, I am prepared to show that standing armies are just as incompatible with liberty in Prussia as Austria."

"*December* 3, 1850.

"Circulars are being issued in favour of a bazaar for the '*League of Brotherhood*.' I do not know exactly with whom it originates, but I venture to repeat an opinion which I expressed last year that the *name* is not well chosen. This morning, at Mr. Schwabe's breakfast-table, the subject was discussed. Both my wife and Mrs. Schwabe objected to the 'League of Brotherhood' as being a name calculated to throw ridicule or odium upon the effort. *Brotherhood* is 'fraternity,' a word dragged through the mire by red Republicans and Socialists, and to adopt it in this country is only to burden ourselves with a needless disadvantage in addition to the abundant difficulties we have already to contend against. I would, therefore, strongly urge our friends, whoever they may be, to call it a Peace Bazaar, or Peace Congress Bazaar.

"By the way, the newspapers report that the *Democratic Party* in America intend to put forward as their candidate for the next presidency General Houston, the conqueror of Texas, and that the choice of the *Whigs* will be General Scott, the invader of Mexico. If this be true, it will be very discouraging, and prove that the democracy of the New World are impregnated with the war-vice of the old ; and it will make me doubt whether the best field of usefulness for our devoted friend Elihu Burritt would not be in the midst of his own countrymen. A well-organized Peace Party in the United States might deter both political factions from putting up successful warriors for the highest *civil* offices.

"What a pity it is that we have no honest daily paper to turn to account the present enormous folly of the German Governments, by showing up the loss and ruin brought upon the people by their prodigious military efforts, all to end in a telegraphic messenger from Manteuffel to Schwarzenburg, inviting a private conference at Olmutz where everything is arranged! But I am not quite sure that we have seen the full effects in Prussia of this calling out of the Landwehr. Probably the terms of the peace if not very favourable to Prussia may lead to internal convulsions."

"*December* 18, 1851.

"I quite agree with you that the way to put down duelling is to put down the conventional cowardice which drives men in nine cases out of ten against their will to stand up to be shot at. . . .

"It is quite useless his troubling himself to write to Lord John Russell about expelling Members of Parliament who fight duels. For ten years, during which I have been in the House, I do not remember to have heard of a duel amongst its Members. It is no longer a practical evil in England."

CHAPTER V

PALMERSTONIAN FOREIGN POLICY

During a large part of the next year (1851) Cobden was chiefly concerned with home affairs, especially the movement which Bright and others were directing for Parliamentary Reform, while the detailed work connected with the arrangements of the Great Exposition engaged much of his energy. But his correspondence with Mr. Richard shows that he was still keeping his eyes open for opportunities of peace work, though two interesting letters written late in the year indicate very clearly the divergence of his own practical peace policy from that of the Quaker absolutists in the Peace Society.

The Kaffir War, which had been smouldering for the last two years in Cape Colony, had taken a more dangerous turn at the end of 1850, owing to a murderous outbreak of the Kosas, and for more than two years a strong force of soldiers, burghers and auxiliaries, was engaged in slowly tracking down the enemy, who were eventually starved into submission. Cobden lays his finger accurately upon one perilous aspect of the provocative policy in our Colonies, where imperial force is profitably utilized for interested colonial objects.

The visit of Kossuth to this country in October was an event of considerable importance and of some embarrassment. Palmerston's friends contended that the withdrawal of the joint demand made by Russia and

Richard Cobden : The Internatioual Man

Austria upon Turkey, for the extradition of the Hungarian leader and his friends who had taken refuge in that country, was due to the vigorous policy of Palmerston in ordering the British Fleet to the mouth of the Dardanelles. Cobden, however, points out in a letter to Mr. Bright [1] (November 13th) that Palmerston himself made no such claim : " You will find on referring to Palmerston's speech on Roebuck's Greek Debate, that in speaking of the entry of our fleet into the Dardanelles, he himself informed us that the Emperor of Russia withdrew his demand for the extradition of the refugees on the arrival of the Sultan's envoy remonstrating against the demand, and before any intelligence had reached Petersburg of the views of the English Government." Cobden's satisfaction at the great reception given to Kossuth is intensified by the slap in the face given to *The Times*, which had conducted an elaborate campaign of vilification against the Hungarian. Cobden seized the opportunity of the incident to expose more clearly than before the value of his non-intervention policy. It did not mean that one nation should not express its opinion about the conduct of another nation, and on occasion make formal remonstrance, but that armed intervention was wrong and unnecessary.

"I remember at the time making the calculation and finding that the newspapers of London and Paris, giving one unanimous expression for all parties and every shade of opinion, of indignation at the attempt of the Northern Powers to violate the Law of Nations in the persons of Kossuth and his companions, reached Petersburg at the same time with the Turkish envoy, and I felt convinced, and I said as much in the House afterwards, that it was that expression of *opinion* from

---

[1] Quoted "Life," ii. p. 105.

Palmerstonian Foreign Policy

Western Europe which scared the despots instantly from their prey. And you are quite right; it is opinion and opinion only that is wanting to establish the principle of non-intervention as a Law of Nations, as absolutely as the political refugee in a third and neutral country is protected now by the Law of Nations."

The following passages are from letters of this year to Mr. Richard:

"*January* 26, 1851.

"I have no means of knowing whether the statement inserted in the *Daily News* about concentrating a great body of troops round the metropolis be correct. But I can easily believe that the old Duke is capable of such a folly, and that the Whigs would not oppose him. Your best plan will be to write to some of your correspondents in the neighbourhood of London, as for instance at Uxbridge, Brentford, *Hounslow*, Kingston, etc., and inquire whether anything is being done to secure quarters for more troops in those towns. If it turn out true, you ought to get up an agitation against it, not only in London, but in all the neighbouring places."

"*March* 13, 1851.

"I don't like the wording of the enclosed resolution. It appears to reserve the alternative of war. But the letter of your correspondent is very interesting as showing the feeling of the leading men at Washington. If anybody but Lord Palmerston were at the Foreign Office, something of the same kind might be done with our ministers. But I have not the slightest confidence in him. I doubt the policy of interfering in the Kaffir business until we have more authentic news. The proper cure for these recurring wars is to let the Colonists bear the brunt of them. This must be done

Richard Cobden : The International Man

by first giving them the powers of self-government, and then throwing on them the responsibility of their own policy. They would then be very careful to treat the neighbouring savages with justice. At present it is the interest of the Colonists to provoke the natives into war, because it leads to a most profitable expenditure of British money.

"In my remarks upon the Navy Estimates on Monday evening, I gave notice of my intention to move a resolution in the House in favour of an explanation with France, with the view to promote a diminution of armaments. This will not go your whole length, but I should be glad to see the principle recognized that it is the policy and duty of a Government in these days to discourage the system of rival warlike preparations."

"*June* 13, 1851.

"I would not take any notice of Girardin. It will be only turned against you. He does not, like Boudet, profess to represent the Peace cause in the Chamber. His inconsistency will surprise nobody that knows him. It is true that troops have been congregated round London, and I believe all parties concerned in it are now ashamed of it. But that is the very reason why you ought to expose it in your paper. The old Duke is at the bottom of it all. The only disturbance created has been by a Captain (Somerset) in one of the Regiments which were brought up from the country to keep the peace. Could you not get from some of your friends particulars of the number of soldiers billeted in some of the neighbouring towns? The effect upon the morals of the towns will not be very favourable.

"Some papers upon the barrack system ought to be

published, showing the evil effects of barracks upon their neighbourhood: the check they put to the growth of towns in their vicinity; the great number of beershops, public-houses, and brothels in their neighbourhood; the reluctance of respectable people to take exercise near them; the comparatively low value of land in their vicinity as compared with other parts of the town."

"*September* 14, 1851.

"Did you observe that in Signor Isturitz, the Spanish minister's communication to *The Times*, defending the execution of the fifty-two American sympathizers at the Havana, he justified the course pursued by the Cuban authorities by citing the example of Rajah Brooke! Here is the extract; pray put it on record, for future reference in the *Herald*. What a compliment to us to be publicly quoted as less clement than the Spaniards! Verily we are a nation of Pharisees, to pretend to be shocked at the minor atrocities of other people and to boggle at no amount of butchery ourselves."

"*September* 19, 1851.

"I send you by this post copy of correspondence which has passed between the Liverpool Peace Society and Lord Palmerston. I have written to Mr. Cooke to say I regret that he should have *thanked* his lordship *in advance* for having shown a disposition to forward the object of the Peace Society, when he plainly tells them in his answer that he will do nothing! Then, as I said to Mr. C., it is to be regretted that he did not send a rejoinder, for his lordship laid himself open to a ready answer. It seems according to his argument that although an increase of the French armament is always held a good reason for increasing ours, yet its diminution does not apply in the same proportion! By the way, what an answer is this letter of the Foreign Minister to such men as Brotherton & Co., who bellow open-mouthed at any one who does not show implicit confidence in his good intentions. I am firmly persuaded that you would have more chance of success with Lord Aberdeen in office, who is capable of an earnest conviction, which is the very opposite of the character of his supple and frivolous rival. *But by dint of dexterous handling of the Press*, Lord P. has contrived to pass himself off upon the Liberal Party, and win the Peace Party, as their devoted friend, and I honestly believe he laughs at his dupes.

"Here is a good article from last Saturday's London *Examiner*. That paper has, with the *Athenæum*, shown a courageous adherence to its convictions—affording quite a contrast to the dastardly *Daily News*. By the way, *entre nous*, I got a letter from a new manager of the latter, Mr. Salisbury, soliciting my co-operation, and offering to make the *D.N.* the organ of the Progressive Party. In reply I told him that I ceased to take in the *D.N.* more than six months ago, and that for the last month I had not seen a copy of it, *and I told the reason why*, not forgetting the backsliding on the Peace Question, and the cowardly desertion on the Borneo Question, and stating once for all my determination to have nothing to do with a paper that was a mere instrument in the hands of the Foreign Minister. I suppose by his writing to me that the paper is not doing well—how could it?"

"*November* 9, 1851.

"I agree with you to the letter in all that you say about non-intervention. I subscribe to every word

Palmerstonian Foreign Policy

of Girardin's logical speech (I wish he were half as consistent in action as in logic), and I venture to say in reply to the question with which he closes his argument, that if England, America and France would proclaim such a law for *themselves* no other Power would dare to violate it. This was my argument at Winchester. Kossuth in his speech had called upon us to say 'Stop' (the word was *his*) to Russia. In my remarks, following him, I said that if England and America would first observe the principle themselves, they might afterwards say 'Stop' to Russia, and the word would *then* have as much force as if uttered with the voice of a thousand cannon. My remarks were a tribute to moral power, the power of truthful example. *The Times* of course perverted it; and such is the terrible power of that paper that I dare say many of my own friends were misled by it. Whilst I go heartily with you on the principle of non-intervention, it appears that this was the proper occasion for public men to proclaim the principle, when we had a guest who inspired our sympathy and respect and who was himself the victim of Russian interference. But there is another reason why a lover of freedom should come forward in support of the demonstration in honour of Kossuth in the attempt made by the most powerful organs of opinion to assassinate him morally on his arrival here. The very honour of our country was at stake in giving him a hearty welcome from the moment that the partisans of Russia and Austria endeavoured to make British soil the scene of his martyrdom.

"This is altogether apart from the Peace Question. But I am afraid your Peace Society has not shown cool judgment in publishing its address. Two questions are mixed up in that address—that of intervention, and

Richard Cobden : The International Man

that of non-resistance; there was an admirable opportunity for making good the former argument, but I must say I think mortal man never chose a worse moment for inculcating the principle of non-resistance. Because, if ever there was an unjust resort to violence it was on the part of both Austria and Russia in their assault upon the Hungarians, who sought only to carry out their own administrative reforms in a constitutional way. It is true the latter were worsted, but that will not satisfy those who were not before in favour of non-resistance that the Hungarians were in the wrong in defending themselves. And then your address lectures the defeated party without a word of censure on the aggressors. I must say that I do think you could not have put forth your peace principle in a way more calculated to give a handle to those who charge you with inviting oppression and injustice. It will, I fear, put all who have been co-operating in the Peace Movement latterly in a false position. There is a great difficulty in acting together on any great public question, unless we are agreed in principle— but I had hoped the Peace Congress party had hit upon an expedient by which men could combine for measures of alleviation, even if they did not all hope for the total extirpation of a great evil. For this end I have always endeavoured to avoid being brought into collision with the 'Friends' principle, and I had thought they were similarly minded towards those who were, like myself, labouring to give practical effect as far as they could to their doctrines. But I doubt whether it will not be necessary for the two Societies to make a more clear avowal than they have hitherto done of their principles. This will be, I think, required not only in justice to those who do not subscribe to the non-resistance principles, but also to those who do. I

Palmerstonian Foreign Policy

fear this may, perhaps, lead to a secession of the Quaker party, and if so I should despair of keeping alive the other movement. I do not presume to say that in the end the uncompromising policy may not be the best; but I am quite sure you will agree with me in saying that if the agitation is to be based exclusively upon the non-resistance principle, it will cease to occupy its present position in the domain of practical politics. I venture to say there are not fifty thousand people in these realms who will sympathize heartily with the first part of your address on the present Kossuth excitement. It may all be true nevertheless, and my remarks must not be supposed as implying anything more than my own opinion as to the policy at this moment of saying so."

"*November* 18, 1851.

"I do not know that anything can be done, that may not be as likely to do harm as good; but it appears to me, with more and more force, upon further reflection, that what is called the 'peace party' are in a false position, and that unless some explanation be given, and some distinct movement be made by the *Peace Congress* Committee, the practical agitation carried on latterly, under the auspices of the latter, must be seriously injured, and the cause itself resume again the position in which it was placed before the Peace Congress at Brussels was thought of. That position was not of a character ever to allow the Peace Party to be more than a passive asserter of the doctrine of non-resistance; because, where that principle is put forward as the bond of union, it admits of no agitation or discussion on secondary details. It merely inculcates this lesson—'don't resist,' and for those who adopt the principle, war is at an end. But the object of the Peace Congress movement, as I understood it, was to

Richard Cobden : The International Man

put forward some plans, the advocacy of which might prepare men's minds, step by step, to look upon the abolition of war as a possible thing. The advocacy of non-intervention in the domestic concerns of other countries was one of these modes. The practical object I have in view in writing is to ask you whether you think it would be well to have a meeting to reiterate our arguments in favour of that principle, called under the auspices of the Peace Congress Committee. It would, I think, be necessary to explain at such a meeting the distinct though not divergent movement of the Peace Society and the Peace Congress; the only stipulation on the part of the former being that nothing should be said or done to compromise their principle. It would not be possible to avoid the topic of the day—Kossuth's visit—but it might be improved upon for the advancement of our agitation. Again I say I don't know whether such a meeting would do good or harm, but we are in a false position."

"December 20, 1851.

"*Now* the French business has turned everything topsy-turvy again, and *that* occupies the front ground of peace questions. By the way, there is good to be got out of it. In the first place, there is a capital illustration of the *use* of an army in a Constitutional State. It is now seen that a standing army can be used by even a mountebank or adventurer, to imprison its own generals, lock up a legislature, and shoot *broad-cloth* citizens in four-story mansions! These are *new* uses of a standing army, which will do more to cure the mania for the military than the slaughtering of tens of thousands of men in wooden shoes or blouses. The *bourgeoisie* have found that the extinguisher has taken fire!"

Palmerstonian Foreign Policy

The year 1852 was signalized by a fresh revival of the alarm of a French invasion, a hasty application of the new Militia Law and a demand for enlarged expenditure both upon the Army and the Navy. The occasion was the *coup d'état* by Napoleon "the Little," by which the office of President to which he had been elected four years before was forcibly converted into "a veiled despotism," first limited by the Constitution of January 1852 to ten years, a few months later converted into perpetuity. The new war-panic, the second of Cobden's "Three Panics," was thus initiated, and the martial ceremonials and sentiments roused by the death and funeral of "the old Duke" in September of the same year poured fuel on the flames. A good deal of Cobden's correspondence with Mr. Richard turned on these topics, while among the imperialistic issues which were never lost sight of, the invasion of Burma and the Rangoon atrocities were matter for his activity both in the House and in the country.

"*January* 13, 1852.

"Men's minds seem to be again in such a state of confusion and trepidation that I fear they are more open to the influence of a vague terror than of cool arguments. I have received many letters from people of whom I had thought better things (George Grote amongst the rest), urging the necessity of increasing our armaments as a protection against the mad designs of Louis Napoleon. It is the old folly over again. In 1847, after seventeen years' reign of the "Napoleon of Peace" and in the midst of the *entente cordiale*, there was a cry for more armaments as a protection against a French invasion. I began my peace agitation by denouncing that attempt. The people refused to have an increase to the income tax, and so there was no

Richard Cobden : The International Man

augmentation of the armaments. In a few months afterwards came the French Revolution, and the Republic, and then folks exclaimed, 'Cobden is a pretty fellow for a prophet. He promised peace, and see what has happened. The French have taken the reins in their own hands, and we shall see them overrun Europe again!' Well, we have had nearly four years of the Republic, and *The Times* and other organs of opinion *now* tell us that never were the relations of the two countries so amicable as during the Republic. 'But now,' say they, 'what will Cobden say, now Louis Napoleon will make an attack on us to avenge his uncle's defeat at Waterloo?' I say again, France will not attack us, if we let her alone. So far from the late election of Louis Napoleon being a warlike demonstration on the part of the French people—it exhibits them, in my opinion, in the very opposite and degrading attitude of giving up every right and privilege of free citizens to the President, on condition that he protects them from disorder and leaves them in peace and quietness to follow their avocations. It is this feeling which prompts M. Sallandrouze and the industrials of Paris to offer their felicitations to the usurping President, and this is the cause of the *rentes* rising 15 per cent. But the prospect of a war with England would convulse their industry, increase their taxes, and diminish their income, whilst the *rentes* would fall to 50. Would this rally the taxpayers, the fund-holders, the industrials, or any other class round the President?

"These shallow and foolish people who talk so glibly about the French going to war with England and making a descent on our shores, seem to have no idea that France is second only to ourselves in the extent of her manufacturing operations and her foreign commerce.

Palmerstonian Foreign Policy

There is no country, excepting England, so dependent for the employment of its people upon foreign commerce, and the supply of raw materials from abroad, which would be interrupted if not wholly destroyed by a war with England, to the destruction of the industry of millions of her population. Yet these silly people who prate about France making a buccaneering descent upon our shores seem to think that she has no more interest in preserving peace than had the ancient Northmen of the sixth century. I wonder if they trouble themselves to take a peep at the French manufactures in the Exhibition.

"By the way, into what inconsistencies do these alarmists stumble. When we advocated an international reduction of armaments, we were told that the armies of the Continent were not kept up by the Governments for offensive or defensive operations against their neighbours, but to repress their own subjects. But now, when half the Continent is in a state of siege, we are told we must prepare against an attack from these same Powers. Again, we were met with the argument that large standing armies are favourable to the preservation of peace—that 'to maintain peace we must be prepared for war.' But now we are told that Louis Napoleon *must* go to war in order to find employment for his troops. I should not be surprised at any folly that may be committed by the old Duke and our weak Government. They talk of a circle of fortifications round London. And at the same time we have a large squadron lying in the Tagus, and line-of-battle ships enough lying useless on distant stations to form a continuous line within hailing distance from Plymouth to the Thames. The Americans have not one line-of-battle ship in commission. There is no cure for all this waste and folly but in the galling load of taxation which it entails upon us. And you are doing wisely in keeping public opinion alive to the cost and iniquitous character of the Kaffir War. Time must work its cure.

"I really hardly know how to recommend you to take any course of action upon the peace question generally, with a view to the general election, in the present confused state of the public mind. But let a peaceful issue result from the present French Revolution, or rather usurpation, and then we shall have the alarmists once more on the hip, and I hope they will be discredited with the public generally; although I must say the said public are gluttons in gullibility. My own opinion is that France is more anxious for peace with England, than we are for peace with her. Time will show—I can't tell you whether it is likely we shall have another election this year, but should say it is very probable."

"*May* 14, 1852.

"I have given notice of a motion upon the subject of the annexation of Pegue, and if I could secure a day for the discussion it would be very useful and important. But I have had my usual bad luck at a ballot and stand third on the notices for June 7th. Still I must be prepared to take my chance; and shall be obliged by your letting me have all the facts you collected for your speeches upon the Burmese War, and any other aid in your power."

"*August* 10, 1852.

"There is little doubt but you are right as to the letter about our bloody work at Rangoon, etc. It is upon a par with the doings of our forefathers in the East. I was told by an East India Director that the war was totally unnecessary, that it grew out of the

Palmerstonian Foreign Policy

violence of the naval envoy; that if a civilian had been employed hostilities would not have begun at all; and that Lord Dalhousie disapproved of the conduct of the Admiral in seizing the ship-of-war. But nobody of any authority will publicly disavow the acts of these fighting men. *Esprit de corps*, the spirit of nationality, and the great social sway of the military class, all tend to sweep us more and more into the martial vortex. If God really rules this earth (as I solemnly believe He does) upon the principle of a self-acting retributive justice, then British doings in India and China involve a serious reckoning with us or our children. And assuredly the day of reckoning will come."

"*August* 24, 1852.

"In a *weekly* overland *China Mail* which has just reached me I find an allusion made in a leading article to another article in the *Bengal Hurkarn* (which, however, does not appear in the columns of the *China Mail*) exposing the pompous pretensions of our fighting men in Burma. In fact, the bulletins of General Godwin in last Saturday's *Times* are worthy of Bombasto Furioso himself *when one compares the talk and the results*. It is quite clear that our so-called battles with these people are nothing but *battues*. They have no more chance against our 64-pound red-hot shot and other infernal *improvements* in the art of war than they would in running a race on their roads against our railways. War has become, like manufacturing and industrial rivalry, very much a competition of capital, skill and chemical and mechanical discovery. Don't forget that the day on which we commenced the war with a bombardment of shot, shells and rockets, which made an eyewitness remark that the natives must have thought it an onslaught of devils, was *Easter Sunday*!

Richard Cobden : The International Man

"I don't know whether any of the papers notice the fact that our ships-of-war being sent to the coast of America furnishes the greatest difficulty in the way of our negotiations with the Government at Washington. Amongst the vessels sent is a ship of the line. The Americans have not one line-of-battle ship afloat in commission. Here, then, one would say, is an occasion for profiting by our superior naval force. No, on the contrary, it is the source of positive weakness. 'Withdraw that insulting force,' say the senators and the newspapers of the United States, 'or we will not negotiate with you.' And so much do we feel the justice of this rebuke that we are hastily yielding the whole question at issue. Where, then, is the use of our great naval armaments? When the Militia Debate was proceeding, I urged the propriety, if we were really in danger of being invaded, of bringing our large vessels into the Channel. 'If you do that,' said Sir J. Baring, 'it will be regarded as a menace by France!' What, then, are we to do with this enormous force, maintained at so much cost? Where shall we hide it? Or is it to be only brought into play against a weak Power such as an Egyptian Pasha or a King of Greece? Alas, then are we bullies to the weak, and cowards to the powerful!"

"*September* 8, 1852.

"I think your article in the *Herald of Peace* upon the Burmese War ought to be reprinted for distribution amongst M.P.'s and influential people. I would, however, cut out all extraneous matter, suppress the animus as far as possible, and give the facts as you have collected them from the Parliamentary Paper. It is a very strong case. The difficulty is to get anybody to look on the *enemy's* side of the question when

Palmerstonian Foreign Policy

the fighting has begun; and then there is always the lurking bribe in the minds of *all* that the game of spoliation, though often foully played, is yet *profitable*. I often wish I had the leisure to do justice to the argument which is always uppermost in my mind, that the modern application of the principles of political economy has destroyed the motive of self-interest which formerly tempted us to wars of conquest. I *could* turn the batteries against the L. s. d. argument most successfully."

"*September* 29, 1852.

"Somebody has sent me the accompanying. Is it possible that Dr. Cumming has uttered these sentiments in the pulpit? When he talks of 'beating back from his country the oppressor when he comes,' he falls into the common fallacy that Wellington's wars were defensive. In my opinion, nothing is clearer than that the whole of the war from 1793 to 1815 was of our own seeking, that it was in fact a war of kings and oligarchs to put down democratic opinions. But, whatever may have been its origin, certain it is that after the Battle of Trafalgar, when Nelson destroyed the French Navy, we were as safe from molestation from Napoleon as if we had been in another planet. Yet it was *after* that naval victory that Wellington made his descent on the shores of the Peninsula, and we spent from that time four to five hundred millions on continental objects.

"By the way, I wish we had a map, on Mercator's projection, with a red spot printed upon those places by land and sea where we have fought battles since 1688. It would be seen at a glance that we have (unlike any other nation under the sun) been fighting foreign enemies upon every part of the earth's surface

Richard Cobden : The International Man

excepting our own territory—thus showing that we have been the most warlike and aggressive people that ever existed. The only way to begin to turn the tables upon such people as the enclosed is by starting with the theory that the English nation has had its energies perverted to war purposes more than any other peoples. By starting from the time of our great aristocratic revolution, it will by and by be seen that the aristocracy has converted the combativeness of the English race to its own sinister ends, and by and by *peace* will become allied to the course of democratic freedom. The history of England must be rewritten —especially the history of the last century."

"*October* 4, 1852.

"We shall do no good until we can bring home to the conviction and consciences of men the fact that, as in the slave-trade we had surpassed in guilt the whole world, so in foreign wars we have been the most aggressive, quarrelsome, warlike and bloody nation under the sun. If the people can in justice show that their Government has been at fault—that their native energies have been perverted to bad purposes by the ruling classes for their own advantage—I care not. But the fact is there, and unless repentance and amendment follow we shall, as a nation, be no exception to the divine law that ' they who take the sword shall perish by the sword.'

"As respects the origin of the last great French War, the best documents to read are those published amongst the ' State Papers' in the *Annual Register* for 1792-3. The ' Pictorial History of England,' vol. 3, p. 273 and following pages (although the work is written in a Tory sense at that time), gives you a good many facts. But one is sufficient—*we withdrew our Ambassador from Paris in August* 1792, *the French*

Palmerstonian Foreign Policy

Minister remained here till January following, and was then driven away on the death of the French King (we having set the example of king-killing a hundred and fifty years before). See Sir Jas. Mackintosh's 'Vindiciæ Galicæ,' and the language of all the liberal politicians of the day.

"October 12, 1852.

"I saw the enclosed and took a note of it. It may or may not mean anything; but of one thing I am assured, that, if the European Governments were to meet together for the purpose of promoting a reduction of armaments, there is not one which would enter upon such a movement with less earnestness or sincerity than our own. You may make what use you please of my communication about the opposition to the Anti Corn-Law League tracts. Buckinghamshire is a bad county in which to have a trial—but you should see that the bill-sticker be well defended. Much depends upon the talent of the Counsel employed in such a case. I confess I am astonished at the impudence of the Government in entering upon such a crusade. Are there not instances of similar handbills having been put forth long ago, in opposition to recruiting for the Regular Army? I would advise you to get the advice of the longest-headed and soundest-hearted lawyer you can find. If we can foil them completely in this attempt, good will come out of it; but on the other hand, if beaten, there will be found, I fear, some snobs even in our ranks who will say, 'I told you so.' If properly managed, I cannot see that anything but good can come out of it."

"HOUSE OF COMMONS (*undated*), 1852.

"I read carefully through the first of the Parliamentary Papers on the Burmese War. I was amazed at the

Richard Cobden : The International Man

case ; I blushed for my country, and the very blood in my veins tingled with indignation at the wanton disregard of all justice and decency which our proceedings towards that weak country exhibited. The violence and wrongs perpetrated by Pizarro or Cortes were scarcely veiled in a more transparent pretence of right than our own report of the outrage at Rangoon throws about those disgraceful transactions. I will certainly bring out the real merits of the case. I stand third for a chance of making a motion on this subject on the 7th. The other motions may be short, and I shall try to come on ; but if not, I will take a Supply night rather than be deprived of an opportunity of exhibiting the matter in its true light. Last Tuesday I tried my chance in a ballot for my disarmament motion, but with my usual bad luck. Yesterday, when another ballot took place, I abstained for this reason.

"There is a great feeling of anxiety about the state of matters at Constantinople. Very well-informed men express their belief that the Russians are there now. A most uneasy state of mind prevails everywhere, and mixed up with the Turkish question is the report that France will indemnify herself for Russian conquests in the East by seizing upon Belgium. I hope there is no truth in any of these warlike rumours. But the question is occupying all minds, and the Cabinet is divided as to the policy of our intervening in the strife. A few days will decide, and in the meantime I would not give any notice of my disarmament motion ; because, if it were met with a continental explosion, it would be alleged against me as a proof of want of practical foresight and sagacity. In the meantime we may be required to put forth all our energies to prevent our being mixed up in a continental war. Six months' experience of

Palmerstonian Foreign Policy

what a war in 1853 is would, I know, bring John Bull to such a state of mind as to induce him to sneak out of the fray in the most ignominious manner. But we must endeavour to open the eyes of Manchester, Liverpool and Glasgow to a sense of what would be the consequence of a rupture of peace with the Continent *before* such an event takes place. I could do it in half an hour, if the public mind were in the full prospect of a war. If, on the other hand, it turns out that France and England have co-operated to prevent Russia from invading Turkey, what a ridiculous position it will place those in who are now drilling the Militia and fortifying our coasts against a French invasion! Whatever course events may take, the Peace Party is sure in the end to gain by it. Being the only true principle, it cannot fail to reap advantage even from the temporary triumph of its opponents."

.   .   .   .   .

The letters of 1853 show Cobden engaged, as his main purpose, in trying "to beat down this most wicked spirit towards France." To this end he composed and published early in January a long pamphlet, " 1792 and 1853, in Three Letters," the method and meaning of which he describes fully in his letter of January 1st. It was a great success both among his private friends ("What a glorious pamphlet you have written!" said John Bright) and with a large and growing public increasingly suspicious of the Palmerstonian alarms. But it did not stay the panic, and the Peace Party found their propaganda impeded and discountenanced by many whom they trusted to assist them. The majority of the influential supporters of the League and its Free Trade policy refused to see the essential connection between Free Trade and a

Richard Cobden : The International Man

pacific foreign and imperial policy, or to recognize how absolutely the cause of sound and commercial national finance was bound up with the control of armaments. In one of his most interesting letters Cobden deplores and comments on this failure of Leaguers and Liberals in general to seize the logical and practical interdependence of the central principles of his political creed, with non-intervention as its foundation stone. This letter may usefully be supplemented by the following passages from a letter of September 19th, addressed to Mr. McLaren.[1]

"In this Peace Conference movement, we have not the same clear and definable principle on which to take our stand that we had in our League agitation. There are in our ranks those who oppose all war, even in self-defence; those who do not go quite so far, and yet oppose wars on religious grounds in all cases but that of self-defence; and there are those who for politico-economical and financial considerations are not only the advocates of peace, but also of a diminution of our costly peace establishments. Among the latter class I confess I rank myself. . . . We cannot disguise from ourselves that the military spirit pervades the higher and more influential classes of this country; and that the Court, aristocracy and all that is apeing the tone of the latter believe that their interests, privileges, and even their very security are bound up in the maintenance of the 'Horse Guards.' Hence the very unfashionable character of our movement, and hence the difficulty of inducing influential persons to attend our meetings. . . . If we add that the character of the English people is arrogant, dictatorial and encroaching towards foreigners, that we are always disposed to believe that other nations are

[1] "Life," ii. p. 144.

Palmerstonian Foreign Policy

preparing to attack England, it must be apparent that in seeking to diminish our warlike establishments, we have to encounter as tough an opposition as we had in our attack on the corn monopoly, whilst we look in vain for that powerful nucleus of support which gave us hope in the latter struggle of an eventual triumph."

But while the panic regarding the aggressive designs of Louis Napoleon occupied the foreground of his mind and political energies, almost absorbing the interest of the Peace Conferences at Manchester in January and at Edinburgh in August, Cobden found time to compile a powerful exposure of the origins of the Burmese War and the damaging reactions of the policy to which it belonged upon the security and finance of India. Letters relating to the abominable conduct imputed to an American missionary, named Kincaid, show that he was fully alive to the shortcomings of other countries than his own.

Though as early as May 1853 Cobden, writing to his brother, noted a growing uneasiness in the Cabinet about Turkish affairs (his letter of September 13th to Mr. Richard indicates the nature of the trouble), there is nothing to indicate the swift change in the political sky which was to bring war against Russia next year, with our hereditary enemy for an ally.

"*January* 1, 1853.

"I am exceedingly obliged by your letter and the contents, and the volume of Mackintosh. I have got so far as to be certain, at all events, of publishing something; but I wish I had had more time. My plan is this: I begin with a letter purporting to be

Richard Cobden : The International Man

addressed to a reverend friend thanking him for a copy of a sermon preached by him on the death of Wellington. The sermon professes, of course, hostility to all but defensive war, but considers the war with the French to have been won, and that the Duke was an instrument of Providence raised up for our defence. I join issue upon the latter, and without disparaging the Duke (but the contrary), I maintain that the war in which he was engaged was provoked by us, and that the French all but went down on their knees to escape it. In my first letter I give some general broad facts in support of this, but without going much into details. In my second letter I begin by purporting to answer a letter from my reverend friend, who wishes me to direct him to the best sources of information upon the origin of the war, and I, in reply, offer to give him the facts, and this will be a long letter with a good many quotations, particularly from the speeches in *Hansard*, and I can most completely show that the war was not only provoked by us, but was in its object the worst of all wars, because it was to put down *opinions* by force. I will prove this from the admissions and avowals of those who would wish to give a different character to it. I have got to the middle of the second letter and have all the materials at hand to finish it. In the *third* letter I wish to make application of the former views to the present state of things, and here I am rather at a loss for materials. I should like to have had the opportunity of turning over all the pamphlets and volumes brought out during the last few years about the invasion. Some extracts would be nice tit-bits to quote. Here you may be of service to me, and I should be very much obliged if you will hunt up some of these productions, and give me at least the *titles* of as many as possible, and

Palmerstonian Foreign Policy

some extracts if you can. When I was last at the Reform Club, I saw a little heap of these warlike manifestos lying on the table of the library. If you will inquire for the librarian, who would feel a pleasure, I think, in accommodating me, he would allow you to see these pamphlets in his own private room—i.e. provided you have no other way of getting at them in a lump. There is one work that you must send me—the reprints of the letters of an 'Englishman' in *The Times*, who would set us in a blaze again. He must be some Brummagem Burke. I don't know where I can get any statistics showing the increase of the manufactures and imports of raw materials into France now as compared with 1793. The statistics of those days are very obscure and not to be relied on."

"*January* 25, 1853.

" It is not possible for me to come down before this evening. I shall see you to-morrow soon after receipt of this. My three *letters* are now being printed, and Ridgway hopes to send 500 by to-night's mail-train. The pamphlet runs to 130 pages or more, and he says it must be sold for 2s. or it will not pay expense, but the 500 for the members of the Peace Congress may, he says, be sold at 1s. without interfering with his sale. I was very anxious it should have been a shilling pamphlet, for really beyond that price nothing sells very extensively. However, when you see it, if you think it desirable, something may be done to give a cheap edition (leaving you to cut it down if you like) for the people. For, after all, our business must be with the masses—keep *them* right, and we can't go wrong. I am glad that you have put a notice on the paper for a discussion of our present relations with France. It seems to me that our whole practical end for this meeting should be to beat down this most wicked spirit towards France; and the only way, depend on it, is the course I have taken in my pamphlet, where I give the statistics of the imports and exports of France, and especially a detailed comparison of the imports of all the great items of raw materials for 1792 and 1853 (furnished me by Michel Chevalier from official sources) to show by comparison what wonderful progress France has made as a manufacturing people. And then I have taken the bull by the horns by telling the people plump that the eight millions of landed proprietors of France do *not* envy us, and that they would be horror-stricken at the proposal to change places with our population! This, with a most conclusive proof that the last French War was got up by our aristocracy, is what I have brought out, and what we *must show to the whole people if we would keep their hands from 'cold iron' again*. A real *exposé* of the comparative economical status of the two peoples *would make ours discontented with their lot*. So much the better. It will teach them to employ their energies at home, and not be carried after every red-herring that designing knaves (for there is more knavery than folly at the bottom of it) draw across their path."

"*March* 8, 1853.

"The enclosed tracts are very good. I have made a few verbal alterations and additions. I send you the Indian statistics you require for the latest time for which it is before the Committee. More than half the expenditure, including interest of debt, goes for the fighting establishments. Yet a friend of mine told me the other day that Lord Hardinge, who sat beside him at a dinner-party, remarked that we have not three hundred and fifty miles of vulnerable frontier

Palmerstonian Foreign Policy

to guard—thus implying that the army is kept up to keep down the population. You may use the facts but not the name. Take care of the money. Manchester has been used to spending great sums, and some of your friends may forget that you have not got the funds of the League. I have seen Chevalier Bunsen, who has no objection to be named as the person to appoint the adjudicators, provided he finds nothing in the wording of the advertisements of the prize which he objects to. We must draw up the terms of the advertisement. I consider that the announcement of the prize in different publications on the Continent will be the best mode in our power of agitating the European mind upon our plans and of making known our organization.

"I was talking to Bunsen about arbitration clauses in international treaties, upon which he seems to take a good deal of interest; and he appeared to think that it was a step forward in the work of diplomacy which ought to be generally advocated. There is, I think, at present one, if not two treaties being arranged between the United States and this country. It occurs to me that it would be well to see to this, and to probably apply to Lord Aberdeen in favour of inserting an arbitration clause, and to set our Peace friends in America to work to enforce the same views upon their Government.

"P.S.—The whole revenue of India in 1850 amounted to £20,275,000.

The Army cost in 1850 ...	£10,098,000
The Navy ,, ,, ...	384,000
	£10,482,000

EUROPEANS IN INDIA.

30,000 Queen's troops.
20,000 Company's European troops.
7,000 or 8,000 Civil employees of the Company.

Richard Cobden : The International Man

"Number of Europeans residing in British India who are not in the service of the Queen or Company—10,006, male and female. Only 317 Europeans reside in the *interior* of British India, engaged in agriculture or manufactures."

"*May* 7, 1853.

"Did you send Lord C. the American report? It has occurred to me to write to him, under the plea of wishing him to return it after perusal, but really with a view of letting him know that I was quite disappointed at finding that he had the least hesitation about meeting the Americans upon the footing of an arbitration clause. Really these Whigs and all that belong to them are an effete, worn-out set. They seem to have fallen into such a decay-that no new ideas can be grafted upon them. It would have been an infinitely more satisfactory matter to have called upon the old colleague of Castlereagh, as we did upon the reduction of armaments question. As for Lord Clarendon, he has a great name with the public as a safe and discreet man. I fear he will never have boldness or originality enough to travel beyond the merest routine of the Foreign Office."

"*August* 20, 1853.

"I have written to Dr. Bailey, of the *Washington Era*, pointing out to him explicitly the very heinous conduct of the American missionary, and begging him to draw public attention to it. I have told him to show my letter privately to anybody connected with the Church of which Kincaid is the missionary. And I have also sent a message to General Cass, saying that whilst I thank him for rebuking us for our wicked misdeeds in Burma, I will thank him in future to give an eye to the meddling American missionaries who incite our military men to war. Can't you get

Palmerstonian Foreign Policy

a formal address from your Peace Society to the religious body of which Kincaid is a member calling on them to disavow his conduct? The fact is, it is high time to put down the arrogant assumption of these people. Instead of the messengers of peace, clothed in the meek garb of Him they pretend to serve, they are firebrands ready to set the world in a blaze to revenge the slightest affront to their dignity. I remember being shocked, in a conversation with Gutzlaff, who spent an evening at my house on his last visit to England, to hear him advocating a hostile expedition to Japan, and I could not help detecting that at the bottom of his resentment towards the people of that country was the remembrance of some slight he had suffered at their hands. There has been a similar display amongst the missionaries in West Africa. Do you remember the circumstance of one of these modern Hildebrands boasting that he was busily employed in casting bullets in a mould for shooting the Ashantees who besieged the town in which he was resident? I send you back the extracts from the papers. There was a good article in the *Preston Guardian*. What a telling and stinging article it is from the *Northampton Mercury*! What can be done to bring an Envoy over here before next session from the Burmese Government? Now that Lord Dalhousie has, oddly enough, declared that we are at peace with Burma (though its Government has never agreed to recognize our right to the territory we have seized), it is no longer an act of treason to hold communication with that Court. I should exceedingly like to be able to prompt them to send over an Envoy, to be here when I bring forward the question in the House; but I do not know how it is to be done, and it could not be done by me. Sturge is capable of accomplishing anything. I wish he could take this bit of diplomacy in hand. Lord Dalhousie & Co. would be terribly alarmed if the Burmese Government would send over an Ambassador to this country."

"*September* 13, 1853.

" I am glad to hear that you are satisfied with the preparation making for the Edinburgh Conference. It is of the utmost importance that it should be a successful demonstration, and to this end we must look to English aid, for Scotland is not a good field of operations. Very few *influential* people are with us in that part of the kingdom. As respects the Burmese question, everything possible has been done from this side of the globe to bring a mission from Ava next spring. Nobody knows but Sturge, yourself, Bright, Dickinson, and myself. You must make Dickinson's acquaintance. He is the Hon. Sec. to the Indian Reform Association, a single-minded devotee who labours like a galley-slave from the purest impulse of benevolence. He is the son of Dickinson the eminent paper manufacturer of Herts. He wrote to you at my suggestion—for I thought you could furnish him with some extracts from newspapers approving my Burmese pamphlet, which he might send out to India as arguments to induce the Government at Ava to make an appeal to the public opinion of England. It is through Dickinson that the communication has been made to India with a view to its being forwarded to Ava. He is to be met with at the *India Reform Society Committee Room,* 12 *Haymarket.*

"As respects the present state of Turkey, several works have been published lately. ' The Turks in Europe,' by Bayle St. John, seems to be written expressly to prove the case of the Mussulman hopeless.

Palmerstonian Foreign Policy

There are several of these 'St. Johns' at work in the interest of the *Greeks in Turkey*. A newspaper is published at 10 Leadenhall Street called the *Eastern Star*—which I suppose must be subsidized by Greeks, many of whom in England are very rich, and have a good deal of national public spirit. I exchanged a couple of short notes with a *Mr. Percy B. St. John*, who has, I believe, published them in the last *Eastern Star*. These people are, I suspect, not at all of our way of thinking on this or other matters. They do not look at it as a question of principle, but would, I suspect, be glad to induce our Government to interfere to set up Greeks and put down Turks. Then they are, I believe, great partisans of Rajah Brooke. *Greville Brooke* of the *Sunday Times* is a *St. John*, and I rather [think] the father of the others. However, it is well to know 'who is who.' There is a work lately published (reviewed a fortnight ago in the *Athenæum*) by *Eyre Evans Crowe*, upon the Turkish question, in which the Turks are given over to the D——l in the most summary way, and their territory disposed of in the same offhand way. Crowe was formerly editor of the *Daily News*. Then there is a new edition of *Spencer's* travels in Turkey advertised. He also goes against the Turks. In fact, there is not a man of the least sagacity who has been in the country who does not see that the Mahometans cannot be maintained in Europe as a governing class in a territory the great majority of whose population are Christians. All that you hear about reforms of the Turkish administration is mere *fudge*. Corruption and immorality reign supreme in every department of the State. You may bribe everybody with the exception of the Sultan; and he is systematically bought through his women and eunuchs. In all probability the present

Richard Cobden : The International Man

hitch in the negotiations at Constantinople has been planned and paid for by Russian agents, who have very likely a majority of the Divan in their pay. On the other hand, the Austrian Government is alarmed at the idea of a rupture, fearing that it might lead to a break up in Hungary and Italy, and they are therefore exerting their influence with the Turkish Cabinet to induce them to accept the terms of the Vienna Conference without modification. In all probability the two parties are bribing against each other, and between the two the *patriotic* Turks will reap a rich harvest. Then, if it should come to blows, expect to see Generals and Admirals going over bodily to the enemy. You will remember that on the occasion of the war between Mahmoud and Mehemet Ali, the latter bought the Turkish Admiral, who carried his master's fleet into Alexandria. It is merely a question of money. Patriotism does not exist in Turkey. There is *fanaticism* amongst the masses, who, there, as everywhere, are in earnest; but they have no faith in their leaders, and the latter have neither faith nor hope in the future. Now not only is all this known to every intelligent traveller in Turkey—it is reported to our Government by its diplomatic and consular agents. One of the members of the Cabinet told me that the reports they got from the interior of Turkey corresponded with what I stated in the House. And yet Lord Palmerston had the impudence to get up and pledge himself to the fact that no people have effected such improvements in the last twenty years as the Turks! And our *Radicals* are bellowing for *Palmerston and Turkish independence.* Is it not time for men of common sense to found a political hospital to cure such idiots?"

Palmerstonian Foreign Policy

"*October* 17, 1853.

"You know my opinion from the first—that you ought not to calculate upon the old Leaguers transferring their Free Trade energies to the Peace cause. People have somehow fallen into the odd notion that, because certain men have achieved a certain result, ergo, they are the people to accomplish anything that remains to be done. It would be about as rational to argue that the tree which has yielded a good crop of oranges must be able to give you some apples also. I have never varied from the opinion, ever since the League was dissolved, that the same men who took the lead in that body would never form the most prominent actors in any other out-of-doors agitation. I was always of this opinion, even when, yielding to the wish of a majority of my old colleagues, I joined in the formation of the 'Financial and Parliamentary Reform Association,' which has really ended in nothing. *Fresh men* must be found for each distinct movement. I therefore am not surprised that you find yourself a little disappointed in the help you have received from Newalls Buildings. I know of nobody in their party who is thoroughly bitten with our questions (I mean amongst wealthy men) but Thomasson and Whitehead. . . .

"I hope you find a sweet odour coming up after our Conference. We seem to be more savagely abused than ever by the London Press, but perhaps their anger is not a bad sign. What would we have given in the early part of our League agitation to have been so much noticed! I hope that nothing was said or done at the Conference calculated to weaken the Quaker zeal in *our* movement. If so, Sturge, E. Smith and the more orthodox of the leaders must set to work to solder the crevices. We are nothing without the 'Friends.' "

CHAPTER VI

THE CRIMEAN WAR

THE long struggle between the Palmerstonian foreign policy and that which may fairly be styled the Manchester policy of non-intervention issued in the declaration of war against Russia in the spring of 1854, and for two years Cobden's public influence and reputation suffered eclipse. Many of his most trusted political friends, even among the free-traders and certain sections of the pacifists, fell away, yielding themselves to the tide of war fever which swept the country and forced Cobden to recognize that the war was not attributable mainly to the machinations of statesmen but in its outbreak had the people passionately with it. He wrote to Mr. Bright (October 1854):

"I am willing to incur any obloquy in telling the whole truth to the public as to the share they have had in this war, and it is better to face any neglect or hostility than allow them to persuade themselves that anybody but themselves is responsible for the war."

The early letters to Mr. Richard are chiefly concerned with the attitude of the Peace Party in the impending crisis when the nation and Parliament were moving towards war. Always he is the advocate of tact and moderation, recognizing how any "pacifist" indiscretion or excess may help the war-makers. So

The Crimean War

on March 9th he fears lest meetings may convey a wrong impression of pro-Russianism. He is himself no more pro-Russian than pro-Turk, reverting in his letter of May 8th to the views of Turkish misgovernment so fully exposed in his early pamphlets.

His later letters of this year are naturally marked by a deep depression. With Bright he was the chief target of popular and parliamentary obloquy, and the former stung him more deeply than the latter. It was far easier to meet the gibes and taunts of Lord Palmerston and his gentlemanly following than to be burnt in effigy by popular gatherings in the market-place of great commercial towns whose interests he had laboured so assiduously and so successfully to promote.

Bowing of necessity before this storm of public reprobation, his spirit was not broken. Admirable is that passage in which his biographer records the courage of the victims of the popular madness.

"It is impossible not to regard the attitude of the objects of this vast unpopularity as one of the most truly admirable spectacles of our political history. The moral fortitude, like the political wisdom of these two strong men, begins to stand out with a splendour that already recalls two great historic types of statesmanship and patriotism. Even now our heartfelt admiration goes out to them as it goes out to Burke for his lofty and manful protests against the war with America and the oppression of Ireland, and to Charles Fox for his bold and strenuous resistance to the war with the first French Republic. They had, as Lord Palmerston said, the whole world against them. It was not merely the august personages of the Court, nor the illustrious veterans in Government and diplomacy, nor the most experienced politicians in Parliament, nor the powerful journalists, nor the men versed in great affairs of business. It was no light thing even to confront that solid mass of hostile judgment. But besides all this, Cobden and Mr. Bright knew, that the country at large, even their trusty middle and industrious classes, had turned their faces resolutely and angrily from them. Their own great instrument, the public meeting, was no longer theirs to wield. The army of the Nonconformists, which has so seldom been found fighting on the wrong side, was seriously divided. The Radicals were misled by their recollection of Poland and Hungary into thinking that war against Russia must be war for freedom." [1]

Part of this popular reprobation was doubtless due to a mistaken interpretation of the non-intervention policy and an association of Cobden with extreme peace positions which were not really his. But Cobden, soon recognizing that reasoning with such madness was of no use, saw that the fever must run its course. He rightly perceived that the military and financial misconduct of the war would gradually help to bring back both people and Parliament to their senses. But letters of this period show that he overrated the pace of this disillusionment, seeing signs of extreme war weariness after a few months of war.

What he was particularly anxious to secure was the complete discrediting of militarism by a failure of either side to secure a military victory with the glory and future perils it would bring.

Here I may quote a passage from a letter (October 1st) to John Bright :

"Let John Bull have a great military triumph, and we shall all have to take our hats off as we pass the Horse Guards for the rest of our lives. On the other hand,

[1] "Life," ii. p. 155.

The Crimean War

let the Czar's swollen pride be gratified and inflamed with victory, it will foster that spirit of military insolence which pervades everything in Russia. But if neither could claim a decisive triumph, and both were thoroughly discouraged and disgusted with their sacrifices, they might all in future be equally disposed to be more peaceable." [1]

One of the most interesting of the 1854 letters to Mr. Richard is that of December 9th, discussing the indiscreet pugnacity of Mr. Bright in handling his critics and opponents. Several letters allude to the plans for the establishment of the new penny paper, *The Morning Star*, by friends of the Peace and non-intervention movement. Mr. Sturge was the chief promoter and subscriber. Cobden himself had no financial interest in the venture, though he and Mr. Bright were consulted about its policy, and it had his warm approval.

"March 9, 1854.

"As respects the desire of some of our friends to get up meetings in favour of peace, I should like to know what course they recommend to be taken before I give an opinion of the project. To hold a meeting *now* merely to enunciate abstract opinions against war would be simply ridiculous. If we deal with the question, it must be in reference to existing difficulties and dangers. It would in fact merely amount to a repetition of all the arguments pro and con which have been reiterated a thousand times to no purpose. And to be honest, we could not deal fairly with the matter without a due measure of censure on the Czar which would be only adding fuel to fire; for (*pace* Jos. Sturge) the Russian Government is not clean-handed, and latterly there have been loopholes opened for it by which it might have

[1] "Life," ii. p. 164.

Richard Cobden : The International Man

escaped from war which have been insultingly repelled. The Czar must, I think, be suffering from the malady of his family. Or there is another solution of his obstinacy—perhaps he is assured of a rising of the whole of the Christian population of Turkey. If some such event occurs, it will vastly complicate the business, and add to the difficulties of our position. *Then* would be the time for the Peace Party to lift its head. But until some *new* phase in the affair presents itself, it would, I think, be not only useless but mischievous to the Peace cause to attempt to hold public meetings. *We have done our duty*."

" *June* 8, 1854.

" I duly received the French book upon Eastern Affairs. It is perfectly true that it would be an ungracious task to hunt out indictments against Turkey at this moment when the *Government* of that country is suffering a great wrong from a ruffianly neighbour, if one's motives were open to the charge of trampling on the weak. But *we* are as a nation apparently committing ourselves to the task of maintaining now and for all time the independence and integrity of the Turkish Empire. Now, if that Empire contains within itself the seeds of decay, we may be attempting an impossibility—nay, we may be fighting against nature, and attempting to thwart that Providential law which reproduces something different out of a corrupt nation as it does out of a decayed animal or vegetable substance. *Therefore* it is legitimately our duty before undertaking to perpetuate the Turkish Empire to learn what its actual condition is. And guarding yourself most emphatically with this proviso-preliminary, you could not do a better service than to gather all the reliable evidence you can from all sources as to the state of Turkey. It will help your friends in Parliament, for the

The Crimean War

only chance we shall have of a hearing will be on the question *what* do we propose to do, and what can we do? And the more evidence you can rummage up for us upon the present and past state of the country the better.

"Observe *The Times* article of yesterday giving testimony to the fact that, whilst the English people have to be kept back from war by the Government, in France Louis Napoleon has to justify himself to the French at every step for going in the direction of war. It has always been so, and the more I think the more I incline to the opinion that we have not told the English people half plainly enough their fault in this respect. Consider for a moment where should we have been if *The Times* had sounded the signal for war six months ago, and thrown its talents and energies into the scale along with the *Daily News, Herald*, etc.? Why, we should have been in the bloodiest campaign by land and sea long ago! It is only by the accident that *The Times* is devoted to Lord Aberdeen's Government, probably, that it is not so."

"*September* 8, 1854.

"I am up to my chin in books, pamphlets and papers —being in the midst of the dirty and tiresome but necessary task of unpacking and stowing away my library. But I sometimes think of you and your poor oppressed friends of the Peace Party; and as we are brethren in affliction I of course think of you with feelings of sympathy. What are you doing, and what can be done? Nothing, I suppose, but await the result of the expedition to the Crimea which may prove a worse affair than even Varna, although, if one may judge of what the Russians can do by what they have done it would seem not to be difficult to beat them. What are our 'democrats' now talking about? There seems to be a commotion in their camp judging by the public meetings that have been held.

Richard Cobden : The International Man

But I see only *The Times*, which does not even notice the fact of such meetings having been held, and this I think is a betrayal of trust as caterers of news. So I wrote to Crawshay at Gateshead, the leader of the mad people who held the Newcastle meeting. He is a Cambridge man (I mean, educated there), and was one of my most devoted Free Trade allies; and enclosed I send his answer, for it is a good sample of the incoherent style of reasoning which the best of these people indulge in. There is really less logic in this so-called Democratic war party than in the cannon-balls they appeal to which do answer to a certain mathematical rule in their courses. Yet there is a good-hearted intention about these people. Is there no way of reaching them?"

"September 22, 1854.

"I hear occasionally from our friend Dornbusch, but he has not alluded to the newspaper project. I am decidedly of opinion that nothing of the kind will answer our purpose until we can get rid of the *stamp*. It must come to terms of peace in the end, but I really don't know how *we* can contribute to the putting an end to the war. Nor do I see what we gain unless we can establish better *principles* than those which guide Government and people at present. If we are to assume the responsibility of keeping the peace and 'doing justice' to the whole world, then we can never with consistency or security reduce our military establishments. With the liability at all times to be called on to enter into armed alliance with the 'weak against the strong,' and recognizing the duty of an armed intervention in every European struggle, we should be illogical—nay, mad, not to be at all times prepared to take up the cudgels in support of our principles. I feel that we have to lay the foundations of a party organization, and that we must adopt for our funda-

The Crimean War

mental rule 'non-intervention by force of arms in the quarrels of the Continent.' To do this we throw off more than half of those (with Baines at their head) who have professed most noisily to be with us. Are there ten men in the House or one hundred and twenty outside (excepting the Quakers) who are to be relied on? What do you mean by the 'historical facts of the case' not being known to the mass of the people? But you are quite right in getting health in Wales. Nobody has a tougher task before him, and you will want all the strength the mountain air can give you."

"*October* 16, 1854.

"Have you any news? Has the madness of the public shown any symptoms of mitigation? Or is the patient suffering as much as ever from the war mania? I can forgive everybody but Baines, 'the Patriot,' and the so-called 'Saint' party. *They* are doing their best to drag Christianity itself through the blood and mire of the field of Alma. Scenes have evidently been enacted there *after* the battle which our most criminal population of the metropolis itself would have shuddered to take a part in. And yet our 'religious' people call God's blessing upon these doings! Why, they have only to become sufficiently general and widespread to make this earth a hell. Faugh! it is enough to make the very heathen and infidel shudder for the dangers of those who mock a Christian's God with such blasphemous cant."

"*October* 21, 1854.

"It is hard to stand still when one feels that the world is going wrong on a question in which one is deeply concerned, but *events* are working out the best arguments for our principles, and if there be any truth in them it will be more fully vindicated by the deeds

Richard Cobden : The International Man

of the Crimea, and *their consequences*, than anything we could *say*. Besides, there is after all a way and time of doing things which with the best intentions may work more harm than good. I remember the first time I attended Doncaster races on the 'Leger' day being struck with this. In walking from the town to the course in a dense stream of excited and eager visitors, I observed some men having the guise of missionaries who were offering to distribute tracts and harangue the multitude against horse-racing ! A plentiful shower of oaths and gibes was all that rewarded them for their pains. Now if we set up our standard and begin preaching peace whilst the bells are ringing for victory or supposed victory, we shall fare no better than the poor men in rusty black and whity-brown neckcloths at Doncaster. If they had waited a few days, there would have been plenty there who lost at betting who would have been in a mood to listen ; and if we take the proper moment there will be in every town and in almost every 'good' family mourners for the loss of friends and relations who will listen to us. I agree with you that amongst the middle class the feeling upon the war is rather that of acquiescence than of enthusiasm. I was struck with the same feeling in the House in the last session. The tone was always very moderate, that House represents pretty fairly the middle class. The Lords were much more pugnacious. In fact the rabble and the House of Peers were the great advocates of the war. I had an idea of addressing a reasoning letter to the electors of Yorkshire. The time has not yet come, but it may come."

"*December* 3, 1854.

"I returned from Lancaster yesterday, and must confess with sorrow that I never paid so unsatisfactory

The Crimean War

a visit to that part of the kingdom. The war spirit was far rifer than I expected and it pervaded all classes, infecting many from whom I had expected better things. It is a moral epidemic, and the only resource I found was in escaping as speedily as possible from it. Once or twice I asked myself the unpleasant question, 'Are we, after all, rational and progressive creatures?'"

"*December* 9, 1854.

"I have written to Bunsen in the spirit you wish. His complaint about Bright attacking the Ministry is a repetition of what I hear from all quarters. Even many of his friends in Manchester, who go with him heartily against the war, are puzzled at his assault upon the Government whom they believe to have been always as a body less eager for war than the country. In a letter which I have just received from Geo. Combe he holds precisely the same language. He says Bright has taken the weakest possible ground. I have often tried in private to persuade our friend to rely less upon attacks on the personnel of the Government, and more on the enforcement of sound principles upon the public—but his pugnacity delights in a knockdown blow at something as visible and tangible as a Minister of State. I wish you would send copies of your edition of Bright's speech with notes to Combe and Bunsen.

"What is the meaning of this Austrian treaty? Is it a manœuvre of the Government's to get out of the war? *All* of them are tired of it, and I am told our aristocracy are sick of the prospect of the spring, when the Queen's Body Guards and all will have to go and take their share of the hard knocks. I suppose you are aware that the poor Duke of Cambridge lost his head at the last battle. I mean the little reason that was in it. My correspondent says the slaughter of his Guards drove him mad. He showed the usual courage of his family, but the excitement was too great for him. If there be signs of an attempt at an armistice, something should be done at once by the Peace Party. You should in that case see Mr. S. Gurney, whose co-operation would be most valuable."

"*December* 29, 1854.

"No *overt* public act can be taken with advantage till it is known publicly that the Government, or at least a part of them, is for negotiating. I mean no step such as I pointed out, having reference to the four points. But everything should be done by sounding friends and preparing for the moment when it comes. I should have no objection to a meeting of friends of peace being called in London, if at the proper moment it was thought that such a step would be successful. I am inclined to think there is some reaction, or at least that the public enthusiasm is cooling. Several letters have reached me from clergymen approving my speech. It looks very much as if the besiegers were gathering up their strength for an assault on Sebastopol. This I have no doubt is the step urged upon *their* Commanders by the French Government, which is alarmed at the prospect of being defeated before the town and thus having the military prestige lowered in its hands. An assault will be attended with a fearful loss of life, and I predict will have but very partial success, and be attended with scarcely any consequence decisive of the war. But the horrors and carnage of an assault may incline some of our *religious* public to favour peace. These *professing* Christians puzzle me exceedingly. In Baines' last

The Crimean War

Mercury he says: 'England and France must send the largest possible reinforcements in the least possible time, and *carry the place at any cost.*' Now I should wish nothing better than the task of cross-examining him in public, with the New Testament in hand, and compelling him to justify himself out of the Book he professes to believe in and obey."

. . . . .

The unpopularity attaching to opponents of the war had not at the beginning of 1855 reached its maximum intensity. At any rate, it was not intense enough to prevent Cobden from addressing a great public meeting at Leeds in January upon the war, in which he expressed his views in the most uncompromising terms and was listened to, if not with agreement, at any rate with acquiescence and respect. Some passages from that speech deserve citation as examples of the tests which Cobden brought to bear upon the great crime of the mid-century.

" My first and greatest objection to the war, gentlemen, has been the delusive, I had almost said fraudulent, pretences under which it has been made popular in this country. I mean that the feelings of the people have been roused into enthusiasm in favour of the war, by being led to entertain the belief that it was to effect objects which I know and felt, at all events, it never was intended to effect. Now, will anybody for a moment deny that, twelve or fifteen months ago, when the first excitement in favour of a war with Russia took place—will anybody deny that that which carried forward the mass of the people of this country in favour of a war against Russia was, that it had for its object to give freedom to struggling nationalities on the continent of Europe, and that it would have for its object to put a check upon the proceedings of Russia—with reference, I mean, to the invasion of Hungary, and the conquest of Circassia, or the occupation of other countries? Does anybody for a moment deny that the prevalent opinion of the people of the country was that, in going to war against Russia, you were going to inscribe on your banners the reconstitution of Polish nationality?"

But turning from pretences to reality—

"It is a war in which we have a despot for an enemy, a despot for an ally, and a despot for a client." "Looking at the war as it really is—a war in opposition to Russian encroachments upon Turkey," he argued that Austria, Prussia, and the whole German confederates were, from their geographical position and their politics, more interested in Russian schemes of aggrandizement than we were. If the Russian policy were so dangerous, these near neighbours would be the first to fear and resent it, and would have been impelled to take action. Either the knowledge and dread of such powerful resistance would have restrained Russia, or by waiting for the more interested parties to move we should have had an overwhelming force to meet Russian aggression. Our interests are too remote, and neither require nor justify our intervention. Nothing but the rhetoric of pugnacity is responsible for the contention that "if you allow Russia to take Turkey, then she will become so powerful, having possession of such rich territories, that she will next come and take other neighbouring countries, and take possession of England also." There is, he urged, no ground for such a supposition or for the feasibility of such an aspiration after European hegemony. "Here is the opinion given by Lord Palmerston upon this subject: 'There never has been a great State whose policy for external aggression has been more overrated than Russia. She may be impregnable within her own boundaries, but she is nearly powerless for all purposes of offence.'"

The Crimean War

The central appeal of his speech was to reality of motive, which can only be gauged by a wider historic survey. "We are taking a position which the world does not recognize in us. I must ask you again to bear in mind that within the last one hundred and fifty years we have taken from a Mahomedan sovereign, the Great Mogul, territory containing one hundred and fifty millions of people—nearly twice as many as the whole Russian Empire; and when you remember what we have done with the Dutch at the Cape, and what we have done with everybody else somewhere or other—when other countries remember that, they don't view us in the same light as we do ourselves—that we are the disinterested, just, and perfect and immaculate people that we allege of ourselves." "I come now to the logical deduction from this—that we find that not only does not Russia acknowledge our authority as a judge, but that the rest of the world does not acknowledge it." In considering this appeal to our national interests it must be remembered that at this time the Suez Canal had not been made, and the charge of Russian intentions to invade India had not been formulated.

In support of Cobden's attribution of sham idealistic motives to the engineers of the Crimean War, I will quote the following passage from a controversial letter written to Cobden in November 1855 by a Mr. X, a friend of Mrs. Schwabe:

"This, then, is my creed. I look upon Russia as the personification of Despotism—the apostle of Legitimacy, and the enemy of Liberty and human progress. In the present state of Poland and Hungary we see her work; and Sebastopol tells us for what future outrages on the freedom of Europe she was making preparation. Such a power can only be curbed by war, and must be so curbed, sooner or later, if Europe is to remain free. We have no right to bequeath this struggle to our posterity. It is a present duty; and if we believe that God wills the liberty and happiness of mankind, how can we doubt that we are doing God's work in fighting for liberty against aggression? There is no fanaticism in this doctrine. I believe that the Russians themselves have as good ground for thanksgiving under defeat as we have in victory; because defeat will, under God's providence, bring to them the national blessings which victory secures to us."[1]

Cobden's early letters of 1855 have several allusions to this Leeds meeting, and early in the year he notes signs of a recovery of national sanity. But his sanguine temper here got the better of his judgment, as he recognized later in the year. By September the public policy and sentiments of his countrymen inspired him with growing disgust. British pugnacity was the chief obstacle to peace; the people was worse than the Government, and the sole hope of an early settlement he was disposed to find in the broken finance of France and the precarious position of Napoleon.

The democratic instinct of Cobden finds expression in his growing concern for the political education of public opinion as the only valid check upon the crimes and follies of Governments, and recognizing that in periods of great national excitement the "platform" which had served him so well in his Free-Trade agitation might be lost, he turned with greater zest to the project of a genuinely free Press. The unscrupulous misrepresentations of *The Times*, the unreliability of such Liberal papers as the *Daily News* and the *Leeds Mercury*, together with the new possibilities opened up by the repeal of the paper duty (1855), brought him to cherish ardent hopes of the new experiment which began in the autumn by the launching of the *Morning Star*.

[1] Schwabe, p. 259.

The Crimean War

"*January* 2, 1855.

"I see no impropriety in your endeavouring to secure signatures to such a memorial as you sent me. My only doubt would be as to the success of the effort. If it be merely signed by the Friends and Peace Congress people it would not be worth much; and I fear other parties of influence would not give their names unless there was a Ministerial demonstration in favour of peace, or at least until it was publicly known that the Government were favourable to negotiations. Such people might argue very reasonably that any strong demonstration on the part of the English *people* might only harden the terms of the Czar in his transactions with our Government. However, I repeat, I see no objection to the trial. I can give you no information as to the state of the negotiations. Unless Lord Aberdeen himself be false, which I don't suspect, I know him to be trying to arrange peace on the terms of the four points with certain modifications. But I am not sure that if it were put to him he would counsel an agitation for signatures to such a memorial as you sent *at the present moment*, nor can I say that he would not."

"*January* 6, 1855.

"I am in a dilemma about the Leeds meeting. In answer to my letter to Mr. Garbutt (chairman of the Reform Registration Society), asking him to arrange for a meeting and to preside for me, he has written to say that after consulting the leading reformers he declines to be a party to my visiting the West Riding at the present juncture. I am not surprised, I confess, for they all are committed, with Baines at their head, to the war, and my appearance could have no other effect but to disturb their equanimity. I have written a conciliatory reply, saying that I shall hope to see them privately, if they will not

Richard Cobden : The International Man

listen to me publicly, for that being about to visit the North of England, I shall make a journey to Yorkshire, but that as respects a public meeting I shall consult those, be they few or many, who share my views upon the subject of the war, and shall be guided by them as to the kind of demonstration I shall have. Now, I am not sufficiently at home in Leeds to know who are the persons likely to co-operate with me. What I want is to be able to hold such a meeting as will afford an excuse to deliver a speech which will be reported in the London and Yorkshire papers. If I was sure of a calm hearing, I would advise that the Music Hall at Leeds be engaged for Wednesday evening the 17th inst., on which day it is disengaged, and that advertisements be inserted in the Leeds papers on Saturday announcing that on that day, and giving the hour and place, Mr. Cobden, M.P., will deliver an address to his constituents. I should, of course, make *the war* my text, but it is not necessary to rouse the antagonism of the War Party by announcing it. Now, can you obtain for me the advice and assistance of some good Peace men in Leeds, who will take upon themselves to act on the best opinion they can form? I do not think I should be liable to interruption or insult in addressing a public meeting. I would, of course, to some extent adapt my speech to the circumstances, and I should not contemplate asking for any vote or expression of approbation. All I should want would be a quiet hearing, and I suspect the war mania has sufficiently cooled to ensure me that courtesy. I have written to Edwd. Smith, Sheffield, who will, I dare say, be in communication with some of our Peace friends in Leeds. It would be well if the 'Friends' were not the only parties to co-operate with me, but they really seem to be the only reliable body everywhere. They may, however, find some influential persons of other sects who sympathize with me. I am not afraid of filling the Music Hall at the shortest notice. My only anxiety is to have a rational audience. It would certainly be a very desirable thing to be able to speak through *The Times* to the whole world from the West Riding at the present moment. But the time for arrangements is very short."

"*January* 10, 1855.

" By the way, apropos of the newspaper Press, I expect the stamp will come off this spring. Could not a cheap daily paper be started to advocate the doctrine of the 'Manchester School' the same as the *Manchester Examiner*, etc.—peace, non-intervention, economy, etc. ? In my opinion, after the present war there will be a reaction which will give a good opening for such a paper. In fact, it is a great unoccupied field in London, the only one connected with the Press not occupied, and I feel convinced it would prove a good mercantile speculation if the business part of the undertaking were well managed. I should like to see your hand in such a paper.

"You did right in telling Sturge not to appear too openly in the Leeds arrangement. I have an invitation from Garbutt to go to his house, but have advised him to let me take shelter at an inn, rather than carry discord into his domestic circle. I don't know whether he will insist on my being his guest after he knows that I am going to hold a public meeting."

"*February* 5, 1855.

"There is a point alluded to in your letter which I thought of writing to you about. I mean the *now* disputed fact that the popularity of the war originally sprung from the belief that it was to be a war of liberation to certain nationalities. I wish if you find time you would refer back to the proceedings of some of the public meetings and see what really passed. There is a moral in this, for it is an illustration of the lamentable fact that when once involved in war we forget the very motives and circumstances which led us into it, and transfer all our enthusiasm to the war itself. People in this state of mind are more difficult to deal with than any other, for they refuse to reason upon the subject, and abandon themselves to their belligerent passions, and are very intolerant of everybody else who does not follow their example. By the way, our Court and aristocracy are gathering their full share of the bitter fruits of war. The latter by the loss of their sons and relatives, and still more by the loss of reputation as a governing class, the former in the embarrassments and perplexities to which it is subjected in the choice of a new Cabinet. Whilst I write I am ignorant as to the result of the Ministerial interregnum, but if the Court is compelled to gulp the Palmerston dose, it will pay a heavy fine for the luxury of the war; and remembering how much the Court is responsible for the warlike passions which were excited by its camps and reviews, I certainly think it is a righteous retribution that it should suffer some part of the penalty. I am very curious to see if after all that has passed the Queen will 'send for' Lord Palmerston. It will be another illustration of how war tends to set up the wrong men and the wrong principles. I suppose there will be an attempt to bully us all into supporting his Government as an act of patriotism during the time he is carrying on the war 'with vigour.' But I shall certainly never own him as my leader, or for any motive be induced to give him any personal support. I still expect to find the negotiations for peace carried out. Surely the Turk will be more anxious to put an end to the war and get rid of the French and English than any other party. If you hear any news, let me know."

The Crimean War

"*February* 7, 1855.

"I don't think that Palmerston is less likely than Lord Aberdeen to make peace. He is a great *sham*, and not nearly so warlike as his foolish dupes of adulators have believed. Unless we have peace soon, the war will, I expect, enlarge its dimensions very speedily. But I repeat, I don't see what Bright and I can do beyond pressing for information in the House as to the present stage of the negotiations and the causes of the delay."

"*May* 1, 1855.

"I cannot see the slightest objection to the attempt being made in Manchester to get the memorial signed by as many people as possible. It is very well worded for catching even the most moderate lover of peace. In fact, it is so very lenient and even complimentary towards the Government that the most determined Whig may sign. I think Bright would hardly like to be known as the author of phrases so like oil upon those storm waves which he dashed against the Ministry the last night of the Session. Still, I think you will not have much success in London until it is known that the head of the Government is bent on negotiations and *The Times* begins to show signs of turning. But you may be feeling your way in the meantime. I will communicate with Bright.

"I expect to hear soon of another dreadful contest in the Crimea. Probably the town will be assaulted by the French. If so we may read accounts of the dead and wounded cumbering the streets to the first-floor windows. *Then*, probably, our 'religious' public will be satisfied!"

"*May* 15, 1855.

"Gibson will assuredly divide. He comes on next Monday, and in all probability the division will be on

Richard Cobden : The International Man

Tuesday. If you can influence any members to support him you must not lose a moment in doing so ; Gladstone and Graham will speak and vote for him, and several of the Tories are going with him. But we shall be in a poor minority, I expect.

"Lord Grey puts off his motion in the Lords, which was fixed for Monday next. He expects to be left almost alone unless the bishops support him, of which, by the way, I should think there is but little chance. He told me this morning that he was trying to influence the Bishop of Oxford. It has occurred to me that it would be a good plan if the Peace Society were to address a short appeal to the Bench of Bishops urging on them, as the exponents of Christian principles in the House of Peers, the duty of supporting Lord Grey's motion for peace. If, as Lord Lansdowne says, 240,000 Russians have been destroyed since the war began, surely it is time to stay the hand of the destroyer. Think of this idea."

"*July* 15, 1855.

"It would be very desirable, I think, to make a collection of paragraphs from *The Times* upon the subject of the war, and more especially respecting the expedition to the Crimea, showing in the first place how much that journal is responsible for the present dangers into which the country rushed at its instigation, and with a view especially to discredit it for the future and lead the people, if possible, to think for themselves. I should like particularly to see some extracts from articles written at the time of the expedition being sent from Varna to the Crimea. These extracts ought to be brought out in the House, or in a pamphlet, or through the pages of a new daily peace paper. The debate on Roebuck's motion would give a good opportunity for some quotations. I wish you would give your very first leisure

The Crimean War

hours to the exploring of the columns of *The Times*. It is an institution of the realm, like Queen, Lords, and Commons, and must be dealt with as such. If it can be shown how greatly it is responsible for an expedition which every rational man now in his heart condemns, it will much impair the force of its war advocacy in future. Bright or I would not hesitate to take it in hand."

"*August* 5, 1855.

"I had not received your letter dated 1st when I saw you in London, or I should have said (what you would gather from my remarks in Ryder Street), that I quite agree with you as to Haly's views, or rather feelings, being by no means identical with ours on the Peace Question. I should not object to one who was more indifferent than ourselves being at the head of a paper, provided the power over the property were absolutely vested in those whom we could trust. I would trust nobody who set up a paper on merely mercantile principles to oppose the current passions or prejudices even for a day. I quite agree also in your view that our paper must have a country circulation. This will come, of course, to a certain extent, but I predict that London daily papers will have less sway henceforth than they have hitherto had in the provinces. The removal of the stamp will set agoing a far more influential *local* Press. It will be worth while for the Peace Party to promote the establishment of good papers in other places besides London."

"*September* 18, 1855.

"You ask my opinion on the present aspect of affairs. I really do not think that any *rational* deduction can be drawn, from any given facts, of the probable course of

Richard Cobden : The International Man

events in respect to our foreign policy. *Reason* has nothing to do with the ebullitions of the war spirit which we now witness and have before encountered in this country. Its manifestations assume the most opposite characters and take the most opposite directions—now against Louis Napoleon, next in his favour, once in opposition to Louis Philippe, then as strongly against those who dethroned him—in fact, a drunken Irishman in a fair never, even in romantic story, was made to pick quarrels, more heedless of all rational grounds, than this great nation has in the last ten years of its history done with its neighbours. But you ask what in my opinion will be the effect of the late success at Sebastopol upon the chance of peace. If the issue depend on the will of the English people, it is clear that we are farther than ever from that happy goal ; for what corner of the Empire offers, amidst the deluge of fierce passions which everywhere covers the land, one resting-place for the messenger which goeth forth in quest of the olive-branch of peace ? I am actually so amazed and disgusted and excited at the frenzy to which all classes—and especially those called middle and respectable—have abandoned themselves, and am so horrified at the impudent impiety with which they make God a witness and partaker of their devilish paroxysm, that I would rather say nothing about it. My only hope is in Louis Napoleon, his interests and necessities. When I saw Lord Aberdeen a few weeks since, he said that his only hope of peace was founded on a favourable issue of the siege at Sebastopol, that if Louis Napoleon could meet with a 'success' to satisfy his army, he would seize the opportunity of making peace. Well, he has now the opportunity, and I have a strong impression (though founded on no facts) that he has sent pacific proposals to our Government, and that this embarrassing message

The Crimean War

is the cause of the frequent and long Cabinet Councils—for how can *our* Government make out a case to their deluded followers to justify a peace which must certainly involve the abandonment of the Crimea ? The danger is that Louis Napoleon, whose one dominant idea is the alliance with England, may yield to Palmerston and the warlike spirit of our people and go on with the war. But he has graver reasons against such a course at home. He will have to raise another army to pursue the war in the interior of Russia—bread is certainly rising in price, and there is an ugly symptom of rottenness in the financial state of France, as illustrated by the *Dr.* and *Cr.* of the Bank of France and the rapid fall of some of the public securities. How does it illustrate the madness of our combative countrymen, when one can only turn with hope for peace to the coercion of a Bonaparte upon the deliberations of our Cabinet! I don't see how we can act with Gladstone in the broad advocacy of non-intervention so long as he professes to be an advocate of the policy of invading Russia. He seems to put an impassable gulf between us by that one argument—for if anything is ever to be done again in favour of peace principles, it must be by persuading the masses, at least, to repudiate the very principle of the Russian invasion. The paper which offered itself to the Peace Party 'for a consideration' has been changed to a penny paper, and has gone right over to the War Party. I send you a copy by this post."

"*September* 29, 1855.

" Have you returned to town ? I have a letter from Sturge about the proposed penny paper. He has been exerting himself according to his wont, and seems likely to raise the money required. But he expresses his doubt whether Haly is the right man to manage, and speaks

Richard Cobden : The International Man

favourably of Collins (Hull) and Hamilton. These are men in whom I should have the most implicit confidence as regards *principle*. But I understood that another safeguard was to be taken that the paper should go right on the Peace Question; indeed, it is still Sturge's main reliance that Wilson, Bright and I are in some way to have a veto on the politics of the paper. If so, I doubt the policy of giving the management to enthusiastic Peace men, for the simple reason that I doubt whether a daily *newspaper* which avowed itself at the outset exclusively or mainly a peace organ would get into circulation at all amongst the general public, and if it fails to do so to the extent of thirty thousand daily it will fail altogether, and entail nothing but loss on all concerned. My idea is that the paper *must*, if it is to live, be in the first place a thoroughly good *newspaper*, and not a mere expansion of the *Herald of Peace*. If the latter is the idea in view it should be by making it a weekly paper. If my idea of a daily paper be carried out, it must not at the commencement deter readers and subscribers by incessantly giving leaders against this war. I should say that at the first the attacks against this policy of the war should appear chiefly in the form of *letters*, and I don't think anybody's pen but your own need be engaged in that direction. In course of time, when the public will read and reason on the subject, the whole principle of foreign intervention must be worked out in its columns in the interest of peace. In the meantime, not only must nothing be said or implied which goes to tolerate this war, but everything consistent with the success of a *daily newspaper* must appear against it. Now, will our friends who are subscribing their money so far temporize as to be willing to see the editor of the paper *postpone* a portion of what can be said in favour of peace until a more convenient season? If they cannot tolerate a little

The Crimean War

of the 'wisdom of the serpent' as a means of promoting the 'harmlessness of the dove,' I don't believe it possible *at present* to establish a daily paper in the interest of peace. The time may come, perhaps, when the reaction will be more decisive for starting such a paper, but it will not be this year. I hear from all sides of the unanimity of feeling for the war. Mr. J. B. Smith, who has been moving about in the North for a month or six weeks, writes to me to say that he has not met with one person who agrees with us. I have been visiting at Chichester, and positively I cannot *hear* of a man or woman in that cathedral city who is against the war. A clergyman actually assured me (I hope libellously) that a wealthy Quaker, whose name I will not repeat, goes with the stream. It is useless our shutting our eyes to these facts, however unpleasant they may be, and however discouraged we may feel. There cannot be a doubt that *The Times* represents most truly at this moment the prejudices, ignorance, arrogance, and combativeness of the middle class of this country. The working class care less than those above them about it, but only because it does not promise to benefit 'nationality' or revolutionality abroad."

"*October* 26, 1855.

"What delirious nonsense *The Times* is writing about our going to war with the United States and still holding our grip upon the Northern despot! And yesterday we were to go and chaw up Naples. This Cockney bluster will in the end make us ridiculous. If the United States took us at the challenge of *The Times*, and presented us with a *casus belli*, there is no humiliation we should not swallow rather than go to war with that country. The lives of people in Lancashire and Yorkshire, to say nothing of their fortunes, would not be worth six

Richard Cobden : The International Man

months' purchase, if we were at war with Russia and America. They would be eating each other up! But I sometimes think a dreadful example of the kind must be made of us to cure us of our pride and arrogance."

"*November* 8, 1855.

"Many thanks for the letters and books and papers. From the number of communications pouring in on me I should think there must be a little awakening of opposition to the war-at-any-price policy. The newspapers will have terrible uphill work to keep up the steam during the winter. Some of them will, I suspect, turn tail. I have no news from India. That blood-cemented edifice will one day cave in like a house of cards. Did you read attentively the article in *The Times* of Monday on my letter. It is worth while to keep a record of its argument. The first position is that the war is popular, next it says that it does not appeal to the strong political sympathies of the people, and that therefore they won't enlist. Next it says that the electoral body, the middle class, are all for war, and that I should be rejected by the West Riding constituency because I am for peace, and then it goes on coolly to tell us that the middle class are much too well employed to enlist. Then the question remains to be asked—*Who is to do the fighting?*

"The *Globe* has put out an article from the Government to show that the recruiting is going on well, but not a word about the age of the recruits."

"*November* 15, 1855.

"I wish you would be good enough to see Mr. Washington Wilks. If you would give him a meeting, he would no doubt contrive to call, and pray say I wrote to you on the subject. I am of opinion that if these

The Crimean War

people can be moved *outside* of the old Peace Party it would be very desirable. You can judge better than myself whether it can be done. There cannot be two opinions, I think, as to the good effects produced everywhere by the fact of public meetings being called and carried by the Peace men.

"I shall be glad to hear the report of your progress in the country. It will be an interesting test.

"I am receiving letters from new men, clergymen and others, urging the formation of a Society to stop the war. I also get letters from *parsons* giving deplorable accounts of the sufferings of the poor from high prices of everything. It is a fact that the Church of England clergy have from the first given more encouragement by their correspondence to Bright and myself than Dissenting ministers! Is not this very strange seeing that the tithes are increased by the war prices?"

"*November* 28, 1855.

"I think the panic and excitement you caused in some places, and the pains taken to defeat you, argue well for the growing strength of your cause. The frantic doses administered in *The Times* seem also to show that the drunken fit can only be kept up by stronger stimulants—but the reaction must follow.

"My object in writing is more especially to suggest a plan which I have often thought of—that of going through *The Times* for about three years and taking out enough for a short pamphlet of its inconsistencies, false assumptions, unverified predictions, and bombastic appeals to the momentary passions and prejudices. You could get *The Times* from Gilpin, at the Freehold Land Society, turn over its pages at your leisure, and mark the passages for extract for your clerk to copy.

Richard Cobden : The International Man

I have a notion that you would get an astounding hash to print under the title of 'These are your guides.'

"Another thing I would like to see done, and wish such a man as Washington Wilks could be launched on it—viz. to go cursorily over the same paper for twenty or thirty years and extract its choice bits or abuse of Palmerston. Such a collection, under the title of 'The Times and Lord Palmerston' would make a capital theme for a lecture. It would be a rich treat."

"*December* 23, 1855.

"Will you cast your eye over the enclosed uncorrected proof and let me have it again. The article in the *Constitutionnel* is certainly significant, and would lead one to suppose that the French Government is determined to have peace, with or without the concurrence of England. But on the other hand what means the article in the *Post* containing the terms offered to Russia? Russia will never, I should think, agree to *them*, and yet the *Indépendence Belge* says those terms were sanctioned by Gortschakoff. I will believe those terms to be agreed on when I see it, and not before. It will, of course, be the policy of Russia to try to separate France and England, which she will try to do by making a show of a willingness to negotiate, knowing that France is for peace. Louis Napoleon is in a desperate dilemma for money next year. The account in the Brussels paper that you sent is about correct. All the people who surround him are stock-jobbers up to their chins in speculation, and all for peace, because it suits their books. Still, I do not see how we are to avoid another campaign."

CHAPTER VII

PEACE AND RECOVERY

By the close of 1855 it became evident that the French nation was both tired and disillusioned in respect of the Russian war. The fall of Kars and the breakdown of the Turkish defence in Asia Minor fairly balanced the success at Sebastopol, and the growing unpopularity of the British alliance inclined Napoleon towards an early peace. The preparatory steps were taken by the Austrian Government in the presentation of proposals to Russia which might form the basis for a general peace. This was the announcement made on the meeting of Parliament, January 31st, by Lord Derby. Though the general feeling in this country was still for a continuance of the war, Cobden's early letters show that he diagnosed the situation accurately when he insisted that Napoleon's peace disposition would prevail. The Treaty of Paris was signed on March 30th, and before the Conference rose it subscribed a statement of great importance dealing with maritime warfare, entitled " The Declaration of Paris." By the abolition of privateering, the protection of neutral goods under an enemy flag, and enemy goods under a neutral flag (excepting contraband of war in both cases), and by a stricter definition of blockade, a considerable step appeared to have been taken towards that doctrine of " Freedom of the Sea" for which Cobden stood.

The peace was not particularly popular when it came,

Richard Cobden : The International Man

and for some time afterwards attempts were made in certain quarters to stir up a renewal of strife. But domestic affairs and certain aftermaths of the war in the United States, and in Italy, soon diverted the attention of our politicians and prevented the threatened disturbance of a "patched-up peace."

Soon after the peace a serious diplomatic strain occurred at Washington. During the Russian War a number of American citizens had enlisted in the British forces. The United States Government protested against this act as violating both American and international law, and adducing evidence to associate Mr. Crampton, our envoy at Washington, with this enlistment policy, they demanded his dismissal. After some attempts at bluff, accompanied by defiance and threats of war from our Jingo Press, our Government made a sort of apology. The American Government, however, insisted on Mr. Crampton's withdrawal, and it was seriously proposed on our side to dismiss Mr. Dallas, the American representative in London. This might easily have led to war. Fortunately we pocketed this affront, as it appeared we were in the wrong, and the affair blew over. Cobden in his letters of the spring sheds a good deal of inner light upon the whole case, and shows how much more real importance attached to the less-discussed issues of our position in Central America, and the projects connected with a canal in Nicaragua and Panama which were already looming in the political horizon.

In the summer the question of the Bourbon dynasty in the two Sicilies became prominent. Gladstone's eloquent exposure of the horrors of the Neapolitan prisons in 1850 had yet borne no fruit. Now the English and French Governments united in a vigorous protest against the cruelties of the Bourbon rule. The

Peace and Recovery

king's disregard of these protests led to a withdrawal of the English and French Ambassadors on October 28th, and the dispatch of a joint fleet to the Bay of Naples. But all was useless. Russia had made a counter-protest against this naval demonstration, pointing out its violation of the principles of the Paris Conference, and in any case the Western Powers were not prepared for the extremity of bombarding Naples on an issue not of "vital interests" but of "humanity." Cobden, as early as July 9th, cuts down to the roots of the situation and predicts the futility of this show of violence.

The other matter of external importance this year which would naturally have attracted Cobden's attention was the war with Persia which broke out in November, in consequence of the siege of Herat by the Shah, probably at the instigation of Russia. The contest was short and the defeat of the Persians complete. Peace was signed in March of the following year. The silence of Cobden on this affair in his letters to Mr. Richard is probably attributable, in part, to his absence from London, in part to the obscurity which beset the affair until the publication of the official dispatches by Sir James Outram in 1857.

His absence from London during virtually the whole of the year was due to the terrible blow which fell upon him and his wife in the sudden death of their bright young son, who had been at school at Heidelberg. The condition of Mrs. Cobden's health for a long time to come was such as to require Cobden's constant presence and care. During the spring and summer they remained at their Midhurst home, later on they spent some time at Bognor, and the late autumn and winter found them farther afield in North Wales, near Bangor. This temporary withdrawal from the House of Commons and

Richard Cobden : The International Man

the platform left Cobden with the pen as his only direct instrument of political influence.

During the latter part of 1855 he had spent some time in preparing, in view of the expected termination of hostilities, an elaborate pamphlet, bearing the title "What next? And next?" This pamphlet, one of his longest and most closely reasoned, was published early in January 1856, at the time when Austria, influenced by Napoleon, was proposing to Russia the terms of peace which resulted in the Conference of Paris. It was an argued plea for an immediate settlement on the ground that we had nothing to hope for in the way of a decisive victory, if we continued the war, and that such continuance would cost us dear in lives, trade and finance, without securing for us any definite political or other object. It opens with the question : "What grounds have we for believing that the success which the military and naval authorities promised a year ago will be attainable by another campaign?" Suppose that, after the occupation of the Crimea (which would require an Allied army to keep possession), our forces proceeded to attack the Danube forts, to occupy Odessa and to seize every place in South Russia, within fifty miles of the Black Sea, what then? Would such a conquest enable them to dictate humiliating terms to the enemy? How? We could not hope by any force we could assemble to occupy Moscow, or to pursue the Russian forces to their destruction within a vast country in which every further advance would increase our difficulties and our dangers. It is evident that we could not subdue her by direct internal military operations. Could we destroy her commerce and so cut off her revenue? Then Cobden marshals his great store of evidence to show that the Protectionist policy of Russia, injurious in so many ways, had this single advantage, that it made her virtually self-sufficing for all

Peace and Recovery

necessary supplies, so that the most complete blockade could not reduce her to submission. The internal communications of Russia by land and river, and the wide distribution of her foods and other necessary supplies in the interior, conspired to render our blockade almost valueless. Cobden turns next to what we should call the psychological factor, especially the patriotic sentiment of Russians and the powerful religious feeling with which it is associated. While it is, he contends, a great delusion to attribute to the Russians any desire to overrun any part of Western Europe, or to pursue any purely aggressive policy, an invasion of their territory, even of the Crimea, will be resisted with the utmost obstinacy. Their Eastern " missions to regain for their religion the ascendancy over these neighbouring countries which were formerly under a Christian Government, and where a large portion of the population are still Christians," he distinguishes from the general aggressive designs imputed to them.

Having thus dealt with the material and moral resources at their disposal for resisting our "will to victory," he addresses himself to the question of finance. By a close analysis of her financial situation, and of the Government banking system, he shows that her inconvertible paper currency, though fundamentally vicious, will enable Russia to avoid for several years to come anything in the nature of a financial crash, a depreciated currency being far less ruinous to an agricultural country like Russia than to a more wealthy mercantile or manufacturing nation, such as England or Holland. On the other hand, our financial troubles must accumulate rapidly if we are to pour in fresh streams of English and French soldiers with their supplies of food, clothing and transport, for a campaign of invasion. Cobden sees a growing difficulty in furnishing the men. Our tough agricultural stuff is very limited, and townsmen, not the best material for such a task, can only be got by letting down our productive trades and disorganizing the delicate mechanism of a subdivided industry. "No, a manufacturing community is of all others the least adapted for great military enterprises, like that in which we have embarked." Our Government and people are not sufficiently united and excited by a sense of vital interests or religious enthusiasm, to be willing to bear such burdens as would be involved in a war to a finish under the circumstances he has described.

In conclusion, he answers the challenge, "What would you do, if you were the Government?" by a definite summary of European policy. He would withdraw every British soldier from Russian territory, and would resort to the policy adopted at the outset of the negotiations, of appealing first to Germany and Austria, the most interested parties, to join us, not in the war against Russia, but in constituting a European bulwark against Russian aggression by means of treaty arrangements which would bring into being a "federation of the States of Europe."

"I should appeal not only to Germany, but to all the States, small as well as great, of the Continent, for such a union as would prevent the possibility of any act of hostility from the common enemy. This is the work of peace; and to this end, with the view and responsibilities of the Government, I should address myself."
"Finally. Not to incur the charge of vagueness, I would not risk the life of an Englishman, or spend another shilling, for the chance of the barren triumphs of extorting pacific pledges from the Russian Government; and having come to this determination there would no longer be an obstacle to peace." [1]

[1] "Political Writings," p. 534.

Peace and Recovery

Some of Cobden's early letters this year were much concerned with the effective publication of this pamphlet. But in March the daily newspaper the *Morning Star*, controlled by persons friendly to his political and economic views, began its career, and Cobden, though not financially interested, was recognized as its chief adviser. He took the position very seriously, and having more leisure on his hands than usual, spent much thought in directing its activities both on the political and business side. Mr. Richard was from the start one of its chief leader-writers, dealing with foreign policy and kindred topics, and Cobden poured through him a constant stream of information, opinions and interpretation of events. He was much concerned to preserve the paper from too close identification with the extreme pacifist party and to make it a good general newspaper, correcting the errors of what he called the "capitalist" Press and yet appealing to the business interests by sound commercial and financial intelligence. Most of his communications were made to Mr. Richard, though he was also in constant though less confidential relations, first with Mr. Haly, who acted for a short time as editor, afterwards with Mr. Hamilton, who took his place. Sometimes he sent items of political or even personal news, but for the most part his letters contained either the material for a leading article, or advice upon the conduct of the paper. Writing on July 25th he says, "I can often give you rapid hints for an article without any trouble to myself if I know that my own language is not necessarily to be printed. When writing *for the Press* I am beset with a fastidiousness that almost paralyses my fingers." It is, however, pretty clear that many of the *Star* articles were in substance and even in literal composition Cobden's, with some slight editing. One letter (December) contains what is avowedly designed as an article dealing with

Richard Cobden : The International Man

the delicate subject of Prince Albert's supposed "influence" upon foreign policy in the German interest.

"*January* 16, 1856.

"The worst case by far of critical profligacy, or of the profligacy of criticism, which I have met with, is in the *Leeds Mercury*, which I found here on my return home. I send it to you, and you will see that the rascal, whoever he may be, has passed sentence on my pamphlet without avowedly having seen it, and has taken its character at secondhand from *The Times*! I have written to Baines, assuming that he did not write it, for another reason, that the article condemns the plan of a mutual and *pro rata* reduction of naval armaments which he again and again publicly approved. But I have told him in as strong language as I can find what I think of the conduct of his paper. I still think you ought to have a sub-committee in Yorkshire to look up Baines's sayings on the war. There is an article in *The Times* of yesterday that out-herods Herod. In the very same column it takes credit for the policy of fighting for Germany and Scandinavia, and threatens to throw them to the "bear" unless they now fight their own battles! Then mark the art with which the whole object of the article is brought in as it were incidentally where it assumes that *nearly all* that the *Western Powers* want is ended! Now what is the meaning of this? Does the paper know Louis Napoleon is decided for peace and *The Times* is wriggling on to the new ground? Read that article again."

"*January* 18, 1856.

"Many thanks for your kindness in sending me the latest news. I am sure *The Times* has misled the Stock Exchange, and that the *Morning Post* has the more correct account in saying that Russia has accepted

Peace and Recovery

the propositions as a *basis* for negotiations. Of course she would any terms. But if *The Times* plays this game, it may be that we shall see its influence a little impaired before long. I am still of the old opinion that Louis Napoleon is quite as much alarmed at the future as the Russian Government, and it is he that will force us to peace. I feel pretty certain it will come, but not in a way to afford a triumph to our papers. They will have a very difficult game to play."

"*January* 24, 1856.

" Peace will come not through the good sense of the English Government or people ; but in spite of them. I feel no doubt that Louis Napoleon has made up his mind for some time to this course. *That* was known to the initiate on the Paris Bourse, and hence the way in which the credit of the Government and the operations of the Bank were sustained in spite of adverse appearances on the face of the French finance. I have no doubt that, to use a vulgar phrase, Louis Napoleon ' tipped the wink ' to the Court of St. Petersburg, through Baron Subach (Saxon Minister at Paris and of course go-between for the Russian Government), as much as to say, Let us get into a peace conference, and I will ' make things pleasant.' In spite of the bluster of *The Times* we must go where he pleases to lead, for what would *leaded-leaders* do for us in the Crimea if the French bayonets were withdrawn ? Press and people in England will have to lower their tone, you will see, for when Kars comes to be set off against some of the terms in the Austrian protocols, there will be precious little left to fulfil the predictions of the fighting party in this country. Is there a rational man even among our War Party that will say that England has gained anything in prestige or glory by what has occurred since

Richard Cobden : The International Man

the last Vienna Conference? And, on the other hand, is there any one out of that party here or abroad that will not admit that we have lost caste even in military rank, and disgraced ourselves by the barbarities of Kutch, etc.?"

"*May* 21, 1856.

"I do not know that any good can follow it, and therefore I am sorry to trouble you, but if you would learn from Cash on what day my pamphlet 'How Wars are got up in India' was published, and look into *The Times* of a day or two after you will see an article strongly condemnatory of the Burmese War. If you will take an extract or two from it and publish it in the *Herald* (there is, I suppose, no other organ of the Press sufficiently in earnest), alongside of the enclosed extract on the same subject from last Thursday's *Times*, I should like to see them in juxtaposition. But *cui bono?* you may ask. I really can't answer your question. I should advise no one who did not wish to reap the disappointment which Burke so feelingly confesses at the close of his career to meddle with Indian politics with a view to the arresting of our career of spoliation and wrong. Still it is well that there should be the whisper of conscience, if only to prevent it from being said, that the nation is unanimously unjust, and therefore I am always glad to read such truthful and *home*-truthful articles as that in your last number against our pharisaical self-sufficiency and self-ignorance."

"*May* 27, 1856.

"I wrote to Henry Rawson a few days ago and advised him to give the paper a very decided tone in favour of non-intervention. I am glad to hear that

Peace and Recovery

your hand is in it. Nobody can give the democratic argument in favour of peace and non-intervention so well as yourself. Indeed, George Wilson and I agreed, whilst talking it over, that you would make a good Editor for the paper. It seems to me that *now* is a most opportune time for taking up the *principle* of non-intervention, for everybody seems at sea on foreign politics without rudder or compass. Everyone is dissatisfied with the past and nobody has a standing ground of *principle* for the future, excepting the advocates of non-intervention. What can be more absurd and illogical than the hue and cry raised about Italian politics? The French Government having violated the rights of independence in Rome, and Austria in Bologna, and Sardinia by way of putting herself wrong in principle having a corporal's guard in possession of Monaco, it is proposed by France (apparently) that there should be an interference in Naples—*the only part of Italy excepting Piedmont where foreigners are not in possession of the country.* And of course the Press of this country, being the great *gobemouche* of the day, following the false trail, raises the cry against the King of Naples—instead of telling France and Austria to recall their troops from Italian soil, and the Sardinians their corporal's guard from Monaco, and to leave the Italians to settle matters with their own Governments. Now this is the line for the *Star* to take—not feebly and occasionally, but boldly and systematically. The *principle* of non-intervention, as a *right of the people* everywhere to self-government, is the line the *Star* should take. If the people fall into anarchy, that is *their* affair, and they will be all the more eager to come to an agreement upon some form of government—for *order* is not only the first law but the greatest necessity of our nature. I told Hy.

Richard Cobden : The International Man

Rawson, too, that I would take advantage of the exposures of the betting world in Palmer's trial [1] to exclude betting news from the *Star*, and, not only so, but systematically attack the betting system and expose the practices and denounce the haunts of these pests of society whether they live in the atmosphere of West End clubs or the back slums of St. Giles. The *Star* will never have the patronage of these people, and it must make itself the organ of moral reformers of every national kind."

"*May* 31, 1856.

"I have to thank you for the *Stars*. Your vigorous pen has vastly improved the quality of the writing. Let me suggest to you now to let the dead bury the dead, so far as the Russian war is concerned, and not to bore people about it (excepting in reference to the state of Turkey) but to give your study to that which is really of vital practical importance — the American question. The *Star* ought to take the lead in denouncing the complications which have led to our difficulties, and in blaming the governing class of this country who are really responsible for every diplomatic entanglement. I say the governing class—for a score or two of families have had possession of the Cabinet during the last thirty years, and have had absolute control over our foreign relations. To deal with effect with the American difficulties you must separate the two disputes, and point out to your readers, so clearly that they can understand it, the difference. Lord Clarendon talks a great deal about the *enlistment difficulty*. Now I know that there is no fear *in any* quarter of war arising out of that question. The utmost that can arise is that the President will give Mr. Crampton

[1] The famous Rugeley murder case.

Peace and Recovery

his passport, and withdraw the exsequatur from three or four Consuls. The business of the embassy will be carried on by a secretary quite as well as now; there will be a little diplomatic pouting as has often been the case between European Governments, and then some other Minister will be named. In fact, we, being in the wrong, shall pocket the affront. As to the Consuls, our merchants will take care that no interruption to their business arises out of the neglect to appoint fresh ones.

"The real difficulty is with Central American affairs, and this arises not merely out of the disputed construction of the Clayton-Bulwer Treaty, but from the complications which the progress of American traffic and adventure has imported into the question. You must take a good map—for it requires a good one to find out the mighty territorial interests for which we are embroiling ourselves with the most powerful State in America—and study the geography of Central America. The last edition of the maps of the Society for the Diffusion of Useful Knowledge will suffice. You will see the English possessions marked red. Now, I have talked the matter over with Sir H. Bulwer who signed the treaty. There is no danger about our claim on Belize, Ruatan and the Bay Islands. *That* would keep. But the real difficulty and danger are in our claim to the protectorate of the Mosquito Coast. We have set up a king of Mosquitia—a savage chief whom we took to Jamaica to crown and anoint and then set up as 'his majesty' over a few thousand wandering uncivilized Indians. Remembering that he is the only king of the Western Hemisphere—that from the icy circle to Cape Horn there is but one crowned king, and he of Mosquitia is the specimen of the order which England sets up for the admiration of the New World,

Richard Cobden : The International Man

what must be said of our tact and judgment as a monarchical nation! Of course he is only a puppet in our hands, and virtually *we* are the rulers of the Mosquito Coast. Now the Americans refuse to acknowledge the king we have set up. They refuse to call Greytown anything but St. Juan (which is certainly more euphonious). And they refuse to recognize our right of sovereignty over the Mosquito Coast.

"The annexation of California and the gold discoveries brought the countries of Central America and the Isthmus of Panama into great importance, and a question which might otherwise have slumbered is now likely to involve serious difficulties and dangers unless promptly settled. The great streams of traffic between the eastern and western shores of the American Union pass by two routes, first, the Nicaragua Lake, and the River St. John which brings the passengers in contact with the Mosquito Territory—and second, the Panama Railway. I believe the latter was generally preferred. But there arises the Walker complication. This adventurer penetrates from California into Nicaragua, thinking that the distracted and anarchical state of Central America will afford an opportunity for the display of his virtues. He begins in Nicaragua by setting up a President (following our example in setting up pretenders in India) that he may become 'viceroy over him.' This fellow seems to have had no friends in the 'States.' He was denounced as a pirate. Two things could alone have made him popular—a massacre of American prisoners by their opponents after the old Spanish fashion, or the English Government taking part against them. Both these incidents have occurred. Lord Clarendon, foolishly coquetting with the Costa Rican envoy here and his qualified offer of some musketry, has given Walker a party in America,

Peace and Recovery

and thousands of rowdies will, if he should hold his own for a few months (which I pray he will not), flock to join him from New Orleans and New York. Then arises our danger. If these men present themselves on their way to Nicaragua at a port in the Mosquito Territory, and we refuse to give them the right of passage, a collision may take place, and we may some morning hear that an American and an English ship have exchanged broadsides. And when our blood is spilt we know how little chance there is for reason and justice.

"I began by complaining of the conduct of our governing class. What is the use of a privileged order if not to anticipate and prevent such complications as these? I have known from successive American Ministers at our Court during the last eight or ten years that the Central American difficulty (particularly that of the Mosquito Territory) would be one day, if not settled, a very serious question. I alluded to the subject in a speech at Bradford nearly seven years ago, and it is reported in the little volume of my speeches. Now what excuse can there be for our aristocratic rulers, who knew all that was passing, not having taken steps to dispose of the difficulty? Our *interest*, as everybody now knows and acknowledges, was and is to clear out of Central America, where we could not possibly gain anything, but where there was every danger of a collision with the United States, whose interests are great and growing in consequence of the increasing traffic between the Atlantic and Pacific shores of the Union. From the moment that the Americans bound themselves by the Clayton-Bulwer Treaty not to occupy any territory in Central America every motive of even old-fashioned state rivalry for our retaining a hold on any part of Central

Richard Cobden : The International Man

America was at an end. Every motive, whether political or politico-economical, prompted an abandonment of the miserable specks of islands, and still more wretched protectorates of the Mosquito Indians—the former might have been given up to Honduras on condition of making them free ports; and as for the Indians, if we could not induce the Yankee to agree to a joint protectorate, better to have bought them all and made them a present of an island of our own in the West Indies and kept them for ever on champagne and venison than allowed them to be the cause of a war between us and the United States. I know from the highest authority that the only real difficulty now with our Government is as to the *point of honour* towards the crowned and anointed savage, and all the rest of our 'possessions' we could agree to give up to one of the Central American States. But how much better could all this have been managed before than now during the pressure of events, and whilst it is known the Americans are demanding the concession. *Yet instead of our governing class preparing for the withdrawal—the Foreign Minister has been for years trying for a triumph in dialectics by proving that by the treaty we are not bound to go!* The question for plain men of common sense was—is it not *our interest* to clear out of Central America? Every man at headquarters now admits privately that it is a pity we ever had any connection with Central America. But why did not they *act* accordingly? If there had been a will there would have been a way of getting out of the dilemma. Why? Because we are not governed by the rules of common sense."

"*June* 1, 1856.

"I wrote the other letter with loose hints upon the Central American business before I got yours this

Peace and Recovery

morning. From what I hear this morning from a well-informed friend in London it is probable the news by the steamer to-day will be that Crampton has been dismissed. This will cause a fall in the Funds, and be looked upon as of more importance than it really is. No war will follow from *that*. I hope you will be prepared to write an article for the *Star* on this subject. I am writing to Mr. Langley at the *Star* office by this post to say how important it is that this American question should be dealt with judiciously and promptly, that *you* can do it better than anybody else; and let me beg *you* will without squeamishness call at the office on receipt of this and be prepared to give them an article for Tuesday. Now this is my view of an article. Keep the readers' mind fixed upon the fact that the dismissal of Crampton has arisen out of the Enlistment and no other question. That on that question our Government have acknowledged themselves to be wrong—but they say they have made apologies and that the American Government ought to have been satisfied. Very likely it is so, and I wish the American Government had been less exacting. But, if the English people find that they are subject to a very unpleasant rebuff in the person of their Minister Plenipotentiary at Washington, then they must settle the matter with their own Government, which has placed them in such a position as to be obliged to put up with it—for it is out of the question that we who acknowledge ourselves to be wrong are to insist upon deciding exactly what amount of atonement we shall make. The Americans say they will not have Mr. Crampton for a Minister at Washington, and we must therefore find another. This raises the question who and what is Mr. Crampton! We know who the Ministers from the United States to England are, for

Richard Cobden : The International Man

they send us their most eminent men. Mr. Dallas has been Vice-President of the Union, Mr. Buchanan has been Foreign Secretary, Mr. Bancroft was their first historian, Mr. Abbott Lawrence the head of their manufacturing interest, and Mr. Everett their most accomplished scholar. These are the men who are sent by America to represent her in England. But who is Mr. Crampton? We never heard of his capacity for public business, and doubt if any public man in England ever heard of it. We believe he is related to Sir P. Crampton, an eminent professional man in Ireland who perhaps has influence with the Government. But what proofs has Mr. Crampton given of his capacity for business at Washington? His latest escapade we leave to be decided by the weight of evidence to be brought on both sides to solve a grave question of veracity in which he or Mr. Clayton (the signer of the Central American treaty) must be found guilty of falsehood. But we know by the confession of Mr. Crampton himself that he forgot to read the whole of a letter of about a score of lines sent to him by Lord Clarendon last *November*—that it was only at the *end of January* that he bethought him to read the whole of it, when he discovered that it contained directions to submit the Central American question to arbitration. Now a man who can treat Lord Clarendon's letters with such slovenly disrespect as this is capable of lighting his cigar with a Government dispatch, or doing any other act of indiscretion or carelessness. This country cannot be at a loss to find a Minister to fill his place, or if the salary be saved and the duties of his office be performed by a secretary, the diplomatic world will not be a great loser. I remember that on a certain occasion when Sir Stratford Canning—now Lord Stratford—was to be sent to St. Petersburg as

Peace and Recovery.

Ambassador, the late Emperor of Russia objected to receive him, having an objection to him personally—yet there was no war in consequence between England and Russia—nor is it likely than anything more serious will follow from the dismissal of Mr. Crampton. These are very rough ideas for an article for Tuesday, whether the news comes of Mr. Crampton's dismissal or not. For if he be not dismissed the *probability* will be very good grounds for an article."

"*June* (?).

"I have not seen the report of the trial in America which brought home the complicity to Crampton. But it has always appeared that we labour under this disadvantage, in denouncing the untrustworthiness of Hertz and Strobel, *that they were our own agents*. The only course to take in my opinion is to denounce the Government and the governing class, and *The Times* and other papers, such as the *Economist* and *Examiner*, which are mixed up with the Government, deserve no better handling. You ask whether I would abandon Central America altogether. There is not a man at headquarters who would not be glad if we had never set foot there, or who does not know that by one means or another we must abandon all claim to possession or protectorate, or ultimately be driven out with discredit. In *private*, all our leading public men hold but one language—that we have no interest in Central America, and the sooner we get rid of all connection with that region of earthquakes and volcanoes the better. But in public, and in their endless diplomatic dispatches, they contend for possession of every rock and islet as if they were of the utmost value. This is the dishonesty of our public men. Lord Palmerston's policy must be attacked. He is the most responsible man.

Richard Cobden : The International Man

Buchanan says in one of his letters that he could have settled the matter with Lord Aberdeen. The *Post* and *Times* are really now making us more contemptible than ever. After holding the most bullying and insulting language, after telling the Americans that we were ready to fight, threatening to blockade their ports and burn their towns and Heaven knows what besides—and pointing to our fifty line-of-battle ships and three hundred gunboats, *now* that the Americans are going to send away our Minister, they are telling us not to be indignant, but to be cool and pocket the affront, and yet all the time assuring us that we have been most insolently and unjustly treated by that Government. Now the proper way to turn the tables is to tell the Government and their organs of the Press that, if we were to put up with all the wrong and outrage they tell us Mr. Pierce and his Government are heaping on us, we should indeed be inviting injustice and insult. But that it is not so, that as between Pierce and Palmerston the former is more in the right than the wrong—perhaps altogether in the right, and that is why our Government submit so quietly to the dismissal of their Minister. But the English people must come to a reckoning with their own bungling ministers, unless indeed they are willing to adopt all their blunders and follies, and confess that they are at the end of their muster-roll of statesmen and that Palmerston is the despotic necessity of the time, and then we must be content to pocket the insults heaped upon him, and consent as a people to be branded as braggarts and cowards."

"*June* 15, 1856.

"Up to the moment when I left I could not learn whether the Government would or would not send away Dallas. They are, I suppose, wavering, and to

Peace and Recovery

judge by *The Times* and *Post* are likely to 'eat the leek.' In *any case*, it will place the Palmerston Government in peril, and the 'parties' in the House are beginning to scent the carcass. But we of the *Star* have no object but peace, and if Dallas be *not* dismissed, and the offer of arbitration be *accepted*, it will close the American difficulty. If there be any vengeance due for the past misdeeds of the present Cabinet, *that* may be left to the tender mercy of political opponents. I see *Little* Lord John is moving. Pray see that the *Star* does not needlessly play into *his* hands. He was more responsible for the *mad* popularity of the Russian war than anybody. And I would not trust him to keep the peace for a day with America if he could gain power by a war with her.

"I suggested that a public meeting should be called. If so, I hope you will arrange the resolutions and speak to one of them. You will of course take the same line as in the *Star*. Throw overboard Crampton and his backers on the Enlistment Question, and go for arbitration on Central American affairs. In speaking of a public meeting, it is on the assumption of course that the final decision of the Government as to Dallas is still hanging in the balance. If the desperadoes at headquarters should send away Dallas, then 'war to the knife' must be the cry of the Peace Party against the present Ministry. If it be known on the contrary that they have resolved not to retaliate in that way, it will take the edge off your meeting. By the way, in dealing with the question of Crampton's dismissal, show how the oligarchical dislike of the democratic power peeps out. *We* were not so stiff with Autocratic Russia, or even wretched Monarchical Spain, under somewhat similar circumstances, for when Nicholas objected to receive Sir Stratford Canning as our

Richard Cobden : The International Man

Ambassador, we yielded and threw him over. And when the Spanish Government sent away Sir H. Bulwer on personal grounds, we submitted."

"*June* 17, 1856.

"I take it for granted that the Cabinet have resolved to throw overboard Crampton. *The Times* follows suit, and will be ready evidently to fling the Government after him if necessary. What a disgusting exhibition of bullying in the first place, and when that fails, of mean evasion, our newspapers are making! Do not fail to rub the nose of *The Times* in its former articles. The *country Press*, which to a considerable extent follows the lead of *The Times*, is really to be pitied—for they have to write once a week only, and during that time their leader sometimes throws two or three somersaults. The braggart Press must be made to eat dirt, as the only mode of putting the country in a right position with the rest of the world —for if we do not avow that, so far as the journals have hitherto represented the facts of the case and the opinion of the public, they have been entirely wrong and the Americans right, what can be said of our 'honour' in submitting now to insult and injustice? We must throw over our Government, *Times*, etc., as the only way of proving that we are not now a mean-spirited and craven people in allowing our Minister, who according to them was in the right, to be returned on our hands. If the Government have pocketed the affront the American Question is of course settled, excepting in so far as there will be a reckoning between the 'ins' and the 'outs.' But there is no party which can in my time govern this country for whose advent to office I would care to take the trouble of walking down Parliament Street.

"The British Liberals should be told plainly that, apart from the merit of any dispute our Government may

Peace and Recovery

have with that of Washington, there is always a latent instinct at work in the breasts of our aristocratic ruling class, which seeks to estrange the two countries as much as possible, and to render the Americans the object of dislike, fear or suspicion to the English people. Our so-called Radical politicians fall pell-mell into this trap, and here you see such papers as the *Dispatch* and *Sun* howling to the same tune as the *Post* and *Times*."

"*June* 18, 1856.

"I doubt the policy of admitting that the Ministry have saved themselves (I allude to the first words of the Summary in yesterday's *Star* : 'Lord Palmerston has saved himself'), for the conclusion I have come to, after thinking the matter calmly over, is that, for the honour of the country and the dignity of the Ministry themselves, the proper course for them to take is to resign. That would save the nation a humiliation, and would be more dignified on the part of the Cabinet than to throw overboard their representative and cling to office, whilst the ink is hardly dry in which they have justified his very act, and when they have gone so far as to say (as Lord Clarendon did in one of his speeches) that neither intentionally nor unintentionally (I think he said 'neither by accident nor design') had Mr. Crampton infringed the laws of the United States. But I am quite sure you ought not to commit us to Baxter's qualified amendment, *approving* the tone of Lord Clarendon's correspondence—that correspondence is quite indefensible, *if Crampton is to be thrown overboard*, for its whole object was to justify him.

"By the way, young Baxter, who comes of a good Free Trade stock in Dundee, and has some talent with a little too much self-esteem, is the same who, in seconding the Address, went out of his way to attack the Peace

Party at the opening of the Session, when he was sure of gaining the applause of the military party in the House, and who declared that we, the Peace Party, would not have been safe if we had gone to preach our doctrines in his boroughs. A gentle rap on his knuckles, or rather a little quiet advice, would do him good, and show that we intend to act on the Scotch motto that nobody will touch us hostilely with impunity. He should be advised to keep steadily in view the example of his great predecessor, Mr. Hume, who never allowed himself to be *used* by the Government or aristocratic parties, but who kept himself free and independent amidst the rise and fall of a score of administrations. There is one cardinal principle of his predecessor's political life which should be especially commended to his imitation—that which guarded him from ever separating himself on light grounds from those who generally agreed with him and who had the same public objects in view. If for the sake of catching the cheers of a military party in the House he goes out of his way to attack those whom he called the Peace Party, he is separating himself from men with whom he will find himself voting in the same lobby in nine cases out of ten—unless the politics of his constituents have changed since Mr. Hume represented them. By the way, apropos of Baxter (who has travelled in the States and published some lectures on the country), you heard J. B. Smith state that he (Baxter) said he witnessed the folly of Crampton in refusing at a public meeting to uncover and stand up when the national air was sung. How can *he now* justify the correspondence of the Government which identified them so completely with that silly person? However——

"Looking to the state of parties in the House and the way in which *The Times*, etc., are committed, and the cowardice of M.P.'s under the threat of a dissolution,

Peace and Recovery

I incline to think they will let Palmerston go on again. He is a dangerous fellow, and in the case of a strong Power like America the whole danger lies in the probable humiliation he may bring on *us*. There is one point to which I can only refer, but will *talk* about to you. We must guard ourselves against being thought a party aiming at peace by any means, and at any price, and without any care for national character, or what some people call 'honour.' The fear of our being so considered came over me as I read the remarks in the Summary yesterday beginning 'Lord Palmerston has saved himself.' We must show as sensitive regard for our national character as anybody, and I doubt whether we do so in meeting so great an affront as the sending away our Minister with toleration to the Government, and without saying that they ought to resign in order to place the *country* in an honourable attitude and themselves in a graceful position towards the Americans. There is no doubt that anybody would have a better chance of arranging the Central American Question with the Americans than Lord Palmerston, whom they do not like. When Buchanan said he could have settled the differences with Lord Aberdeen in half an hour, everybody knew that he meant more than he could express, and that he has a very different opinion of his prospects with Lord Palmerston. You cannot do wrong in bringing out these points. *He* never was and never will be *our* Minister.

"I see no objection to your denouncing the ruffianly attack on Sumner [1]; I am writing to him to do so. But I would avoid *on principle* going into the question of their 'domestic institutions.' I have always acted on the rule that *non-intervention* should be observed morally as well as materially. I speak of myself as a politician, and

[1] Cf. p. 340.

Richard Cobden : The International Man

I would observe the same rule in the *Star*, which is a secular organ. *Religious* organs are different. In my opinion you ought at once to denounce the sending more armed ships to America. We doubled our force on that station in November last. What good has it done? What pretence have we? As to the protection of our interests in Central America, you will perhaps see by the article in the *Economist* that we have little interest there. The Americans have not augmented their fleets in Europe, *where they have far more trade than we have with all America.* The English people should be told that this is only done as an excuse for employing ships-of-war and furnishing a pretence for keeping up a large force. There is really no dignity in sending fleets and at the same time allowing the Americans to send away our Minister."

"*July* 9, 1856.

"Apropos of Italian affairs, you ought to be prepared with a good article to follow the debate on Lord John's motion. The point to press in your argument is this: What does Lord John, and what do our aristocratic politicians who have our foreign policy in their hands, propose *to do?* Do they intend to set up the peoples of the Italian States to *force* their Governments to give them Constitutional freedom? If so, are they prepared to help them? No, a thousand times no, must be the answer of all who know what our Government is. But the Italians may be deluded and incited by the vague reports of what will reach them of the proceedings of our Parliament, and, through our *foolish Press*, into premature plot and insurrection, which will again lead, as they have before, into proscription, exile and death. Protest against such delusions, which betray ardent patriots to their doom and lead only to broken hearts,

Peace and Recovery

ruined fortunes and every species of misfortune. But our aristocratic rulers will probably exert their *moral influence with the Government* of King Bomba and the Pope to ensure better government! Does any rational being suppose that with the tone of their Press and of such tricky politicians as guide it our Government will have any influence whatever in the way of friendly advice? The truth is, it must be again and again told the English public and the world that our aristocratic politicians make political capital out of the Italians, Poles, Circassians, etc., for purposes of their own, and not with any serious intention of promoting liberty anywhere. And this game will go on so long as the English public allow them to parade their sympathies for the grievances of foreigners instead of *doing the work* of liberty at home."

"*July* 10, 1856.

"When does the Reform Club banquet to Williams come off? Either on that or some other occasion you should read a lecture to our so-called Liberals and Reformers upon their warlike and military tendency. They ought to be rallied in good round terms. The Reform Club seems to have grown more martial than the United Service. One would have thought that their escapade with Charley Napier would have been enough in that line. But to what is all this to lead? What is the policy, what the principles of the Reform Party? We know what the professed principles of the Whigs were down to the time of their advent to power in 1830. Peace, economy and non-intervention were the words inscribed on Lord Grey's banner. We know that the leaders of the Whig Party had for half a century denounced the military tendency of the Government; and at the close of the French War they advocated a reduction of our army down to the old constitutional standard with

Richard Cobden : The International Man

a vehemence quite refreshing to those who study the pages of *Hansard* from 1816 to 1822. Not only did the leading Whigs—Grey, Tierney, Mackintosh, Brougham, Lord John Russell, etc., denounce the large standing army of the day (much less, by the way, than now), such statesmen as the Marquis Wellesley and Lord Grenville joined in the same tone. It is true the Whigs have turned round upon their followers and are now worse than the Tories, but what are the principles of the so-called *Independent Liberals*? There were formerly eighty to one hundred men in the House who professed to be more economical, liberal and progressive than either the Whigs or Tories. Where are they now and what are their principles? Are they represented by this frenzied spirit of hero-worship and love of military glory exhibited at the Reform Club? If so, do they think they are in the track of peace, economy or non-intervention? They are playing the game of aristocracy, privilege, high taxation and all their attendant evils to the millions whose interests they profess to serve."

"*July* 18, 1856.

"*The Times*, with its Cockney ignorance, in an article yesterday on Emigration winds up by expressing a hope that the emigrants in future will go to Canada and not swell the number of our enemies in the States, as if their feelings to us would be different wherever they might be. I should not write a *long* article on the Canadian view of the question, but still people might be told to pause and inquire before they assumed that the Canadians would fight for our diplomatic blunderers as if they had an interest in the matter. The point you mention of the Canadians having *talked* of sending a representative to Washington is significant, as showing which way they think their interests are gravitating. In fact, since a free

Peace and Recovery

trade in *native produce has been established between Canada and the States, there is far more intercourse between America and Canada than between us and Canada.* We must show better reasons than the support of our diplomatists in their chicanery, *in which Canada has no voice*, before she will embark in a war with the best customer at her doors."

"*July* 28, 1856.

"Put the enclosed into your own language. I have purposely written it on both sides to compel you to rewrite it—for I can often give you rapid hints for an article without any trouble to myself if I know that my own language is not necessarily to be printed. When writing for the Press I am beset with a fastidiousness that almost paralyses my fingers.

"What have you done about the *Star* editorship? Let me advise you always to try to make your articles apropos of some topic of the hour—otherwise they look like treasured-up essays, which to daily-paper readers always seem misplaced. For instance, a line or two connecting your article of last week on Turkey with Layard's speech at Aylesbury would have invested it with the prestige of *ready writing*. You must come to the *democratic* view of the Peace Question. Apropos of Spanish affairs, it might be stated once for all that the creed of the *Morning Star* is that where large standing armies exist rational liberty cannot live. Work out this view in a succession of short, sharp articles all apropos of something."

"*July* 30, 1856.

"I cannot too strongly express my regret at the language used in a letter in the *Star* of yesterday on Italian affairs. Gladstone's pamphlet is attacked and poor Poerio assailed. Surely ordinary generosity, if not policy, ought to have held the hand of the writer when speaking of a man who is now in a dungeon and in irons. Depend on it, our principle of non-intervention will be suspected to mean an alliance with despotism all over the world if such indiscreet excuses for tyranny be allowed to have prominent place in the paper. Read this to Hamilton."

"*July* 31, 1856.

"I am not dogmatical on the Education Question. How could I be, when I find myself opposed, on economical grounds, to the opinions of Bastiat, and to yours in a theological or ecclesiastical point of view? But here is my creed in the matter. My political sympathies are with the *masses*. They in this country are still under the hoof of feudalism. The middle class is to a large extent the accomplice of the privileged order, and eager to be admitted within its charmed circle. The only chance for the workers with their hands is in their greater intelligence. Compared with the United States, Switzerland, or any Protestant State there is no population half so ignorant as our own. Among the other perversities of Baines is his attempt to show that we are 'not so very bad,' and when we adduce the large proportion of married couples that don't sign their names, he argues that many who can write yet prefer to make a mark, as if the argument in the eye of any unprejudiced person did not lean the other way, and warrant the inference that if so large a number cannot sign their names, *how much greater number cannot write anything else*, for the pride of a man, especially when being married—an occasion which draws forth all his love of approbation—would impel him to write his name even if he could not pen another syllable. Well, the ignorance of the English masses being so great, how is it to be best removed? I say, try the New England machinery—a local *voluntary*

Peace and Recovery

organization which has borne the test of time and experience and has enabled its people to govern itself and prosper. By comparison, our so-called voluntaryism has undoubtedly failed, and in my opinion, instead of being in the way of making up our lost ground, we are being more and more distanced in the race every year. I have nothing to say for the *present* system in England. But I confess I can hardly see how the question can be ignored with a view to securing something better. However, it is not at present the question before the country.

"I did not write because I was really not in a position to advise you, not knowing what terms were to be offered. I hope you will undertake the office of editor-in-chief, with an absolute veto over the leading articles. And I hope you will be put in a position to *exert an unquestioned authority in all departments of the Star office.* I agree with you as to Hamilton's eccentricities, and they will grow apace if he be left to himself. But there is so much moral goodness, and such an originality of genius and power of intellect, about the man, that it would be deeply to be lamented if he were not utilized to the utmost. But it will require tact and gentleness to bring him back to his former post of second in command. You can do this better than anybody else, because he has faith in your sincerity of purpose. Let him know that if you are put at the head, it has not been from your own seeking; on the contrary, that you have taken the step with reluctance, that it is the act of *the Quakers*, who wish not to be disturbed about details any more, but to be able to throw all responsibility on your shoulders as a person whom they know and who they think knows them, and what will satisfy them. Count on my co-operation in every possible way."

Richard Cobden : The International Man

"*August* 1, 1856.

"I observe the subject of trade unions treated in to-day's *Star* paper. The desire of the writer to speak in a conciliatory spirit to the workpeople, which is right, leads him, I think, to speak in a tone of concession and compromise which may be misinterpreted. So far as the wages view of the question goes, I think the only sound and honest course is to tell the people plainly that they are under a delusion as to their assumed power to regulate or permanently influence in the slightest degree by *coercion* the rate of wages. They might as well attempt to regulate the tides by force, or change the course of the seasons, or subvert any of the other laws of nature—for the wages of labour depend upon laws as unerring and as much above our coercive power as any other operations of nature. There is a desperate spirit of monopoly and tyranny at the bottom of all these trade unions, for they begin with regulating the numbers to be brought up in their trades, refusing to allow unlimited apprenticeship, thus excluding the children of the unskilled labourer from sharing their advantages. Then how entirely they ignore our foreign trade, and forget that liberty of commerce which puts it out of the power of the working class of one country to dictate the rate of wages which employers shall pay. To treat this question *au fond* you must have writers very strong on political economy, and yet do not let them write in the abstruse technical and unsympathizing style of some of these political economists. It is not enough to show that the labourers are wrong in their particular efforts to improve their condition, but we must show that we are their friends and try to point out to them on what their welfare really rests ; and this opens up the whole field of social and political questions, including our own Peace Question.

Peace and Recovery

For it might be shown that it is impossible to waste a hundred millions on a war without the working classes feeling it in increased pressure on them, and that if they are to still preserve the same share of comforts as before, it can only be by increased labour, for it is out of their toil that the taxes are directly or indirectly in great part paid. Then it might be shown that, if the Americans remain at peace and their people are comparatively untaxed, it is impossible that we can compete with them unless we are content with less wages and less profit of capital than they. In fact, it is a world-wide question—but the great point is to start from *sound ground*. The people who write these topics must *read up*."

"*August* 8, 1856.

" I paid a visit on Wednesday to my neighbour, the Bishop of Oxford, and met Lord Aberdeen, Roundell Palmer and some others. The old Earl was even more emphatic than at the same place a year ago in lamenting to me that he had suffered himself to be drawn into the Russian war. He declared that he ought to have resigned. Speaking of the authors of his policy he said, ' It was not the Parliament or the public, but the Press that forced the Government into the war. The public mind was not at first in an uncontrollable state, but it was made so by the Press.' He might have added that Lord Johnny had something to do with it. I really could not help pitying the old gentleman, for he was in an unenviable state of mind, and yet I doubt if there be a more reprehensible human act than to lead a nation into an unnecessary war, as Walpole, North, Pitt and Aberdeen have done against their own conviction and at the dictation of others. By the way, between ourselves, he told me that he had told the Queen he thought she was playing too much at soldiers, and that she

Richard Cobden : The International Man

laughed and said, 'You know I am a soldier's daughter and must take care of the Army."

"*August* 20, 1856.

"The Americans must be backed up in their view of exempting private property at sea from spoliation. It is a most important principle—tends to rob the spoiler of his prey and make war a game of blood and bruisings without the attractions of plunder and prize money. Hurrah for anything that tends to make war a mere duel between professionals, for it will make the calling less profitable and therefore less popular. Don't forget to quote prominently a passage where the American Foreign Secretary condemns large armaments as being hostile to freedom and the interests of the people. That's the way a Government speaks which really represents the people."

"*August* 26, 1856.

"Don't omit your foreign topics—but what I meant was to let the *Star* have a due mixture of home questions. It is too true that the public mind has been so blaséed with Sebastopol that it can't attend to its own affairs—but that is too unnatural a state of things to last—and besides, let us recollect that it is our mission to show the evil of such a tendency in the public mind. *You* can write on any home topic you choose to take in hand quite as well as on foreign questions. I liked your article upon the state of parties—follow it up—you are quite right in putting down Whigs and Tories in the same category. I should like to know what distinctive ground the most decided Whig would claim for his party as against the Tory. Certainly not for being the party of Peace, non-intervention and economy, for on these questions neither Fox nor Lord Grey would any longer own their party if they could again revisit this scene. But in dealing with these two

Peace and Recovery

aristocratic factions, avoid on the other hand the tone of the Tory-Chartist—i.e. the active advocacy of the restoration of the Tories as a means to better government. All that I would say in this direction is that we need not be frightened at it—for the Radicals are a much more useful and honest party in the House when in opposition, and the Whigs never make any progress excepting in that invigorating atmosphere."

"*September* 5, 1856.

"The Slavery Question is working to a crisis in the United States. I have a strong suspicion that these Southern bullies, who bluster so loudly, when they find the opinion in the North go against them, as I hope it will do by a decided vote in the Free States for Fremont, will draw in their horns. If not they will find themselves given over to perdition, for if once the North is fairly roused against the South it will be short work with the latter. Northern races are less impulsive and may therefore sometimes seem to be at first run down by the South, but they always win against lower latitudes when fairly brought to bay. I wish you would tell them as much in a short *quotable* article in the *Star*. It helps the good cause in America. The way in which you can legitimately take up the subject is to refer to the threat sometimes thrown out by Southern newspapers that the Slave States will form a union of some kind with England. Tell them they can have no idea of the feeling in this country or they would not look in this direction for sympathy, that before they can be admitted to a union with England they must not merely give up the extension of slavery, which is all their fellow-citizens in the States wish them to do, but must first emancipate every slave they possess, for that if they were subjects of the Queen of England they would be every man of them felons, and liable to the punishment of transportation for owning slaves. Tell them there is not a man in Europe, unless it be a kindred despot who likes to see republicanism brought into disrepute, who does not cry shame upon them. They must be given up to the madness which precedes a fall or they would not challenge the attention of the world to their odious institution so out of time and out of place in a Christian and democratic community."

"*October* 1, 1856.

"It seems to me that the present is a most favourable opportunity for vindicating our principles in the *Star* in reference to the Neapolitan business. I am writing constantly to Dunckley at Manchester, and to Hamilton, offering them hints and stimulating them to an energetic advocacy of non-intervention views. I wish you had been in London. It is at such a moment as this that the *Star* ought to put forth all its strength in the vindication of its views, and to endeavour, as it did in the American business, to make its influence felt. But this can only be done by a daily reiteration of its arguments. But to do this as *The Times* does, without boring its readers, requires the resources of several pens. All parties should bring their minds to bear on the great topic of the day. It seems to me that we are more thoroughly wrong in joining Louis Napoleon to coerce the King of Naples into good government (bless the mark!) than ever we were before, and that is saying much. But the Cockney Press, as usual, is running full cry after this false scent. Not only the London papers, but the Whig provincials as usual, and our friend the *Mercury* taking the lead. I send you a paper with an atrocious article calling for the *cannon*, and at the same time avowing ignorance of what the demands of the Allies are! Then there is the inconsistency of wanting only to make despotism safe and

Peace and Recovery

preventing the spread of insurrection into Hungary and Poland. But I have underlined several of the absurdities and not the least the last. I wish you would give a gentle rebuke to our *religious* friend for his reckless advocacy of sanguinary measures on all occasions. He richly deserves it. Is not this a monomania? The only way I can account for this course invariably taken by a man who pretends to the highest regard for the interests of religious morality and education is that he is over-endowed with the pugnacious organs even to a point of deformity."

"*October* 15, 1856.

" There was an excellent and very suggestive article in the *Star* about the physical force tendencies of the Anglo-Saxon race. If it was Hamilton's tell him what I say, for he will not take it as a worse compliment coming through third hands. But tell him it would have been better without the first paragraph about the 'enlightened foreigners.' And pray call all your contributors together and forbid them ever putting an *exordium*, *Times* fashion, to their articles. *In medias res* must be the motto for the beginning of your articles. It is old-fashioned and impertinent to dally with your readers over an exordium, and they resent it by not reading the articles.

" It seems to me that we ought to take some opportunity of showing the political philosophy of *our* non-intervention policy. I mean that it must not be allowed to appear as a sterile principle. But we must show that the intervention principle is against the interests of our people in a variety of ways, as in distracting attention from home politics, adding loads of debts and taxation which keep down by their presence the working class and prevent them from rising in the social scale and *therefore* from rising politically. This should be brought out—or otherwise we appear to be merely fighting for a sentiment."

Richard Cobden : The International Man

"*October* 19, 1856.

"I have seen Bright twice; we have had long walks, played at billiards, and fished together, and have talked incessantly for hours, not always keeping clear of the forbidden field of politics. I could perceive little difference except that he is twenty pounds thinner and his tone and aspect are much more gentle and subdued. He found himself none the worse for our interview. He says he can talk politics with me or any one who agrees with him without inconvenience, but if he is *opposed* it makes his head ache and gives the sense of fatigue to his brain. I am thus far relieved by what I have seen of him after an eight months' separation that I have no longer the horrid fear of his falling into a state of mental imbecility, a fate far more dreadful than death. If he follows the good advice of Sir J. Clark and others and goes abroad for another year, I feel sure that the risk of any active and permanent disease arising from the present attack may be averted. But whether he will be ever able to take again a position in public life when he is to bring to bear the same fervour of feeling and the same herculean energies as in times past is a question which I hardly dare ask myself. However, I am thankful that at all events the health and happiness which are consistent with a moderate exertion of his mental powers are within his reach. He has quite made up his mind to go abroad within a month.

"Don't omit any chance of utilizing Faucher. I told him you were anxious to do what you could. Now pray be candid with him. Tell him he must not only give all his powers to the paper for the time engaged, but that he must have tact and conciliatory manners at the office to everybody. Tell him that it is natural that there should be a little awkwardness between him a foreigner and an

Peace and Recovery

English staff. It would be so in any walk of life. But it must be his business to surmount this difficulty. I have not heard from him since I saw you. Of his knowledge, at once comprehensive and exact, of continental politics, and of his unswerving devotion to sound economic and peace principles I am quite able to speak with confidence. I send you. in strict confidence of course, the enclosed note from Bright to show what is doing about the proprietary of the *Star*. *I* shall not take a pecuniary interest. I am too sensitive, whilst in the public arena, to be a proprietor of a London daily paper. I tell Bright, a *partner in London* to manage the business department is in my opinion a *sine qua non* of success. I see no objection but the reverse to the names he mentions."

"*October* 21, 1856.

"It appears to me that the fact that the English public have to learn for the first time what their Foreign Office is doing and what use the Admiralty is about to make of their ships-of-war *through an announcement in the* '*Moniteur*' ought to be bitterly commented on. Then mark with what care the French Government announces that they don't intend to promote revolution. After this will the geese and donkeys in this country who profess to believe that Palmerston, the partner in this intervention, really means something serious against the rule of the Bourbons still continue to delude themselves? But bear in mind that when the *Moniteur* tells the world that revolutionary movements will not be encouraged, it really means that they will not be permitted. The only serious menace in the article in the *Moniteur* is against the republicans and Mazzini. It is evident that the King of Naples has nothing to fear.

"An occasion ought to be taken (but do not mix up too many branches of the argument in *one* article) to refer

Richard Cobden : The International Man

to the maddening articles which appeared in the London Press (and don't forget the *Leeds Mercury*) when this intervention was first announced. Quote these articles. Look at the *Daily News*—it was one of the worst. How these papers invoked the indignation of the country against the *King* of Naples ! The *Leeds Mercury*, you will see, distinctly says he is an 'assassin' and 'murderer.' It was with these phrases that these papers, relying on their former impunity and forgetting that there is now a real competition in the Press which will always tend to their swift exposure, only a few weeks ago endorsed this act of intervention and inflamed the minds of their readers, leading them at the same time to expect that proceedings commensurate with the alleged misdeeds of the wicked king would be carried into execution. Well, now, what has come of their thunder. A proclamation from the French Government that not a hair of this alleged 'tyrant,' 'murderer' and 'assassin' shall be touched ! These newspapers seem every few months to be holding themselves up to the ridicule and contempt of the whole civilized world by their bombastic threats and abortive performances. Who will trust them for guides in future ?

"Another topic. Some of these papers, wishing to be logical even at the expense of every sentiment of morality and humanity, when pushed home in argument and compelled to avow a theory in harmony with their warlike policy, boldly avow, like the *Leader* in the enclosed paragraph, that they look on wars and revolutions like lotteries in which though blank after blank may be drawn yet somehow and somewhere liberty is to emerge out of the bloody cauldron. If these parties are honest and not blinded by self-conceit, one would not despair of convincing them that every step they take in this path of warfare or preparation for war between crowned heads and despots

Peace and Recovery

leads directly back from the goal of freedom they profess to seek. Increased armaments, more young men put under the yoke of the drill sergeant and made a part of the machine of despotism, heavier taxation keeping down the masses, and last, not least, the attention of men diverted from the more important question of domestic policy to be scattered and wasted in the maze of diplomatic squabbles. And do such simple folks as their writers in the *Leader* expect that out of this liberty is to grow? Do they suppose that some day the armed tyrants will forget their cunning, and that this military machine of theirs instead of despotism is to turn out by accident and against the will of its masters the friend of freedom?"

"*November* 2, 1856.

"It appears to me that you have a good opening now for a home thrust at the Government Press, and those who have stunned us with their praises of Palmerston for having saved the country, rescued us from dishonourable terms, and secured a peace of twenty years at least by showing Russia how utterly powerless she was, etc. Well, now, what are these same journalists with *The Times* at their head telling us? That the terms of the peace are not being fulfilled, that Russia is not subdued, that she is at her old work again, precisely as before the war, that in fact Palmerston's peace is a failure. But then what becomes of all the merit claimed for Palmerston? He went on with the war after the Vienna Conference, spent us another thirty or forty millions, sacrificed of French and English troops some one hundred thousand men and all for what? Read the articles in the Government papers and they tell us the work must be done over again. But what is more serious we are to do it single-handed. *The Times* is now at its old work of bluster again, 'in

Richard Cobden : The International Man

the name of the people of England,' telling Russia that we are as ready as ever for war. Stop a bit, *Mr. Times*. If the people go to war again it will not be for objects such as now seem to be the ground of quarrel—the Serpents Island or a few square miles of morass and lake in Bessarabia. Without pretending to speak for the country, it may safely be said that it will not again be led blindfolded by *The Times* or trust itself once more to the genius of blunder who is at the head of the Government. Every word these parties utter against the late peace is a condemnation of themselves, and a proof that the people ought not again to listen to them in any grave matter of foreign politics. The public feel that the power even for mischief of *The Times* is gone, destroyed by its own reckless immorality—for its bluster now ceases to affect the Funds which actually rise in the face of such leaders as that of Friday. You must really pile a little scorn and indignation on this topic."

"*November* 4, 1856.

"Do you suppose one person in ten that buys the *Star* reads through such an article (apropos of nothing) as that upon *knighthood* the other day? These essays, wanting in aptness, give a poor idea always of the practical talent about a paper. Depend on it that the penny Press must not only go to New York for its printing-machine but also for its model of management. There must be the same vigorous *aptness* in all that is written, and as much news and correspondence eventually (when the paper duty comes off) as in the *Herald* or *Tribune*. Your writing may if you please be more classical and in milder taste, but it must be equally *direct* and *apropos* to the business of the hour, and you must not get into the way of one formal leading article, but give sparkling little leaders as they do. Bright agrees to all this."

Peace and Recovery

"*November* 7, 1856.

"So we are now to have an Austrian alliance! Turkey and Austria are our only European friends. If I could afford it I would pay a person of sufficient industry to go constantly back for a few years over *The Times* paper and reproduce the articles which it would wish to have forgotten just at the moment when it was perpetrating a new act of tergiversation. Now pray do hunt up one of its diatribes against Austria and print it. Is there no way of stinging the public in the Liberal Press into self-respect on this subject of a foreign policy? Our newspapers are obtaining for us the scorn and contempt of the reading world by their total disregard of consistency and their kaleidoscopic suddenness of change to suit the views of the Foreign Office; and the worst of it is that both the old political parties are so much in the same vein and expect some day to have their turn in the same convenient game that it is almost impossible to establish a sound principle which shall put an end to their doings.

"There is one party that I should think might be brought to repudiate the old policy altogether, I mean the phil-Hungarians, the Italian-liberation Society, etc., in fact the party of the 'nationalities.' But unfortunately they have *their* scheme of foreign intervention, the wildest and most anarchical of all, for it sets aside the allegiance to treaties and international obligations and would set up a universal propaganda of insurrection and rebellion. But surely these parties who are honest, if they be logical, will be open to this conviction *now*, that any attempt to serve 'nationalities' whilst the policy of the 'Balance of Power' is all-powerful and overrides every other consideration, even to the extent of defending Austria against Russia, is an utter delusion. There is something most offensive to reason and common sense in seeing great

Richard Cobden : The International Man

popular demonstrations in favour of Kossuth and for the Italians in this country, whilst the people who move in these meetings are utterly powerless to prevent their own Government from giving its support to the oppressor of these nations. One would think their first business should be to get as much power over their own Government as would prevent it from *helping* the Austrians. I shall certainly have something to say about this when Parliament meets."

"*November* (?), 1856.

"No Power gives more advantage to the Government of Austria in this way than England, for it is needless to add that first and foremost in all continental intrigues and diplomatic imbroglios is the Foreign Office of this country. And none is more ready to hold up European treaties between the *Governments* as a discouragement or menace in the face of the struggling leaders for independence than our present Prime Minister. Ask not merely M. Mazzini, whom it is the fashion to blame as impracticable, but M. Manin, the temperate but heroic defender of Venice, or M. Kossuth himself, what answer they got from Lord Palmerston even after they had driven every Austrian from their territories. Why, they were coldly reminded of the Treaty of Vienna, and told bluntly enough that no other authority could be recognized in Vienna or Hungary than that of the Austrian Government.

"Now we recommend a course, a principle of action, which will tend to leave their Government more at the mercy of the people they are oppressing. We would keep aloof from the blood-stained oppressors at Vienna. We would have no compliments passing, no secret diplomacy, no dependence in any way on that central authority; we would cultivate friendly intercourse and

Peace and Recovery

trading relations as far as possible with the people throughout all the Austrian Empire, and we would be on a courteous footing diplomatically with the Government. In a word, we would take as much as possible the same ground as that occupied by the people of the United States towards Austria. Now here is a programme of foreign policy; will our Liberal politicians, our Radicals and democrats, as they profess themselves, join us in this policy? If it can be carried out, depend on it we shall do more than by any intermeddling to bring the Austrian Government upon a proper footing of dependence on its people. It will be far sounder and more successful than meddling in Italy or any other country *through the same diplomatists who are binding us hand and foot to Austria.* Will our Liberals embrace this policy? If not—why not? Are we to be told of the Balance of Power, that Austria is a part of the system of Europe, and if she were removed from the scale then we should not be safe from the encroachments of Russia, etc.? Then we are in league with the murderers of 'Ciceroacchio,' and it is for *our* safety that the oppressors of Hungary and Italy are to be maintained in their sanguinary rule at Vienna."

"*November* 20, 1856.

"I observed what you said about the Greeks. They are very clever fellows. All my sympathies are with them. I like the race, for I never met a stupid Greek. But you must always have a certain watch and reserve on yourself in your political relations with them. They are very ardent patriots, and sometimes their zeal is apt to get the better of their discretion. The best way is to do them justice at all times but not to give the *Star* the aspect of their advocate. They ought to be able to give you early information sometimes. The resuscitation

Richard Cobden : The International Man

of the Greek race and the wonderful development it has made in commercial enterprise and wealth during the last thirty years is one of the most remarkable signs of the times. That race will yet play a part in the destinies of the East. If we could see the Italians turning to industry and commerce it would give us better hopes of them. But whilst they leave the trade of their ports to foreigners and do nothing but whine to other nations for help I have little faith in their destiny. With their long seaboard and numerous ports they ought to have a commerce which would put down Austria by sea."

"*November* 30, 1856.

"I have been moving about, but see the *Star* regularly. The writing is good, but the 'reading' still execrable. The enclosed from the *Manchester Guardian* is very good. Do you think it would do for the *Star*? Robertson Gladstone suggests that London would be a better place than Manchester for a first meeting about 'Foreign Policy.' If any meeting be held I am inclined to that opinion. Manchester has never been more than the ghost of its former self in the agitations that have been attempted there since the League shut up shop. And we always suffer by a comparison with our former selves. It is perhaps contrary to human nature to expect that the same community which has won one great triumph should be the first to re-enter the political arena for other victories. People naturally feel a wish to enjoy what they have been for seven years fighting to obtain. Besides, the truth must be told that people in Lancashire are growing conservative and aristocratic with their prosperous trade. London in my opinion would be more likely to turn up new blood. What do you say to this? I have written to Sturge. Let it be private."

Peace and Recovery

"*December* 1, 1856.

"I have often thought of referring to the subject but have not time by this post to do more than offer a word of caution. There is, I see, a man arrested at Berlin, and he seems to point to a *Court* enemy in England as the author of his arrest. As I never see the Cockney papers except *The Times* (which to do it justice never has lent itself to the party) I don't know what they are now saying upon the subject, but I have always observed that the *Advertiser* and other papers are ready to be let slip upon Prince Albert and the 'Germanism' of the Court at every opportunity. Now I suspect all this to come from the inspiration of a high quarter. There are not two men perhaps of exalted political rank capable and dexterous enough for playing this game. It is to retaliate upon the Court, and especially Prince Albert, for checks which a certain ambitious politician has had at the palace that these attacks are made. They don't spring from a Radical or Chartist inspiration, but from the opposite end of the political scale. You will understand. All I wish now is to guard you against giving any countenance to this strategy. It is not on our side but to favour the arch-enemy of our principles."

"*December* 4, 1856.

"Pray write a sharp indignant article upon the one in *The Times* yesterday about Wallachia and Moldavia. Read the last paragraph where we are distinctly told that our object is to sustain the rights of the Sultan even against the *people* of those provinces, and as it is known that the population are for *union*, *The Times* is now ordered by our Foreign Office, which has taken its line against it, to vilify beforehand the people as unfit to decide for themselves, and to denounce their decision as being only the work of Russia. And so we are to put ourselves in opposition to the people and to be the ally only of that Turkish minority which, to use *The Times's* own simile, lies like the lava of Vesuvius upon the Christian population. And yet we are indignant with Americans and Russians because they will not call our Eastern policy the defence of 'liberty'! But what can possibly result from this line but disastrous failure? The population of these countries—the Christian and progressive element—will be more and more our enemies and more and more the friends of Russia. Who can doubt that it is in the end the intelligence, wealth and numbers of the Christian population that will rule the East, and the utmost that we can do to retard it is by tying ourselves for a few years to the corpse of the Ottoman despotism to be ultimately compelled for very shame and decency to turn upon it and aid in its overthrow. In the meantime where are those Liberals among our warlike politicians who have always advocated the union of these principalities, because they know *that* is the wish of the people?"

"*December* 5, 1856.

"I think you would do well to put forth an article calling the attention of the public to the necessity of a *Reform in our Foreign Policy*, and inviting your readers to set to work to accomplish it in the only way in which reforms of any kind can be effected in England, viz. by association and agitation.

"The necessity of some change in our diplomatic procedure is now all but universally admitted. Outside of the Foreign Office scarcely a human being can be found to defend the mode in which its affairs are conducted. The practicability of some agreement on a new *principle* of foreign policy is the only question to be

Peace and Recovery

discussed. *That* can be solved only by a conference and a discussion, perhaps more than one, between honest men of various shades of opinion who agree as to the necessity of *some change*. The Liberals all profess the principle of non-intervention. The Tories do not oppose them in this view. Mr. Roebuck says to Mr. Hadfield at Sheffield, 'I am for non-intervention, but then I am for making other people conform to the same principle.' Well, there is little difference of opinion on this subject. We all wish to see the principle universally adopted. But there are some who think that the first step is to act up to our own professions, and thus try, at least in the first instance, what *moral means* can be adopted to carry out our views. Mr. Roebuck is all for force, for cannon and squadrons, and regiments and fleets—let us try in the first place the force of a good example and of an honestly expressed opinion. England will never speak in vain when she has moral power to back her, but Mr. Roebuck will allow that whilst our Foreign Office is ready to approve the French intervention in Rome, and excuse the Russian invasion of Hungary, and become a party to an occupation of Greece, to say nothing of the threatened intervention in Naples—we can have no *moral* standing ground for appealing to Austria to put an end to the occupation of the Papal Legation or the Danubian Principalities. Our policy seems studiously devised to give an excuse for all that Austria, Russia and France have done and are doing in the way of intervention."

"*December* 20, 1856.

"If I were going to put out an advertisement to reconcile the gentility of the land to penny newspapers, I should lay stress upon the advantages which steam and the electric telegraph give, and which allow cheap papers *now* to place themselves on a par with the richest old

Richard Cobden : The International Man

high-priced journals in the power of obtaining important facts. I would admit that those facts must be given in a compendious form—but then I would argue that to nineteen-twentieths of readers—to all indeed who have something else to do than read newspapers—it is preferable to have news in the briefest form. I should admit that twenty-five years ago, *before* steamboats and locomotives and electric telegraphs had been brought generally into use, it would have been impossible to have had a good penny paper able to compete with the old capitalists. For instance, *then The Times* would bring, in a postchaise and four from Liverpool to London at an expense of fifty pounds, a copy of the American President's message to gain twenty-four hours' start on its rivals. *Now* the same message is brought in a parcel by railway in six hours for three shillings, and at such repeated times of starting every day as to prevent the possibility of any advantage to any paper from hiring an express. Besides, the electric telegraph anticipates the substance. *This* line of argument applied to the Continent—to the Indian mail from Marseilles, the dispatches from Paris, Vienna, etc., is what I should carefully and accurately elaborate to convince sceptical minds that the cheapness is a necessary result of the steam and electric telegraph."

" Saturday.

" I am scarcely to be trusted when writing about this too successful charlatan. I get out of temper more with my generation than the man.

"Here is what I have written. Adopt it, or reject it, alter it as you please—but if it appears it must be on your own responsibility and therefore as your own. Don't mention me to Hamilton or anybody in connection with it. But something of the sort should be

Peace and Recovery

done. It will attract attention in high quarters, and it is the honest thing to be done."

"What is 'Germanism'? Where shall we find the 'Coburg influence'? Will anybody be so good as to enlighten us about the 'German element in the councils of St. James'? We ask for this information that we may unravel the innuendoes which are going the periodical round of a certain portion of the Press, insinuating that Prince Albert is conspiring with foreign despots to thwart the policy of a Liberal (!) Government.

"Sometimes these mysterious revelations are made to originate at Paris, and sometimes at Berlin or Brussels, where 'our own correspondent' discovers the secret springs of intrigues going on at Buckingham Palace, intrigues quite concealed from the vigilant eyes of the denizens of Westminster. The latest discovery of Coburg treason has been in connection with the Belgrad affair. Listen to the following alarming specimen from the Paris correspondent of a daily contemporary. . . . This startling piece of intelligence is much too good to be monopolized by the diurnal Press, and so the hebdomadal journals join in the cry; and under the head of '*Postscript*,' in large capitals, and with the exciting addition of 'Friday, 12 o'clock,' we find the following in a weekly contemporary. . . .

"These attacks against Prince Albert are always found in the same prints—not the first-class journals, be it remembered, for *The Times* and the most intellectual of the weekly papers refuse to notice them—and they are always in some way or another associated with the espousal of the cause of Lord Palmerston. Now, from what inspiration do these attacks emanate? It is much easier to give a negative than a positive answer to the question. They certainly do not spring from any prejudices in the popular mind which crave for grati-

Richard Cobden : The International Man

fication at the expense of the Court. A democratic orator who had no better programme for a Chartist meeting at St. Andrew's Hall than to charge the Prince with thwarting Lord Palmerston in his Liberal tendencies would be laughed off the platform. In the manufacturing districts the Prince is known only as the ready patron of education, science and art. There is not even a tradition among the Radicals of this metropolis which keeps alive any sense of grievance against a German influence at Court adverse to Liberal principles. The oldest frequenter of the most dingy bar parlour who muddles himself every evening with tobacco smoke, beer and the *Advertiser's* politics, never heard of anything of the kind. How should he, when for more than a hundred years there has been no German political element known at Court? George the Third, whose reign commenced a century since, when he determined to rule in opposition to his advisers, was always more English than his Ministry. If he played off one part of the aristocracy against another with success, it was by knowing how to conciliate the prejudices and the virtues of the British people. Whoever heard of a German element in the political conflicts of the fourth George, or of William the Fourth. Besides, the rough-and-ready logic of the million naturally asks—what are the opportunities and where is the power which Prince Albert possesses for swaying the policy of the Government? He attends no Cabinet Councils; he utters no argument and gives no votes in the Peers; and we never heard of his being able to influence a single vote in the Commons. He owns no pocket boroughs; nor does he possess large landed estates which give him the power of influencing the county elections. The Duke of Sutherland, or Bedford, or Lord Derby, could buy all the land possessed by the Prince and pay for it with less than a year's

Peace and Recovery

income from either of their rentals. The masses know all this, and hence we never hear them alleging that he is responsible for wrongs which they sometimes lay at the doors of the aristocracy, the Church, the middle class, etc. Seeing, then, that they do not spring from popular prejudice or feeling, whence emanate these attacks?

"We will not imitate the conduct we are reprobating by making charges which cannot be substantiated. We do not therefore presume to say that a certain personage is the instigator or approver of these systematic accusations merely because they have always happened to be made in his interest and behalf. It is notorious enough that these attacks have always turned up just at the critical moments when a scapegoat was indispensable to atone for some conspicuous failure of the present Prime Minister, to cover his retreat from an untenable position, or to revenge his temporary fall. The unhappy fact is also notorious that mutual confidence and esteem must be wanting between the Sovereign and her present Prime Minister; for there is on the records of Parliament that terrible letter which Lord John Russell read to the Commons of England, charging Lord Palmerston with want of candour to one who is the essence of womanly purity and truthfulness. But forced upon his Sovereign as he was by a bewildered Parliament and people, not a doubt has ever been whispered of the perfect loyalty and frankness with which his official services have been accepted. And we absolve him from the charge, the base charge of suborning or conniving at anonymous slanders of the Court to which he beyond all others owes a frank allegiance. But we give this absolution on one condition. These charges and insinuations, reiterated, specific and public, are of a character which can only be effectually silenced by Lord Palmerston himself. They speak in no

Richard Cobden : The International Man

equivocal terms of unconstitutional influences exerted over *him*, and they charge *him* (and it is no light charge) with succumbing to those influences. So tangible and specific have been these attacks that Lord Aberdeen and Lord John Russell have felt themselves called upon to defend the Prince in their places in Parliament. But not one word has Lord Palmerston ever uttered to contradict accusations with which his name as an aggrieved party has always been impudently associated. We trust when Parliament meets a member will be found to give his lordship an opportunity of silencing for ever these attacks, and if, as we trust, he hates foul play as cordially as we do, he will be grateful for the opportunity which will be afforded him of covering with scorn and reprobation those truculent prints which have been making such free and unworthy uses of his name."

December (?).

"If what is now said of the murder, by the Austrians, of 'Ciceroacchio' and his two sons, one of them a child, be true, it ought to be denounced by the *Star* as heartily as any paper. When I was at Rome in the spring of 1847, and the Pope had just begun to evince a spirit in favour of Reform, there was a great excitement in the Papal States, and a considerable latitude of speech and Press. The most remarkable man in Rome for his influence over the populace was a tradesman of decent character (I believe a coachmaker) whose powers of oratory got him the sobriquet of the second or little Cicero. I can speak to his character, for I had indirect communications with him. At that time the Marquis Massimo D'Azeglio, since Prime Minister of Piedmont, a man of every modern accomplishment, grained with the purest patriotism and an antique courage and disinterestedness,

Peace and Recovery

was living a refugee at Rome. I was in constant intercourse with him, and he was in private communication with the Pope on the one side and the people on the other through 'Ciceroacchio.' It was thought best that I should not *see* the latter in an interview, but owing to my being fresh from an anti-aristocratic triumph in England, I found myself a very great authority in matters of tactics with the leaders in Rome, and my opinion when communicated through D'Azeglio had, as he told me, great weight with 'Ciceroacchio.' I was thus in the thick of the agitation and knew from day to day what was going on, and can vouch for it that the above-named orator was always on the side of order, morality and moderation. If that man and his sons were murdered in the way alleged by Garibaldi, the Government of Austria ought to be gibbeted and denounced till it is made to answer before the opinion of the world. It is, if possible, a worse outrage than hanging the Hungarian General officers in cold blood. The Government of Austria is and has been for generations remarkable for cruelty and cold-blooded treachery—the result of cowardice owing to its really precarious hold on the people. In my opinion that Government has been a nuisance to the cause of progress and freedom in Europe any day since the fall of Napoleon. And what is it that perpetuates and will continue to sustain such a despicable rule? *Why, the State system of Europe which goes under the name of the Balance of Power.* This it is which alone preserves the integrity of the Austrian Empire, and deprives the nationalities of a chance of overthrowing the incubus. It is because the other Governments of Europe consider it necessary at whatever cost of internal misgovernment to keep intact a great member of the states system, rather than allow it to suffer disruption and take a new form, that these tyrannies propped up from without seem to threaten to be eternal. And never perhaps was diplomacy more busy in weaving a web, the meshes of which tie together in almost indissoluble bonds under one pretence or another the different Governments of Europe, than during the last two years. Every treaty to which Austria is invited to be a party —every time she is called in to mediate and arbitrate between such Powers as England, France and Russia— a new lease is given to the House of Hapsburg, and the Hungarians and Italians feel an augmented load of central despotism weighing them still deeper in the dust."

"*December*, 1856.

"I wrote to Hamilton advising him not to take sides in the Neuchâtel quarrel, which nobody understands, but to urge on both parties the absolute duty of submitting the question to arbitration, and to denounce whichever side should first appeal to arms. But prima facie the case is against Prussia, for her adherents were the first to resort to armed insurrection. If called on to offer an opinion, I should say that your leaders in the *Star* (not meaning your own) are still wanting in the *ad hominem* and *ad rem* quality. They are generally *essays*, which might have been written two hundred miles from the office, and would have been as opportune a week before as after the time of their appearance. Right or wrong see how *The Times* pounces on the topic of the hour, see their unfair but appropriate article yesterday on the Robertson Gladstone manifesto. It is by thus hanging their articles on the peg which presents itself that they are more sure to be read than any others. Look at the

Peace and Recovery

New York cheap Press, see how they sparkle with full or short leaders on the living and moving drama of public life. It is thus, too, that a paper can alone make itself felt as a power. Hit hard, but with a polished weapon all of sufficient mark who directly or indirectly assail our principles."

CHAPTER VIII

THE CHINA WAR AND THE INDIAN MUTINY

THE year 1857 opened quietly. The country was settling down to a period of peace and prosperity. Cornewall Lewis at the beginning of the Session of Parliament took off the "war ninepence" from the income tax, reducing it from sixteenpence to sevenpence.

But trouble soon arose in connection with the bombardment of Canton by British men-of-war. In the October of 1856 a merchant vessel, the *Arrow*, owned by a Chinese merchant and manned by Chinamen, but commanded by an Englishman, was boarded by a local mandarin, who carried off the crew on a charge of piracy. It had been a custom for the British representative at Hong-Kong to grant registers to Chinese vessels, giving them certain trading privileges and authorizing them to carry the British flag. The *Arrow* had held one of these registers, which had, however, expired some time before the seizure of its crew took place, so that in point of fact the *Arrow* was not in any sense under British protection, and did not in fact carry the British flag. Sir John Bowring, the British representative (a personal acquaintance of Cobden and actually a member of the Peace Society), resented the Chinese action, insisting that the *Arrow* was for the time being a British vessel and that the Chinese had insulted Britain by hauling down her flag.

The China War and the Indian Mutiny

He demanded the release of the crew and an apology. On being refused he directed Sir Michael Seymour, in command of the British squadron, to enforce the demands. Seymour seized the ports guarding the entrance to Canton. The Chinese thereupon surrendered the crew of the *Arrow*. But Bowring then put forward further demands, including the opening of Canton itself to British subjects. The Chinese refused these further claims, and in November Seymour bombarded Canton. The Chinese made reprisals, setting fire to foreign factories and murdering a number of Europeans.

Such was the beginning of a long and costly war which had early reactions upon home politics. Cobden was unsparing in his denunciation of the conduct of Bowring, and when the papers were laid before the Houses of Parliament, Lord Derby moved a vote of censure in the Lords and Cobden in the Commons. Though the Government secured a majority in the Lords, Cobden carried his resolution in the Commons by a majority of sixteen and Palmerston appealed to the electorate.

The elections were held in the latter days of March. Abandoning his seat for the West Riding, when he was convinced he had no chance, Cobden took up his candidature for Huddersfield. But the combination of Tories and Palmerstonian Whigs outvoted him. Palmerston's victory was complete, and the Manchester School was almost destroyed. The defeat of Bright at Manchester especially aroused Cobden's indignation, expressed in trenchant terms in a letter of March 25th. Fox also lost his seat at Oldham and Miall at Rochdale.

Several letters of this period to Bright and others discuss the causes of the collapse of sound Liberalism on the one hand and upon the other the failure of the new democratic appeal in Lancashire. Of special

Richard Cobden : The International Man

interest is a passage from a letter to Mr. Palmer [1] (August 9th) comparing Birmingham, the home of the rising mid-Victorian Radicalism, with Manchester.

"The honest and independent course taken by the people at Birmingham, their exemption from aristocratic snobbery, and their fair appreciation of a democratic aim of the people, confirms me in the opinion I have always had that the social and political state of that town is far more healthy than that of Manchester; and it arises from the fact that the industry of the hardware district is carried on by small manufacturers, employing a few men and boys each, sometimes only an apprentice or two; whilst the great capitalists of Manchester form an aristocracy, individual members of which wield an influence over sometimes two thousand persons. The former state of society is more natural and healthy in a moral and political sense. There is a freer intercourse between all classes than in the Lancashire town, where a great and impassable gulf separates the workman from his employer. The great capitalist class formed an excellent basis for the Anti Corn-Law movement, for they had inexhaustible purses, which they opened freely in a contest where not only their pecuniary interests but their pride as 'an order' was at stake. But I very much doubt whether such a state of society is favourable to a democratic political movement."

Cobden was not sorry to be absent from the servile Parliament now elected. His wife in her ill-health needed much of his attention, and his farm and garden life at Midhurst strongly appealed to him, especially at a time when his personal influence in politics was eclipsed. Many of his letters to Mr. Richard are concerned with the corruptness of the Press and its evil

[1] "Life," ii. p. 199.

The China War and the Indian Mutiny

control over public opinion. Even the *Star* sometimes he finds 'too soft and mealy-mouthed.' All through this year he is continually feeding the *Star* through Mr. Richard and others with material, chiefly on foreign and imperial affairs. On July 5th we get his first allusion to the outburst in India and the horrors of the Mutiny and its repression. Writing to Mr. Ashworth in October, he draws from the terrible episode the larger lesson of imperialism. "I am, and always have been of opinion, that we have attempted an impossibility in giving ourselves to the task of governing one hundred millions of Asiatics. God and his visible natural laws have opposed insuperable obstacles to the success of such a scheme. But if the plan were practicable at the great cost and risk which we *now* see to be inseparable from it, what advantage can it confer on ourselves?"[1]

Almost the only important personal incident of his quiet life this year was a short visit from his American friend Charles Sumner, of whom he writes: "He is nearer to *our beau ideal* of a politician than we could pick up in any other man of his calibre."

. . . . .

The following extracts from his correspondence with Mr. Richard furnish his commentary upon the foreign policy of the year :—

"*January* 3, 1857.

"You have taken the right view of the Canton business. It is not clear that we had any right to claim the protectorate of a vessel built, owned and manned by Chinese, but at all events it was the act of unreasoning violence to refuse to discuss that point. What other course was there left for the Chinese

[1] "Life," ii. p. 206.

Richard Cobden : The International Man

Governor but to withdraw in despair and give up everything to ruin, or to affirm by his own act what he believed to be an injustice and invasion of his country's right and thus bring down on himself the vengeance of his own Government ? What right have we to register vessels, to which there is not one title according to the rules of civilized nations ? Now in all cases a certain title either in the origin, i.e. the building or ownership or manning of a ship, is necessary for registering a vessel and entitling it to carry a flag. But what other end could be aimed at but embroiling ourselves in war in thus taking Chinese vessels under our protection ? I say this on the assumption that the vessel in question was built, manned and owned by Chinese. Is not 'lorcha' a Portuguese word ?

"But my object in writing is to suggest an inquiry, What was Sir John Bowring doing all this while ? He is commander-in-chief and representative of the English Government in China. He has an establishment in Hong-Kong costing a very large sum with Secretaries, Judges, and all the paraphernalia of state. Why did Mr. Parke, a young and inexperienced man whose only exploit that I have heard of was the bringing home the treaty with Siam, presume to call up the Admiral, and why did the latter undertake to act without the formal and regular and step-by-step intervention of Sir John Bowring, who is the accredited representative of England in China and who was at a few hours' steaming distance from Canton ? This is a point I think to bring into question—not in the way of blame to Bowring, for I expect he is treated as nobody."

"*January* 18, 1857.

"You have not sent me a *Gazette* containing the correspondence about Canton. I have reckoned on your doing so.

The China War and the Indian Mutiny

"I should be very glad if you could get any evidence of the failure of the late war so far as the *missionary* efforts are affected. God help the *Christians* who think of making their religion acceptable in the rear of an opium war, for surely nothing but an interruption of the laws of human nature by especial divine interposition could ever have that result! Pray give me the extract from Davies's correspondence with Palmerston in which he says he has more difficulty with the English at Canton than with the Chinese."

"*January* 1857.

"I send a copy of a letter (not for publication) which I have forwarded to Mr. Gregson, the Chairman of the East India and China Association. He is a good man, and I am sorry he has put his name to the memorial—which, by the way, is not honest so far as it puts down the enormous import of silk last year without noticing that it arose from the extraordinary demand owing to the failure of the crop in some parts of Europe. But I wish you to say something about our commercial gains from the last China War, when everybody in England was fully persuaded we should have an enormous increase of our exports if we could only gain access to the northern ports. When the terms of the peace were known there was a general throwing up of caps. I remember that even such staid men as Porter caught the enthusiasm and his 'Progress of the Nation' gives a great improvement in our trade. One of our Manchester manufacturers I remember got excited and delivered himself of a calculation that if every Chinese man only bought a cotton nightcap a year from us it would add 20 per cent. to the demand for our staple manufacture. So far as our exports are concerned it has proved a complete disappointment. I send you by this post a Parliamentary Paper in which you will see a table of our exports to China for fifteen years, and I have added in the margin extracts still farther back from Porter. Observe that we have gained scarcely anything in the way of customers for our manufactures. Indeed, some of the years since the war have been less favourable than before. ˙We have obtained more tea and silk, it is true, but nobody pretended that there was ever any difficulty in procuring those products without a war. It is the opium, and not our manufactures, that serves as a means of payment for the additional supply of tea and silk; and it is the opium trade, and not the exclusive policy of the Chinese, which, according to the best authorities, stands in the way of our increasing our exports to China. I advise you to give some of these figures of our exports as a table in your leader, apologizing and saying, 'We are not in the habit,' etc.—but figures are sermons in this case, for they teach us not to rely on violence and bloodshed again for the extension of our trade. The Chinese have always set Europe an example of low duties on imports, and when our old sliding scale on corn was still the law of the land the Chinese not only admitted rice free of duty but exempted vessels filled with that staple of their food even from port charges. It is not therefore from protectionist or restrictive legislation that our trade is suffering.

"At present it is obstructed by the revolution—that revolt according to the highest authorities having been occasioned by our last war, which destroyed the prestige of the present Government. Who can tell what may be the effects of another war? Certain expense—we keep now a ship-of-war at every port, and they will be largely increased now. Before the last war we never had more than a vessel or two at Canton. Then there is a costly establishment at Hong-Kong. I am writing in haste, but here is *verb. sap.*

The China War and the Indian Mutiny

"Suppose we force our way to Pekin and that France, England, and Russia each has its Stratford de Redcliffe intriguing and interfering with the affairs of China as we now do in Turkey—what shall we gain? etc.

"The increased cost of our establishments at the five ports—at Hong-Kong, and our increased number of ships-of-war must amount to at least 20 per cent. on our exports, and it has all failed to increase them."

Subjoined is a copy of the enclosure, a letter addressed to Mr. Gregson (*January* 14th):

"I am sorry to see your respected name appended to the memorial from the India and China Association. Not that I am opposed to the object you have in view, in trying to open still further the Empire of China to the commerce of the world. (I wish, by the way, our trade with the continent of Europe were as free as with China, and that we had five ports or even one in France where the Chinese tariff was in force.) But what I much regret is that you should put forth your claims as a sequel to the late proceedings, of our authority in China, without offering a word of censure or comment on those base and cruel transactions. It is very like attempting to enter a house in the rear of a burglar and offering to transact business whilst some of its inmates are weltering in their blood and others still struggling with their assailants. You are a free-trader, and I am proud to remember how friendly and warm have been your commendations of my efforts to emancipate our trade. All my best sympathies are with the mercantile class; but this makes me the more jealous of their fair fame, and I do not think it will be raised in the estimation of thoughtful and good men by becoming in any way identified or associated with the outrageous acts to which I allude. If you have read the dispatches, as I have done, you will have seen that in Sir John Bowring's first letters to the Consul at Canton he

Richard Cobden : The International Man

confirms the statement made by Yeh that the lorcha, about which, and *which alone*, as appears in the correspondence, the dispute arose, was not, when boarded by the Chinese, entitled to hoist the English flag; but he goes on to add that the Chinese authorities did not know that the register of the *Arrow* had expired, and he authorizes the resort to violence in support of the allegation of our Consul, *which he knew to be false*. A more nefarious paragraph than that penned by my old friend Bowring was never given to the public eye. And the attempt now to change the issue to a totally different question, in which we may be right, ought not to be tolerated. I repeat I am sorry to see your name appended to a document which has this object in view."

"*January* 27, 1857.

"I got a note from Parker on Saturday saying he heard in high quarters that the Persian affair is to be settled—that the Persians will knock under. In a letter which I received yesterday from Bright, dated Genoa and written in his usual spirits, he says he passed a day or two at Nice amongst such folks as Ellice, the Ashburtons, etc., and he was told by them that the Persian difficulty would be settled before the meeting of Parliament. Be on your guard then in dealing with this question. Our privileged oligarchs can do as they like, and as Palmerston, their real tool, has for a couple of months distracted public attention from home matters by holding the Persian war *in terrorem* over us, it is not unlikely that in a week or two his flunkeys of the Press will be taking credit to their master for having saved us from a war! Be prepared for this. The Chinese affair is a much more uncertain matter, and I am told the Government intend to stick by their tool.

"There are two symptoms in the *Star* which I observe,

The China War and the Indian Mutiny

or perhaps only fancy I perceive, viz. a tendency to systematically quote from the *Press*, and a proneness to praise and champion Gladstone. The first is Disraeli's organ, a sneerall of the Press, without a heart, plan, sympathy, or conviction. Nothing in *our* direction can be hoped from that quarter, and I would not care to be the vehicle for its factious attacks upon the Government with no other object than that those who are no better may fill their places. Of course I only say this against systematically quoting from that paper in a way to identify you with its objects. I approve of your plan of quoting from *all sides*.

"As respects Gladstone, what right have we to reckon on his aid to carry out our views of foreign policy? He was a party to the invasion of Russia, and to this day defends the policy of sending a British army to the Crimea. And I believe he was an obstacle to Lord Aberdeen washing his hands of the guilt of the war after the Turk refused the award of the first Congress of Vienna. In my opinion every member of the Cabinet who was a party to the Crimea expedition ought to be considered to be for ever separated by an impassable gulf from us unless he renounce the policy which dictated that step and profess another policy for the future. I don't see what right we have to hope better things from Gladstone. His retirement from the Ministry, you must remember, was not on the plea that he was opposed to the war, but on the ridiculous and unworthy ground of Roebuck having carried his motion for a parliamentary inquiry—thus in fact setting up for a claim to administrative impunity. I have the highest opinion of Gladstone's powers. He is the most eloquent and impressive speaker we have, and, now that Bright is absent, exercises an influence with his speeches to which no other member can pretend to even a comparison.

Richard Cobden : The International Man

His sway is owing mainly to the stamp of earnest conscientiousness which is impressed on the man at the moment he addresses you. But his conscience has not yet taken him in our direction, or if so he has failed to follow its dictates. And indeed I fear he sometimes entangles his conscience in his intellect. I have heard him defend 'protection' with such sophistical arguments that I have doubted whether he was more than a reasoning machine for the moment, with his moral sense put in abeyance. I am afraid he is not even yet committed to any broad and intelligible principles, and if so he may be only invested with powers of mystification by the praise you lavish on him. Lord Grey is the only man of the Cabinet Minister stamp whose conduct can be honestly endorsed by us."

"*March* 7, 1857.

"Is it not time to open fire upon some of those papers which support Palmerston and call on them to explain the *public* grounds on which they do so? There is not the least doubt that Palmerston has, as Disraeli said the first night of the session in reference to his use of the Press, *made greater use of that means of creating an artificial public opinion than any Minister since the time of Bolingbroke.* It might be worth your while to refer to his speech and get the exact words. *He meant a great deal more than was expressed.* I have thought a good deal about it and have talked the matter over with several persons, and am convinced that we shall have to come to an overhauling of the London Press with a view to expose the system by which they preserve the anonymous to the public and drop the mask to the Government and the governing class. It is a totally different state of things to that in the provinces, where the newspaper proprietors and conductors are all known to their neigh-

The China War and the Indian Mutiny

bours. The way to break ground is to ask how it is that *The Times*, which for twenty years was the persistent assailant of the present Prime Minister, should, as soon as he comes into power, become his unscrupulous advocate and the truculent assailant of everybody opposed to him. There must be some reason for the change other than of a *public* character, for Palmerston is the same man as ever, and persevering in the policy which *The Times* formerly opposed. The question to ask is, What is the present connection between the writers in *The Times* and the Government? Then there is the *Advertiser*, which professes to be strongly for the ballot, extension of suffrage, and short parliaments, and is a stout opponent of Church rates. How does the *Advertiser* account, on *public* grounds, for its championship of the Prime Minister who is opposed to all its principles? To make the matter more difficult of explanation in this case, the *Advertiser* is opposed to the Chinese War, and has put forth some of the best articles that have been written in condemnation of that war. How, then, on *public* ground can the editor of the *Advertiser* continue to advocate the cause of Palmerston and denounce all opposed to him? There is a virulence about its support of the Prime Minister quite inconsistent with an impartial attitude. What is the ground, the *public* ground, for this suspicious course? Some explanation is due. Promise to recur to the subject, and give notice that whilst public men are freely commented on, the public Press must not expect to be allowed an immunity from public censure.

"If you would open out on the London Press in the way I have tried to indicate, and promise to return to the subject, and intimate that you will not hesitate to tear the mask from a system which is nothing better than political deception, it will excite much interest and sympathy, and we may by and by rip up the matter with a thorough exposure. I am quite sure there is a great case."

"*March* 16, 1857.

"An article is sadly required on the following point: The rank and file of the electors must be warned to look after their self-constituted leaders, who are everywhere very busy in disposing of and trafficking in seats. Wherever the choice of a candidate is left to a 'committee,' as it is called (which is generally a few busy-bodies self-elected), it will be jobbed to please the Ministers or their creatures. Some strange doings come to one's ears. But the City of London is the most glaring case. Mr. Dillon, and a few other pompous gentlemen who are never heard of when any work is to be done less ostentatious than disposing of the representation of the City, summoned a meeting of two hundred or three hundred persons, who very coolly exclude the public, put a sentry at the door to prevent the intrusion of inquisitive people, and then pass a resolution that Mr. Raikes Currie shall take the place of Lord John Russell as representative of London. Wait a bit, Mr. Dillon, and see whether the electors will endorse your arrogant fiat. These 'committees,' as they are called, sometimes dwindle down to a deputation of three, who come from a provincial borough to town and disport themselves as great men at the clubs, see Mr. Hayter and Mr. Coppock, cross-examine their member if he should happen to have shown the least signs of independence, and probably end by making choice of a candidate from the list of names at the Reform Club. The first notice the great body of the electors have of their doings is probably in the resignation of their member. One would like to know the circumstances under which that

The China War and the Indian Mutiny

most excellent and conscientious representative of the people, Mr. Lawrence Heyworth, was induced to send his resignation to the electors of Derby. I venture to say they know as little of the reason of his doing so as we do. I have heard of the case of a northern borough represented in Parliament by a right honourable gentleman, an ex-Cabinet Minister, whose name was on the back of the Reform Bill of 1854, which Lord Palmerston resisted even to resignation, who was lately visited in London by a 'deputation,' and required to give a pledge that he would in a new Parliament agree to a vote of confidence in the present Premier. He refused, and his seat has been offered, under the advice of the deputation, to another. Will not the electors have something to say to this?

"The body of the electors must everywhere be on the alert, and must put good men of their own forward. Never mind the cry of 'you are dividing the party.' There is no Liberal Party so long as its only principle is confidence in a man without one Liberal principle. This 'Palmerston fever' does not infect the healthy mass of the electoral body. It is only the cliques, clubs and committees that are brought within the range of its influence. They excite and chafe each other, and persuade themselves that all the world is in as great a fuss as themselves when all the world is in a quandary what it is all about, and more than half inclined to believe that it is a hoax."

"*March* 17, 1857.

"I am launched for Huddersfield. All the help that can be given I shall be glad to have. Can you send down immediately a few thousand copies of the tract on the China War and have them immediately distributed by trusty hands in Huddersfield? There is not a moment

Richard Cobden : The International Man

to be lost. I am very much alarmed at the state of things in Manchester. There is terrible rottenness and apathy, and desertions almost by streets. The results can alone show, but I fear very much the chances are all against us. We are to have a great meeting this evening. The cause of the mischief is, I think, less a change of opinion than of feeling towards those who are alleged here to be attempting too long to wield the defunct power of the League. There ought to have been a reorganization on a new basis long ago. However, it is useless to talk about the causes of the mischief now. Our only business is to win if we can. Say nothing about this to anybody, for it oozes out. Pray see Morley and try to what extent he can help Lord John for the City. His defeat will be a triumph to Lord Palmerston, his success a rebuke to him. I hope he and Graham will get in.

"I wish you would let the enclosed be *rewritten* and insert it in a prominent place in the *Star*."

"*March* 25, 1857.

"I made an engagement to return to-day to Manchester to speak this evening at the great meeting at the Free Trade Hall. It is unfortunate, for I am not equal to the task. I have overdone it here,[1] and am brought to a standstill. Canvassing all day and speaking twice at public meetings yesterday, once in the open air, have upset me. I am suffering from giddiness, and have the fear of Bright's fate before my eyes. What to do, I know not; but am very much tempted to cut the cable and separate myself absolutely from politics for a season. Do not be surprised if I should not go to the poll here. I have decided nothing yet. The contest is a very unpleasant, harassing affair, for although I have all the

[1] Huddersfield.

The China War and the Indian Mutiny

Liberal leaders with me, and no open secession of any part of the constituency, yet it is *too small* for me to work on it by any public demonstrations. The 'people' are all right, but the electoral body is to a certain extent under influences which may baffle all calculations. My friends are active and hopeful, but it is not possible to foresee the result. I wish I could stand aside for a year for many reasons. I fear you must be prepared for the worst at Manchester. I am going there this morning according to my promise, but shall not make my appearance at the Free Trade Hall."

"*March* 26, 1857.

"It will, I hope, draw down on Manchester a hiss of scorn if it rejects those men to return two nobodies. In Bright's case it is particularly disgusting, for they have no right to quarrel with *him* over the war, knowing when they elected him he was a Quaker. Under the circumstances in which he is placed, with his health impaired whilst in their service, cutting the connection with less ceremony than we use in getting rid of an invalided horse, it is one of the most revolting cases of public ingratitude I ever met with."

"*April* 5, 1857.

"I am in a fair way to be as well as ever in a few days. My old medicine, *sleep*, comes to my aid. It seems as if I am never thoroughly awake. The only trouble I have is in the number of good people who think it necessary to write to me and whose letters it will be necessary to answer. They seem to have generally a notion that I must be very dispirited and want consolation now. There is perhaps no one on earth who depends so little on external circumstances as I do for cheerfulness or contentment. I don't know that I am warranted in assuming that I have reached that enviable

Richard Cobden : The International Man

point described by Pascal when he says : ' Whoever finds the secret of taking satisfaction in good, without uneasiness in disappointment, has made a great achievement. It is a kind of perpetual motion!' But at least I may say that, my object in public life being to advance objects which I believe to be true, and therefore certain to be triumphant, I never feel that kind of discouragement in temporary defeat which men must who have only personal ends in view."

"*April* 13, 1857.

" I concur in what you say about the extension of the franchise. It does not follow that we should be nearer the realization of our pacific principles if we had universal suffrage to-morrow. In the present general election the most warlike returns have come from the most popular constituencies, the least warlike from the most aristocratic counties. I have said this to Sturge, not as an argument against the most liberal extension of the franchise, but to show that our work of conversion to a more humane foreign policy would have to be performed under any change of the electoral system. I have faith in great multitudes when appealed to perseveringly and honestly, and am willing to take my chance with the million, not shutting my eyes to their want of instruction which we should be all the more eager to impart to them, if, as in America, owing to a wider extension of the franchise, our destinies were in the hands of the democracy. But as respects your advocacy of another Reform Bill in the *Star*, I don't see the necessity of launching a shibboleth ' complete suffrage' or even of ' household suffrage.' I would avow my belief that all restrictions upon the exercise of the vote ought as far and as fast as possible to be got rid of. And as a step I should advocate the ' rating suffrage' —i.e. to give the vote to those who are rated for the

The China War and the Indian Mutiny

relief of the poor. This is the principle already recognized with some modifications both in the election for Guardians and in that for municipal corporations. It is far more than Lord John will propose, who will, I expect, stick at his £5 *rating*, which is equal to £7 10s. *rental*—being only £2 10s.—under the present franchise. Don't be drawn into any dogmatic theory about 'complete suffrage'—it is our friend Sturge's bantling, and he has an overwhelming love for it."

"*April* 13, 1857.

"The enclosed from my old acquaintance Bowring, which I received last week, seems to have been written with a presentiment of what was coming. Let me have it again, for I suppose I must answer it. Apropos of this Chinese business, I presume from the preparations making that there will be a bloody reprisal made either at Canton or elsewhere for the imaginary wrongs done us by Yeh. Now the line to take in the *Star* clearly is to prepare the public for this, and to prevent its appetite for vengeance from being whetted by any speculations about the difficulties of the task, or the probable resistance to be encountered from the Chinese. Let it be again and again assumed, and shown by reference to the former war, that the Chinese with their bows and arrows and matchlocks, and cannon which will not move, and their painted shields and petticoated officers, have no more chance against our Minié rifles, our 13-inch shells of two thousand yards' range, our steamboats and our pivot cannon, than the Peruvians had against Cortez and his men-at-arms. It is not war, it is a *battue*, a massacre, or slaughter, an execution—call it anything but war—which really means a manly encounter where each side has some chance of success or at least of escape from destruction. Warn the people against being irritated or deluded by

Richard Cobden : The International Man

fanciful proclamations put forth in the name of the Chinese authorities, threatening the English with extermination. We have lately seen how easily these things are fabricated for electioneering purposes. The question should be steadily asked—What do we propose to gain by the war? We may compel the Chinese Government to pay all our expenses; *that* they must do if we demand it. But our professed object was to gain a free access to the city and neighbourhood of Canton. Does any rational being think that we are any nearer the attainment of that object? Does anybody suppose that Englishmen will be safer in the interior of China after these slaughterings and burnings than before? Are we prepared to land forces and occupy a country eight times as large as France and ten times as populous? If so, look to the expense, look for jealousies and possible collisions with America and other Powers. Is the object to gain a freer commercial intercourse with China? There is no great empire where our trade is a quarter as free. The Liverpool China Association, in their notorious memorial, signed by their president, that arch-protectionist, Mr. Charles Turner, insists upon our having free access even for our ships-of-war to all the rivers and harbours of China. This would of course lead to endless collisions but not necessarily to increase of our exports—for always bear in mind that the former war with China, whilst it has added enormously to our expenditure for ships-of-war on the Chinese station, for consulates at the five ports, and for our Hong-Kong establishment, has disappointed those Manchester fire-eaters who expected a large increase of exports of cotton goods to China.

"Can't you coax or bait the anti-opium trade agitation into activity? Their movement would do more than anything to discredit the mercantile party with whom, and not the landed aristocracy, this Chinese War originates.

The China War and the Indian Mutiny

"Did you see the speech delivered by the Bishop of Victoria in Manchester at a meeting of the Society for Propagating the Gospel abroad, in which he spoke of the obstacle which the opium trade offered to the missionary efforts? It was little more than a month ago. You will find it, I suppose, in the religious papers, and it should be copied into the *Star*."

"*April* 15, 1857.

"The *money power*, created by the vast sums voted for the support of the standing armaments of Europe, is the great difficulty we have to encounter in trying to reduce those peace establishments. The Peace Party in England raise £5,000 a year to maintain a contest against a system which is subsidized every year by the State to the amount of 15 or 16 millions sterling! There must be great pluck in the men who dare enter the lists in such an unequal contest. And yet we are gaining upon the enemy's position; he is more and more on the defensive; and we have cast off his supplies during the last three years to the extent of four millions—I will back time and the £5,000 of the Peace Party against the remaining fourteen and a half millions voted by Parliament for Army, Navy and Ordnance."

"*April* 17, 1857.

"I can undertake to lead no agitation requiring platform speaking. My throat or lungs fail me, and I am always beset with a hoarseness. I fact, I am nearly twenty years older than when I began my former labours, and no man can repeat himself—if he has done anything in his prime—in the decline of life. I have also had symptoms both at my head and heart which warn me that I cannot bear the same tension as of old. I must give way to younger men, and

Richard Cobden : The International Man

it would be only misleading the public to give any sanction to the notion that I can lead a suffrage agitation. Between ourselves (and I do not write for other eyes), I think those friends who would sanction my rushing into the streets with a new Reform Bill, because I am not elected to Parliament, take a rather low estimate of what is due to oneself under such circumstances. Besides, even as a matter of policy, I must say that I think the very worst step for the interest of reform which could be taken is that a few disappointed M.P.'s should inaugurate a movement of the kind. If it cannot be made to originate with more disinterested parties, it is a proof that there is no great desire for reform. But this applies perhaps more strongly to myself than to many other ex-M.P.'s, for *I* have never taken a strong and continuous line on questions of organic change. I repeat my advice—do not tie your paper to any shibboleth on the suffrage question. It is far better to show a generally liberal and confiding spirit towards the masses, and evince your friendly animus by making quotations from other papers of articles favourable to the democratic principle —*if you can find them*—for it seems to me that never before was there so little political life among the masses and so little of the democratic style in newspaper articles. The secret is that prosperity has made half-Tories of the whole people. And depend on it we shall see this state of feeling bear fruits of a retrograde kind. Let me suggest that whilst you hold your own pens upon the China Question, and abstain from systematic assaults on the Palmerston insanity, you should give extracts from other papers, which appear like echoes of yourself, and therefore give strength to your own opinions. I enclose one from a Kent paper. In fact the newspapers are doing their

The China War and the Indian Mutiny

work well. In all parts of the country there are journals which repudiate the Palmerston imposture, and it strikes me that many of those who go along with the stream do so without much heartiness as if they were leaving open a retreat. In your articles on the Press, don't fail to lay the foundation of a just tribute to the independence of so many journals. This is necessary to shield you from the charge which will be attempted of your being an assailant of the entire newspaper Press."

"*April* 22, 1857.

"I have been thinking about the *exposé* you contemplate respecting the illicit and secret connection between the Government and the Press. The way to inaugurate the topic, in my opinion, is this : write a leader, taking for your text the correspondence which has appeared in the columns of the *Star* about anonymous newspaper writing, in which, after a compliment to the Press generally and an expression of confidence in the future of a Press now for the first time for a century and a half really free, and after declaring for perfect freedom to all the world to publish their opinions either anonymously or with their signatures as they please, refer to one point which comes out of the controversy, viz. the practice that has grown up in our day with the conductors and proprietors of certain papers almost exclusively confined to the metropolis of connecting themselves with the Government whilst preserving a strict incognito as towards the public. In other words, they wear the mask to all their readers excepting those who have the power to reward them for their subserviency. There is reason to believe that this system has been carried out to an extent little dreamed of, and if thoroughly exposed it might account

Richard Cobden : The International Man

for some of the great changes that have taken place in the tone and politics of some of our journals. Mr. Disraeli hinted in delicate phrase at the part played by the present Prime Minister in this system of gaining over the Press when he said in his opening speech of the last Session that he (Lord Palmerston) had known better how to create public opinion by artificial means than any Minister since the time of Bolingbroke (refer back to his speech for what he said : it was in reference to the Belgrad humbug). But Lord Palmerston is not the only Minister. He was exposed, and unanswerably proved to have hired one American or Polish adventurer, Wikoff, to write up his *Peace policy*. But we know by the records of a court of law and the debates in Parliament that Lord Clarendon when in Ireland was not above suborning a newspaper writer. In all probability other Ministers and Governments have been as bad, though there are reasons for doubting whether Sir Robert Peel lent himself to such a policy. However, as a matter of principle, a system of secret connection between the Press and the Government cannot be defended. Open writing as by law in France, where each writer is compelled to sign his name, or, as in the United States, when the name of the proprietor and editor of the paper (who is a leader of his political party and rises to the highest ranks of office) is published on the frontispiece of the journal, or anonymous writing as we *profess* to have it in England, may be either of them good if honestly carried out. But a pretended anonymous system which preserves secrecy to the public on the plea that it is necessary for the maintenance of purity and independence, and then discloses names to the Government and sells the influence thus obtained by false pretences over the public to the highest bidders—such a system cannot be defended, and ought to be exposed by every one who wishes to see the practice of anonymous writing preserved.

"Now as a matter of public principle the *Star*, which seeks no concealment and asks no quarter for itself, will not hesitate to expose every instance of Government patronage being extended to the writers and proprietors of the periodical Press. We hold that they have no right to shrink from any publicity of the kind. If a public man takes office the fact is known. Why should not the same rule apply to a public writer? We do not say this for the purpose of preventing public writers from taking office. They are generally the best informed and most competent men, and therefore the very men who ought to be held eligible to fill posts in the public service. All we stipulate for is that it shall be done openly and aboveboard, and for the promotion of this end we shall not scruple to use whatever facts come to our knowledge, and we have already some which may afford materials for another article."

"*April* 26, 1857.

"I would not advise you *at present* to give up any of the space in the *Star* to such a general appeal as you speak of to the working classes 'showing the bearing of the present war system on their condition.' It would be much better to let striking facts come out incidentally—apropos of something. A series of letters such as you speak of would give too decidedly the character of an advocate of abstract peace views to the *Star* to be advisable at this moment. Besides, there is enough to do on special topics; and this brings me to remark that you must not haul down the flag and give up opposition to the Chinese atrocity. If you abandon the field, it will be the signal for those papers in the country who look to our leading them to follow the example. The late news from Washington should be alluded to. I stated in my speech and in my reply that I had reason to believe that the Government of the United States would have joined this country and France in a pacific representation to the Government of China in favour of greater commercial facilities or rather a freer intercourse with that Empire, but I expressed a strong conviction that the Government of Washington would be no party to our violent proceedings founded on the Canton massacre. (I think I told you that Dallas read to me confidentially a letter from Marcy to this effect.) You will recollect that Palmerston, in his speech on my motion, also stated that before the Canton affair our Government had been in communication with that of France, and was contemplating also applying to that of the United States and that he was in hopes he would have succeeded in inducing those Governments to join us in a representation to the Chinese Government. Well now, then, will the toadies of the Government tell us that their great negotiator at the head of the Government who has had all his own way for the last few months has given us another diplomatic triumph at Washington? By the late advices from America it oozes out that Lord Napier has been instructed to invite Mr. Buchanan to join us in our hostile proceedings, and the answer he has received confirms the statement made by Lord Palmerston as to the probability that the Government of Washington would have joined us in a *moral* demonstration if we had applied before the Canton slaughter, but it leaves no doubt that that Government refuses to identify itself with the sanguinary operations perpetrated and contemplated against the Chinese people. Here then we are again presented to the world as unsuccessful suitors at Washington. The Minister whom we are called upon

The China War and the Indian Mutiny

to fall down and worship for his infallible wisdom in foreign affairs—or if not for wisdom for his 'luck'—has afforded General Cass an opportunity of snubbing us and sending us a lecture against filibustering before he has fairly got possession of his office of Secretary of State. And here is a reason sufficient, if any were wanting, for condemning Sir John Bowring's hasty and violent proceedings—always supposing he acted on his own impulse and not from private hints from home. Those proceedings have prevented our having the alliance of the United States. They leave us to perform the part of butchers and executioners of a mob of defenceless Chinese, and in the end America will step in for the full participation in any concessions we may extort from that people, retaining a friendly footing which we shall have for ever lost with them, and which their merchants and citizens will turn to account in their future intercourse in China. And all this might have been avoided if Sir John Bowring could have repressed for a few months his monomania for entering with cocked hat and feathers the gates of Canton."

"*May* 15, 1857.

"I quite agree with you as to the propriety of the *Star* keeping manfully to its colours. It is the only way, even in a mercantile point of view, to insure any success. I concur also in the view you take of the ferocious spirit in the country which requires repressing, and the mission of the *Star* was undoubtedly to repress that spirit. But even in this you must use so much tact as to prevent the paper sinking as a newspaper and becoming a daily *Peace Herald*. The first and only condition of *any* success is to establish the *Star* as a *news*paper. I am more and more convinced that this war spirit has been generated and kept alive by our career in the East. Our Asiatic morality has come back to plague us. We are whipped with our own pleasant vices. Recollect we have never been free from the excitement of bloody campaigns for more than three or four years at a time, and those battles of the Punjab in particular were on a scale almost to equal in slaughter some of Napoleon's great engagements.

"As respects the *Examiner*—as it is the worst and most barefaced offender, it ought to be attacked the first, and certainly nothing could be more glaring than its subservient wheel-round on the China question. Observe how manfully it keeps to its old Radical opinions upon the ballot, which is not a pinching question with the Ministry. If it were, it would bully its advocates for endangering the Ministry. The course they take is just that of a class of politicians in the House who enter it with ultra professions of Radicalism and vote accordingly when there is no chance of succeeding, but shrink away directly the Ministry is likely to be put in the minority."

"*June* 16, 1857.

"Jemmy Wilson was a worker in connection with the League. He wrote dull pamphlets and made duller speeches, but still he showed some Scotch pertinacity in keeping alive the agitation in the metropolis. When we dissolved our organization and gave up the 'League' weekly organ, a lithographed circular was sent to all its subscribers recommending them to support the *Economist*, which he had previously started, and Bright and I, George Wilson and others, signed this circular. This was the foundation of Wilson's fortune, which was in a sickly state previously. The *Economist* became the stepping-stone to Office. When Wilson entered the Ministry, Mr. William Grey became a leading contributor and a sort of *locum tenens* for the proprietor, with whom he was on intimate terms. After a while Wilson,

The China War and the Indian Mutiny

as Secretary of the Treasury, became a dispenser of Government patronage, and he presented Grey last year with the appointment of a Commissioner of Customs, a post involving so little occupation that it will not interfere with his literary labours, but for which he pockets £1,200 a year. Thus the two principal contributors to the *Economist* having secured, the one £2,000 a year and the other £1,200 from the public purse, what so natural as that the paper should be the obsequious servant of the Government, or that the *Economist's* pages should be employed in assailing the two men who laid the foundation of all this success, if they happen no longer to be in favour with the dispensers of patronage? You may bring out these facts in any way you like. But I think a lively, brief, touch-and-go style of showing up these people is the best. Put it in a short quotable form, and not as a solemn argument. And it might be said that there are some other papers which are now so zealously devoted to the Government and so busily assailing all who are not equally devoted to the powers that be for whose conduct equally substantial reasons may by and by be produced. *There is far more corruption going on in connection with the public Press than in any other walk of political life.*"

"*June* 20, 1857.

"Lord Goderich allows the accompanying to be published, he having made such suppressions as to remove all trace of the writer. Be good enough to see that it be correctly printed, especially as regards the proper names. I think you should give prominence to it by leaded type and then draw attention to it in a leader printed in the same paper. Begin your leading article with 'We invite the attention of our readers to a letter, not penned with the view to publication, in

Richard Cobden : The International Man

another column, written by one who, from his long residence in the country and his perfect knowledge of the language, ranks among the highest authorities on Chinese affairs.' Then comment in this fashion : There are two very important statements in his letter, one a matter of fact, and the other the expression of an opinion. The writer says we have been dealing in something very like falsehood in our official correspondence. 'From all sides,' says he, 'I learnt at Hong-Kong that the *Arrow* lorcha had no flag flying at all. Of course the Chinese know this still more certainly than the English, and will have little faith in our official averments in future.' Inasmuch, however, as our Government have determined that this falsehood shall be made the pretence for an attack upon China, the more practical question now is—what will be the result of the war? On this subject the writer of the letter assumes that a force will be sent to take possession of Canton. Nothing more easy. A few thousand troops occupying the high ground and approaches to the city, and it must open its gates to escape being blown up or starved. What will then happen? According to this well-informed writer, it will be the signal for a general rising of the disaffected throughout the still tranquil portions of the south of China, and the whole country will be thrown into a state of anarchy worse than any merely internal troubles could have produced, and it can hardly fail to end in the Manchoo power being definitely destroyed in Kwangtung and Kwangsee (two provinces containing a population of perhaps forty millions). And if we go on with a sufficient force we are told by the same authority we shall 'clinch the fate of the Imperial Government' and throw an empire of four hundred millions into a state of anarchy out of which in the course of a generation or two a successful

The China War and the Indian Mutiny

pretender may arise to fill the throne of the Tartar dynasty. But how is all this to promote our interests as a commercial people? We see *The Times* gives prominence to the communication of a correspondent who recommends us to hold possession of Canton and —drain it! We rather think the war will be accompanied by a drain of a more serious kind in the demand for specie which will arise in consequence of the insecurity and hoarding which always accompanies a state of civil war and confusion. Already the demand for silver to remit to China is seriously affecting the European money markets. Not only the maritime trade but the overland traffic through Siberia seems to be diverting large amounts of silver from its ordinary channels. We see it stated in the Russian accounts that the Chinese traders at Kiachta will accept nothing but specie in exchange for their teas and silks. As soon as it is known throughout that vast empire that we have landed an army and taken possession of Canton, followed as we are told it will be by fresh successes of the rebels, the effect will everywhere be to cause a disappearance of the precious metals. The people will be anxious to put aside, probably under ground, as much silver as will insure to themselves and their families the means of subsistence whatever may happen. The merchants and agriculturists who have been accustomed to deal with foreigners will be more eager than ever to sell off their stocks, but less disposed than ever to take anything in exchange but hard cash. The expenditure for the war will cause also an increased export of specie to China. At first the eagerness to sell on the part of the Chinese may keep down the prices of their produce, but ultimately, if the rebellion in the interior should, as is predicted by the writer of the letter, assume a state of prolonged anarchy, it may by

Richard Cobden : The International Man

checking production lead to a scarcity and rise in the value of tea and silk. How all this is to benefit our merchants trading with China, who we are told are clamorous for the war, we are at a loss to understand. We have a shrewd suspicion that some of the Canton houses who pocketed the millions of dollars which were extorted from the Chinese Government for 'compensation' at the close of the last war are looking to a like source of profit on the present occasion. But if the appearance of our fleets and armies on the coast of China should lead to the consequences indicated by the letter-writer, there may be no Government with which to treat—who knows but we may be step by step drawn into a participation in the civil broils of that vast empire ? And all this in support of our authorities whose first quarrel, according to the admission of all parties at Hong-Kong, was founded in no better plea than a falsehood ! "

"*July* 5, 1857.

" No man on earth can tell what the result of the Indian events will be, for as they spring from ignorant panic, their direction or tendency cannot be foretold by any process of reasoning. There is, no doubt, a slumbering discontent everywhere in India among the poor Hindoos, but it has no political bearing—it expends itself on the nearest policeman or tax-collector. The remote consequences of this outbreak are by far the more important. All Asia will prick up its ears when it hears that our 'extinguisher has taken fire.' Persia and Afghanistan will 'harden their faces' towards us and Russia will think of old grudges. I am curious to see what the effect will be on the Burmese when they hear of the news and learn that our force in Pekin has been weakened. The Burmese have never acknowledged

The China War and the Indian Mutiny

our right to that province in any treaty. Then there is Oude, of which we have heard but little, and nothing from Scinde."

"*July* 12, 1857.

"You are a dreamer to talk of my being ever in an official situation of influence. My views separate me more and more from the *practical* statesmanship of the day and render it less probable that I shall ever be in office. I hardly think Sumner is in a way to be very differently situated in his country! I admire him the more because he has not subordinated his conscientious convictions to the ordinary ambition of the politician."

"*July* 16, 1857.

"Beware of allowing a tone of exultation over the Indian troubles to appear in your articles. I thought I perceived such a spirit in the *Star* article yesterday. The public are not prepared for such a tone, and it will be put down to want of patriotism or even to a corrupt motive. You and I are sufficiently cosmopolitan to see that *our* doings in India deserve a retributive visitation. But the dear self-complacent people of England persuade themselves that we take all the trouble to conquer the Hindoos for *their* benefit, and to spread the light of Christianity among them, and that they are very ungrateful to rise against those who are their disinterested friends! The only process by which we shall be disabused of this comfortable delusion is that which is now going on in India. There will be constantly recurring troubles and difficulties in our path, and in the end people will begin to ask themselves—what benefit do *we* derive from the 'possession' of India? and it will then one day be looked upon as the worst 'bad debt' the nation has on its hands. Meantime unhappily

Richard Cobden : The International Man

we are rooting out these elements of self-government in India and by the time we become disgusted and throw up the impossible task there will be nothing left in the way of a governing class or authority, and we shall abandon the nation, as Rome did our ancestors, to intestine anarchy and foreign conquest."

"*July* 23, 1857.

"By the way, there was an article against the discordant proceedings in the House on Friday, and calling for some restrictions on the right of members to moot questions on the motion of adjournment till Monday. That article was well written, but it struck me that it might have been the production of a *new* M.P., for the views were not such as from my longer experience I should have taken of the subject. It *appears* very irregular and disorderly to talk of Persian wars and Isthmus Canals, etc., on the motion that 'the House at its rising do adjourn till Monday next,' but the party chiefly inconvenienced is the Minister of the day, and the parties who profit by the practice are independent members, and the Opposition, and, through them, the public. Almost every other mode of bringing forward a subject on a given day to meet an emergency has been taken from individual members, whilst the Government has acquired a constantly increasing power over the proceedings of the House. Formerly a member could make a speech and raise a debate on presenting a petition, and Lord Brougham has declared that in this way he achieved some of the greatest triumphs for the people. Then still more lately it was possible to raise an amendment to reading the orders of the day. These opportunities are now no longer available. The old privilege of moving an amendment to going into Committee of Supply has been retained, but even this

The China War and the Indian Mutiny

has undergone some restriction. Now all these restrictions, though they seem to facilitate business, are curtailments of the popular influence in the House, and afford a convenient shield to the governing class. As respects the question more immediately at issue—the right of speaking on the question of adjournment on Fridays—I have known most damaging results to the Ministry of the day arise from those brief discussions, and I should be very sorry to see the opportunity for firing an occasional shot at the Government abolished. The Liberals are putting their heads into nooses laid by their 'betters' in all directions, and nothing will surprise me in that way. But beware how you lend yourself in the *Star* unconsciously to such proceedings.

"I was glad you fired that shot at Thackeray, and still more so to find that it helped to bring him down. Those sentimentalists are very unreliable politicians. Look at the greatest of the class, Lamartine: after all his magnificent mouthings about national integrity, justice, and liberty, see how he was prepared to imitate Frederick or Napoleon in his treatment of Italy. There is nothing after all in a politician like the stern logic of a Jefferson or a Calhoun. They may sometimes start from wrong premises, but when once started you always know where they are going."

"*August* 13, 1857.

"It appears to me that, being on the spot where information can be had, you ought to be able to rip up with a trenchant blade such affairs as that of the Principalities. It is clear to me that the facts are these: The English ambassador, as usual, has leave for bullying down all opposition at Constantinople. He was encouraged up to a certain point to go with Austria and Turkey against the Union. Tricks were

Richard Cobden : The International Man

resorted to to obtain a simulated expression of opinion at the elections in opposition to Union. These tricks were detected and exposed by the representatives of the four Powers. Still, as usual, Lord Stratford encouraged the Porte to persist in *his* views and to resist the representations of Russia, France, Prussia and Sardinia. Then comes Louis Nap. to Osborne knowing our Indian straits, and I am told the substance of what he said to Palmerston then amounted to this: 'I have sacrificed two French Ambassadors to the arrogance of your representative at Constantinople, but I'll see you d——d before I offer up another victim to the same impracticable temper.' Then Palmerston, of course, draws in, but he dares not throw overboard Lord Stratford, who knows too much and has him in his power, and so then the only question is how he shall mystify the public, and by the aid of the truculent *Times* beat a retreat without exposing his defeat; and so the Conference is to meet again at Paris. This is, I suppose, agreed to by Louis Nap., just as he did in the silly Belgrad business, because it plays the game of his British colleagues, with no loss of prestige but rather the contrary to himself, for it is another excuse for a Conference at Paris, and the more of them the better it pleases the Parisians. But now comes the transparent and childish character of the whole game. For if four of the parties to the Conference are already known to be on one side, and only three on the other, everybody can see what the decision will be without the seven men meeting again at the same table. If one could believe that anything will restore us again to a reign of common sense and ordinary morality in our Foreign Affairs, surely such displays of childlike folly as these might bring a better state of things. But I fear the big baby of a British public is only to be amused by such rattles and straws as Palmerston knows how to exhibit to him."

"*August* 14, 1857.

"*The Times* is adding to the difficulty of our forces by threatening wholesale slaughter in case we succeed. What is this but inviting the Sepoys to fight to the last with no risk of loss even if they are slain, for that will only save them from the scaffold? But the most senseless part of this tomahawk style of writing is that it really means nothing but sound and fury— for even the editor of *The Times* himself does not propose that the eighty thousand Sepoys who are in revolt shall be hung or shot, as would undoubtedly be the case if the mutiny had been confined to half a dozen. Even the fire-eaters themselves would make some difference in deference to the numbers involved. They would act as a matter of policy upon the soundness of the late Sir Charles Napier's dictum in a similar case when he said, 'Punishing by wholesale makes hatred, not obedience.' These writers know right well that there is no difference of opinion as to the propriety of punishing unsparingly those wretches who tortured and slew women and children. *That* is not the question at issue. But when they call for the destruction of a town like Delhi or the indiscriminate massacre of Sepoy prisoners, they prove themselves just as unfit to guide the conduct of government even in matters of policy as they are to be the guardians of the country's character for religion or humanity."

"*August* 27, 1857.

"There is one thought ever recurring to my mind. How is it possible that we, a Christian and a superior race, can have been for a century in close contact with

Richard Cobden : The International Man

this people and produced no better results than these? Has not our conduct been such as to imbue the minds of the native population not only with hatred but contempt for us? I fear this is in part the solution for the otherwise unaccountable outrages and barbarities inflicted upon the British. We do not read of such vindictive and merciless traits in the mode of warfare in India generally. Take the case of all others most likely to present the natives under the influence of the most ferocious passions—that of the invasion of Afghanistan. We don't find Shah Soojah and Akbar Khan cutting our women and children who fell into their hands to pieces. Even among the Red Indians of North America, those tribes who have been for a generation or two in close intercourse with the whites (such as the Seminolis, Cherokees, etc.) are incapable of such 'horrors.' It is only the Comanches and others who have hardly been brought in contact with Christians who are sometimes accused of adhering to their old barbarities to their prisoners. How can we account for these unnatural cruelties among our fellow-subjects in India upon any theory which is not a mournful reproach to ourselves as the conquering and dominant race? And having had this revelation of the state of the population in Hindostan, what a perspective of sacrifices, difficulties and dangers does the future government of such a people offer to a reflective mind!"

"*November* 23, 1857.

"What does Miall mean by so ostentatiously proclaiming that he would recover our dominion in India at 'any cost'? He is not the man generally to use phrases in a vague and parrot fashion. But surely he has never fairly considered *his* position in this matter.

The China War and the Indian Mutiny

He acknowledges the criminal means by which we got possession of that Empire, and makes *that* the plea for holding it at any cost of life and treasure—for cost in war means men as well as money—for the purpose of benefiting the people of India. But what right has he to assume that we shall govern that country well? Take the very test which he himself applied to that of the State Church principle. He declares that he would be against our holding India if it were to be followed by our enforcing the endowment principles there. But after sanctioning any amount of waste and slaughter in reconquering India, what guarantee has he that this principle will not be carried out? *Can he prevent it there any more than he can here?* Does not he know that there is a religious body in this country, ten times as potent as he and his party, in favour of Government propagandism there? Doesn't he know that the principle is in full operation, bishops and all, in Hindostan? Does not he know that every chaplain for every regiment in India is paid his yearly salary out of the hard earnings of the Hindoos, and that crowds of retired Christian clergymen and *their descendants* are living in England on pensions annually remitted from the same source? And yet he would sanction the waste of any amount of blood and treasure in reconquering India *on the plea of setting up the voluntary principle!* Was ever self-delusion so powerful in blinding a really acute and logical thinker?

"But Miall knows surely when he speak of 'India' as a whole that he uses a word which has a very indefinite sense as applied to our relations with the peninsula of Hindostan. With some of the territories of India he might fairly argue that it would be impossible to resign our authority into the hands of more rightful rulers than ourselves, inasmuch as there are no descendants of some of those sovereigns who were deposed by our earlier conquerors in that region. But he knows that this does not apply to our latest acquisitions to Scinde, Burma, the Punjaub (whose rightful heir is a visitor occasionally at our Court), and above all to Oude—the latest and worst of all our violations of right and justice. What would he do with these if the whole of them should rise as Oude has done against us? He was in the House when Lord Dalhousie returned red-handed from more extensive if not more flagitious acts of spoliation than had been perpetrated by any Governor-General who preceded him, yet he was rewarded by Government with the tacit assent of Parliament for his acts. And now, *when by the admission of all*, the whole population of Oude is up in arms fighting for their rights, fighting with as much title to the rank of patriots as was bestowed on Swiss or Dutch in their wars of independence, Mr. Miall, who has not a syllable to say in defence of our rights in the first place to depose the king of Oude and seize his territory, would now sanction the conquering of it at any cost. That which was not justifiable five years ago must now be perpetrated *because of that injustice!* But then Mr. Miall will indemnify the people of Oude by preventing the Government of this country from establishing the endowment principle in Oude—if he can?"

" Wednesday.

"Let the essay style be avoided in the *Star*. I can illustrate what I have to say by reference to the article yesterday upon foreign policy. The *first paragraph* would be good for a magazine article—it is an exordium preparing one for an argument and the reader is warned

The China War and the Indian Mutiny

to compose himself for a course of instructive reasoning. Now this is precisely what the readers of a penny paper don't want—or rather they must not be told that they want it, or they skip away to something else. The article, good in itself, would have been far better if it had commenced with 'Nobody in England except the dozen noblemen and gentlemen,' etc. All that precedes gives a repulsive heaviness to the aspect of the article. I can never too strongly impress on you the necessity of making everything *ad rem* or *ad hominem*, and plunging at once in the outset into the midst of the subject. It is in newspaper writing as it was with our League agitation. I used always to lay it down as a rule that the audiences at our meetings must be taught without their knowing it, and that a course of amusement and excitement must predominate over the labour of learning, *or the same parties would not come to a second meeting*; and as I knew we should want them year after year to listen, work and pay, I was obliged in all my popular harangues to throw in a spice of amusing ingredients which I used to call 'eating fire, pulling ribbons out of my mouth, or standing on my head' for their amusement, like the clown at the fair. I remember how I was often ashamed at reading the reports of my lighter passages in the paper next day, but there was no alternative. If I had confined myself to a process of reasoning in which instruction was the obvious end in view, the audience would not have followed me through and would certainly never have come to hear me a second time. Here is a confession and a lecture for you.

"Observe the accompanying figures showing the great increase in the circulation of the *Leeds Mercury* consequent on the war. The same rule will apply to all newspapers, and it shows the interest they have in keeping it alive. It is amusing to see the *Mercury* taking to itself the merit of having always displayed the '*warmest attachment to Peace*'! Why, it is notorious that there has never been a war, even including the Opium War, that it has not defended, and you know it was by a mere accident that I was in time to stop it from joining in the cry of the French invasion.

"These newspaper statistics must be turned to account by and by, as a warning to the public how they follow guides who may have an interest in misleading them.

"The *Mercury*, like all the other 'religious' papers, is a good lover of peace in the abstract."

CHAPTER IX

AN INTERLUDE OF PEACE

AFTER 1857 Cobden's epistolary intercourse with Mr. Richard grew less frequent and less full, though never long interrupted except during his visits to America and France. Out of the House and living in retirement at his country home, with only occasional visits to London, Cobden found comparatively little in 1858 to arouse him to activity. The settlement of India, the China War still lingering, and relics of the Borneo affair are chief topics in his letters to Mr. Richard, and his intercourse with Mr. Bright and other correspondents was slighter than usual. In addition to this lull in public affairs, much of Cobden's attention this year was necessarily absorbed by the critical condition of his private finance. A large proportion of his resources had been invested in shares of the Illinois Central Railway, which, though a sound concern and destined to a career of great prosperity, was yet an infant requiring constant supplies of fresh financial food, in the shape of 'calls' upon share capital. At the close of the year Cobden sailed for his second visit to the United States, going on behalf of English shareholders to examine on the spot the railroad and its management. Needless to add he used his eyes, ears, and understanding to take in a large fresh stock of information and of opinions, and was greatly cheered by the signs of progress which he everywhere detected. "It is the universal hope of rising in the social scale which is the key to much of the superiority that is visible in this country. It accounts for the orderly self-respect which is the great characteristic of the masses in the United States. . . . All this tends to the argument that the political condition of a people is very much dependent on its economical fate."[1]

During his absence in America in the early months of 1859 Disraeli's Reform Bill led to the defeat of the Government and the election of a new Parliament in May. Cobden was returned without a contest for Rochdale, and on his return to England at the end of June was greeted by a letter from the Prime Minister (Lord Palmerston), offering him a seat in the new Cabinet as President of the Board of Trade. His refusal of this offer, strongly urged upon him by many of his closest friends, and the motives which actuated him, made this incident the crowning point in a career of principle which to the ordinary politician of his day, or ours, would appear quixotic. The negotiation with Palmerston is particularly interesting in showing that the centre of Cobden's policy was not Free Trade but foreign policy. The tempter put his lure with great astuteness. "You and your friends complain of secret diplomacy, and that wars are entered into without consulting the people. Now it is in the Cabinet alone that questions of foreign policy are settled. We never consult Parliament till *after* they are settled. If, therefore, you wish to have a voice in these questions, you can only do so in the Cabinet."

Though, doubtless, Cobden's decision was affected largely by the dislike of sitting in the Government of a man whose whole character and career he had persistently distrusted and assailed, and of the misunderstand-

[1] Letter to John Bright ("Life," ii. 224).

An Interlude of Peace

ings to which his entrance upon office under Palmerston would inevitably give rise, the final determining motive of his refusal lay deeper still. He did not wish to form part of a bad system of secret Cabinet diplomacy. He was "out" to break that system and to insist that Parliament and public opinion should be the governing forces in foreign as in domestic policy.

But though thus determined not to undertake the proffered ministerial responsibility, Cobden did not refuse a public work of a supremely important task which presently presented itself, and which formed a principal episode in his public career. It will be convenient to give a separate chapter to this work, merely placing here on record the letters to Mr. Richard which fall within 1858 and the earlier part of 1859.

"*January* 8, 1858.

"I wrote to Sturge yesterday, suggesting that O'Neil should bring the case of *Oude* before a public meeting and try to obtain a vote in favour of a restitution of that piece of stolen property. I am quite sure I could carry the majority of a body of working men in favour of justice to the people of Oude. I am by no means sure that I should be equally successful with a middle-class audience, or with an assembly of so-called Evangelical Christians. I want to ask the latter, point-blank, who told them that God gave us India in trust for religious purposes? The presumption of that class is astounding. If I had all the Blue Books and pamphlets relating to Oude, I would put the case in a clear shape and rub John Bull's nose in it. The newspapers would of course call me a Sepoy.

"By the way, is it so clear that we are going to recover our former position in India? The hot weather will be again on us in a month or two and our young unseasoned troops will die like flies in a frost. Our armies may occupy central places, and flying columns may sweep all before them, but all beyond the British cantonments will be in open or secret revolt, and how is the country to be reorganized without the aid of the native army? All the hard work has been done by the Sepoys: midday and midnight sentry duty, the escorting of treasure, the police service—all, in fact, requiring hard labour and exposure as distinguished from actual fighting with the enemy has been put upon the natives. I doubt the possibility of Englishmen performing their duties, and therefore I can't see how we are to reorganize the country. By and by we shall see the impolicy of the indiscriminate vengeance which we have shown to the native troops. We have made every Sepoy a desperado and furnished him with the strongest possible motive to become a hero—for the only chance of escaping the pollution of the halter is by selling his life dearly in the field. In the end, when too late, the policy of pardon and conciliation will be tried. The arrogance of this people may yet be subjected to a rebuke at the hands of these despised Asiatics."

"*January* 14, 1858.

"An admirable article in the *Star* from, I believe, your pen, on the Evangelical movement for converting the Hindoos, gave me infinite pleasure. This mustering of the black coats to step into the breach opened by the red coats is to me ten thousand times worse than old Charley Napier 'sharpening his sword' or Kars Williams deprecating the neglect of the art of war. It is a wonder these people who read the New Testament backward are not afraid of bringing the devil himself into their midst and thus realizing the old popular superstition. Their doings are enough to make atheists of us all,

An Interlude of Peace

i.e. if we are to take them as the accredited exponents of Christianity.

"I want you to give another short article about China. Did you see the letter from *The Times* correspondent at Hong-Kong in yesterday's paper? It is desperately immoral. Sneering at Christian morality! Can we play the game of fraud, violence and injustice in Asia without finding our national conscience seared at home? May we or our children not see the bloody appetite which we are encouraging in Hindostan and China satiating itself on each other? In fact, is not our national character already changed? Observe with what callous indifference we read the Gazette returns of the killed and wounded in India, and compare it with what we felt when the first bulletins of our losses in the Crimea appeared. Like the Romans at the Amphitheatre, or the French populace in the first Revolution, we acquire a habit of enjoying scenes of carnage, the only difference being that we look at them through the columns of the newspaper. And hence 'our own correspondent' is sent to the seat of war to deck out in pictorial phrase, for the amusement of the reader, the scenes of slaughter and wounds and agony which we peruse with precisely the same zest as if we were witnessing a mimic battlefield at Astley's. Observe the eager levity with which *The Times* correspondent at Hong-Kong is urging on the fray, calling for the 'opening of the ball,' and threatening Lord Elgin with a recall if he does not execute his behests. In due time we shall hear of our forces having at a safe distance with their superior artillery bombarded and burnt the crowded city or terrified the population into submission. And all this in support of a quarrel into which our vain and foolish representative plunged us without a tittle of right or reason. And whose war is this? Not the war of the House of Commons, for a majority of that body stigmatized it as an unwarrantable aggression on our part, and every man of high intellect or commanding position who was unconnected with the Government gave solemn judgment against our own functionary, and the greatest legal authorities proclaimed that law and justice were on the side of our opponent. Yet in spite of all this it is now assumed by the Government that the middle class of England have by the last election endorsed the wicked acts perpetrated in our name in China, and now the representative of the newspaper which was the foremost abetter of the Government laughs at the idea of applying the maxims of Christian morality to the Chinese. The Greeks and Romans became vitiated in character by their contact with Asiatics—are we to suffer the same fate ? The bishops are inviting us to more strenuous efforts for the conversion of the heathen —are we not in need of all their care to prevent our being ourselves converted to heathenism ? Have not our acts in that largest and most populous quarter of the globe been characterized in a majority of cases by a pagan disregard of the precepts of Christianity ? "

"*August* 18, 1858.

"Nobody has a greater horror, scorn and detestation than I have for the doctrine of an irresistible law or destiny impelling to brute violence and injustice. *That* may be the law for wild beasts, but it is because we are something better than wild beasts that it ought not to be our law. What I meant was this: that when a *Government* plants its power and authority among an inferior race (I don't like the word, but there are inferior climates for the development of man), the very superiority, whether intellectual, moral or physical, leads to an extension of its power and influence over surrounding barbarism. This may be a desirable state of things if the ascendancy be

An Interlude of Peace

a moral one, *providing the governing intruders be capable of taking root with the indigenous population and amalgamating with them*. Thus it was a good thing for Penn to set up his moral-force sway over the North American Indians, because he and his colonists could live and multiply their species in the same latitudes as the red men, and there was no reason why they should not be fused into one community. But my doctrine is that it would not have been desirable for Penn to have colonized Borneo, and set up a form of government for white men who could not perpetuate their species there or follow the pursuit of agriculture. If he had gone there, and all the neighbouring tribes had come to volunteer to submit to his rule, or at least—which I maintain would have been the case—his moral power should have extended its influence to neighbouring tribes and they had in some degree acknowledged his authority—still it could not be a Pennsylvania, inasmuch as no white child can be reared on the Equator. The white race could only hold power by a constant succession of adult visitors which is the most unnatural and worst of all governing powers, and the more widely it is set up the greater will be its fall, to the confusion and injury of the governor and governed. If you want to benefit the races who properly belong to such regions as Borneo, India, or Africa, send your missionaries, both religious and secular, teach them what you know, and try to inspire them with the ideas of a better social and political status, and the desire for a better government. But don't attempt to govern them or to exert your influence through the Government. Do, in fact, as St. Paul did!"

"*August* 21, 1858.

"I doubt the policy of Mr. Wise interfering personally. It gives the occasion for such friends of Brooke

Richard Cobden : The International Man

as old Drummond to raise the cry of persecution. Everybody knows that Wise and Brooke have had a deadly personal quarrel. His facts and arguments had better be used through others. Why, for instance, should not he send a letter to the *Star* with an assumed signature exposing the blunders in the article from the *Leeds Mercury*? I send you quite a tit-bit from one of Molesworth's speeches. Put it in the *Star* as a paragraph. This China news will be made the test for hallelujahs over our criminal policy in the East. The striking success of our arms flatters the self-love and gratifies the combativeness of our people, whilst the cupidity of our merchants is excited by the prospect of fresh ' openings ' for our trade. *Our* case can only be proved by a long course of experience which will show that trade does not gain, whilst our tax-payers lose, by this process of forcing markets open at the point of the bayonet."

"*November* 28, 1859.

"There is a leader in to-day's *Daily News* about Borneo, the writer of which is evidently well informed upon the subject, and I have no doubt others will follow. The case for the Peace Party and the Aborigines Protection Society is strong enough upon the simple ground that here you have a slaughter unparalleled in its character since the massacre of the feeble Mexicans by the Spaniards in the sixteenth century, committed upon a race of barbarians upon no other pretence than that they were living in a state of uncivilized warfare with neighbouring barbarous tribes. No attack was made or contemplated upon Englishmen or Europeans—no attack was possible ; for mark the features of the case : *The Times* says one thousand five hundred or two thousand were blown to atoms, and we do not find that there was as much opposition to the British force as to cause the loss of a

An Interlude of Peace

single life to an Englishman. This fact constitutes it the most wanton, cruel and cowardly butchery of modern times. I believe that fewer lives were sacrificed at the Battle of Trafalgar. I have thought in vain upon the subject, to bring to mind any parallel atrocity perpetuated upon sea or land by a so-called civilized nation upon an uncivilized people in our day."

CHAPTER X

THE FRENCH TREATY

COBDEN's mission to France in 1859-60 for the negotiation of a commercial treaty with Great Britain was not in its first intent a business mission. It was a peace mission. The alliance for the Russian War, like most war-alliances, was an ill guarantee of lasting amity. The atmosphere of mistrust, which the Russian enterprise interrupted, again closed round the Governments and nations soon after peace was restored. The outbreak in April of the Franco-Austrian War, arranged in the summer of 1858 between Napoleon and Cavour and concluded by the Treaty of Villafranca, in July 1859, in which Savoy and Nice were handed over to France, aroused great indignation in this country. Though Palmerston was regarded both here and in France as friendly to Napoleon, the continental disturbances were used by the Government as grounds for increased expenditure on armaments, and on both sides of the Channel suspicions and antagonisms began once more to be inflamed.

Such was the situation when Mr. Bright, speaking in Parliament, asked why the Government did not approach the French Emperor with a view to establishing free commercial relations between the two nations as a pacific and a mutually profitable policy. The distinguished French statesman and publicist, M. Michel Chevalier, struck by the opportuneness of this suggestion, wrote to

The French Treaty

Cobden urging the experiment, and shortly afterwards, on a visit to this country, pressed him personally to undertake the conversion of the Emperor to a Free Trade treaty, so far as that policy was immediately practicable.

The only member of the new Ministry likely to be in full sympathy with such a large proposal was Mr. Gladstone, now Chancellor of the Exchequer. Cobden visited him at Hawarden early in September and discussed both the political and the fiscal feasibility of a treaty for the mutual reduction of duties upon articles of commercial exchange between the two countries. Though both were alive to the dangers to which treaties of commerce are always exposed, as compromising the sound general principle which bade each nation adjust its own fiscal policy to its own interests, unhampered by express arrangements with other countries, both were equally convinced that, as Lord Morley puts it, "An economic principle by itself can never be decisive of anything in the mixed and complex sphere of practice," and that diplomacy may be called in to assist the actual process of applying such an economic principle.

Cobden's first proposal, that he should utilize the opportunity afforded by a visit to Paris which he had previously arranged, to make a private inquiry into the matter, was changed into something more definite. If anything was to be accomplished, it was felt that some position of at least informal authority must attach to such a mission. He therefore consulted Lord Palmerston and Lord John Russell, the Foreign Minister. He did not find them strongly sympathetic, for their sense of the political proprieties had been gravely upset by the alleged intention of France to take a bit of territory from Morocco. But still he was accorded a permission and the friendly services of the Paris Embassy.

The situation was felt at first to be one of extreme

delicacy, as indeed it was. It could hardly be expected that Lord Cowley, our ambassador at Paris, would view with entire favour an irregular envoy thrusting himself into important relations with French Ministers and professing to carry some great unmeasured authority. On the other hand, Cobden was equally insistent that he was not to be regarded merely as a pushful commercial traveller seeking the expansion of French markets for British wares.

The following letter to M. Chevalier, written just after his return from visiting Mr. Gladstone, indicates his feelings :—

"*September* 14, 1859.

" It would, of course, be agreeable to me to see your Ministers of State. But I attach very little value to such interviews : for there is always a latent suspicion that I, as an Englishman, in recommending other Governments to adopt Free Trade principles, am merely pursuing a selfish British policy. Thus my advice is deprived of all weight, and even my facts are doubted. But, on totally different grounds, I should be glad to see a removal of the impediments which our foolish legislation interposes to the intercourse between the two countries. I see no other hope but in such a policy for any permanent improvements in the *political* relations of France and England. I utterly despair of finding peace and harmony in the efforts of Governments and diplomatists. The people of the two nations must be brought into mutual dependence by the supply of each other's wants. There is no other way of counteracting the antagonism of language and race. It is God's own method of producing an *entente cordiale*,[1] and no other plan is worth a farthing.

---

[1] " C'est la méthode de Dieu lui-même pour produire une *entente cordiale*, et tout autre système ne vaut pas un liard." This is perhaps the first recorded use of the expression *entente cordiale* as applied to the desirable relations between the two nations.

The French Treaty

It is with this view that I hope to see our Government greatly reduce the duties on wines and other French products, and it is only with this view that I feel any interest about your following our example. If I thought I could promote a similar spirit in the minds of any of your statesmen, I should be very glad to have an interview with them. But to have any chance of success it is necessary that they should previously understand that I am not a *commis voyageur* travelling abroad for the sale of British fabrics.

"I don't like the tendency of affairs on the Continent. Every year witnesses a greater number of armed men, and a more active preparation in the improved means of human destruction. *Depend on it, this is not in harmony with the spirit of the age.*"

On October 18th Cobden arrived at Paris, and, after an interview with Lord Cowley, was brought by M. Chevalier into close intercourse with M. Rouher, the Minister of Commerce, a man fortunately of strong Free Trade professions. It was soon made clear that all depended upon convincing the Emperor, and a long interview was arranged, at which M. Rouher presented Cobden. There are several accounts given by Cobden of this interview, in a formal letter to Lord Palmerston, a letter to Mr. Bright, and a very full account in the private journal, from which long extracts are given in Lord Morley's "Life."

The first hour of the conversation turned entirely upon the sore subject of the suspicion and dislike which the Emperor found in the English Press and Parliament everywhere and always directed against him, though his own acts had been continually dictated by a desire to be on good terms with England.

Writing on December 26, 1857, to his French Free-

Richard Cobden : The International Man

Trade friend, M. Arles Dufour, Cobden uses the same language : "I have had the opportunity of talking a little to the Emperor on the great question of Commercial Reform, and have tried to persuade him that *ours* is the only reliable *entente cordiale* between two great nations. Free Trade is God's diplomacy, and there is no other certain way of uniting people in the bonds of peace.

"I then turned to the question which I wished to talk upon, and urged the necessity of bringing the two countries into greater commercial dependence on each other. We talked for a full hour on the subject. My only fear is lest I talked too much, and may have sometimes forgotten that I was not speaking to the same gentleman with whom I had breakfasted at Mr. Milnes' three days after his escape from the château of Ham. But he is an excellent listener, and from every remark which fell from him he seemed to be favourable to Free Trade. (I have heard this even from his enemies.) But I came to the conclusion that he is very ill-informed on the subject, and that, as a consequence, he has a great fear of the Protectionists, whose numbers, power and influence he greatly exaggerates. Of course, I did all I could to take this party down in his estimation. He told me that a large majority of the Legislative Body and the Senate were determined protectionists, and that the only way in which he could effect a change would be through a treaty with a foreign Power, the provisions of which would then become law by his simple 'decree,' and he asked me whether England would enter into a commercial treaty. I explained that we could give no exclusive advantages, but that I was sure your Government would be glad to make some simultaneous changes in our tariff and embody them in a treaty, if that would facilitate his action in the same direction ; and

The French Treaty

I explained how it might be possible next year for Mr. Gladstone to co-operate with him in this reciprocal reduction of duties. I told him I thought we could abolish all the duties on the *articles de Paris*, and enable him to say to the Parisians that everything they made would go as fully into London as into Rome. He seemed pleased at this idea. He remarked that he was under a promise to the manufacturers not to abolish the prohibitive system before 1861. I told him that if the treaty was entered into next year it was not necessary that it should wholly take effect in one or even two years; that, if spread over three years, it might be as well for all parties. All that I wanted was the moral effect of the fact that the new commercial policy was adopted. I took this opportunity of explaining, in very emphatic terms, that England did not want customers; that we had already more markets than we could supply; that in a large number of our mills and manufactories the machinery was standing partially idle owing to the want of hands, whilst there were large orders in hand beyond what could be executed. He asked me how I should go to work if I were in his place. I told him that I should act precisely as I did in England, by dealing first with one article, which was the keystone to the system—in England that article was corn, in France it is iron; that I should abolish totally, and at once, the duty on pig-iron, and leave only a very small revenue duty, if any, on bars, plates, etc., and that I would buy off the opposition of the iron-masters by appointing a commission to afford them an indemnity out of a loan to be raised for the purpose. This would render it much easier to deal with all the other industries, whose general complaint is that they cannot compete with England owing to the high price of iron and coal. (I am told there is not much difficulty in making coal free.) He made me repeat to him these last remarks. He asked me to furnish him with a list of the articles imported into England from France upon which I thought we could reduce the duties. I promised to give him a general idea, which I have since done through M. Rouher. He asked whether the repeal of the Corn Laws had thrown any land out of cultivation, and when I told him it had had the very opposite effect—that in nothing had Free Trade been so completely triumphant as in the improvement it had effected in agriculture—and when I described the great veneration in which Sir Robert Peel's memory is held by the people, he remarked, 'I am charmed and flattered at the idea of doing the same work for France, but the difficulties are very great. We do not make reforms in France; we only make revolutions.' He alluded to the way in which he had been thwarted by the protectionists in some small measures of reform, such as the admission of iron for shipbuilding and the removing of the sliding scale. I was struck with his repeated allusions to the opposition he had to encounter and his evident fear of a mere handful of monopolists. I tried every argument to convince him that, instead of injuring the protected interests, he would render a greater service to them than any other class by subjecting them to a little wholesome competition. But he seems, like almost every Frenchman I know (excepting my friend M. Chevalier), to be very deficient in moral courage. The result of my interview was a conviction that, if left to himself, the Emperor would at once enter upon a Free Trade policy, but I am by no means certain that he will do so, and encounter the dangers which he imagines are in his way."

The French Treaty

The urgency of the situation, if a fresh anti-French panic was to be averted, is well indicated in the following letter to M. Chevalier:—

"PARIS, *October* 13.

"My interview with the Emperor was so far very satisfactory that he put pertinent questions and listened to me patiently. But, of course, he did not lead me to expect what his policy would be. I had no right to expect so much. I must return to London in a week to meet an American gentleman on private business, and shall not be back in Paris again for some days. I wish you could leave your vines and sheep at Lodene and come and see me before I go. What shall I say to Mr. Gladstone? I am not sure that the Ministers of the Emperor appreciate so fully as I could wish the importance of doing something to convince the world that he is going to do the work of Sir Robert Peel rather than that of the first Napoleon. M. Persigny feels this because, being on the spot, he knows what the state of opinion is in England. The alarmists and the incendiaries have got complete possession of the public ear. The feeling in England is now worse than ever. Not a voice is raised on the side of moderation. I met, at Messrs. Rothschild's counting-house, Meyer Rothschild, the M.P., from England, and asked him what news he brought from the other side, and his answer was, 'There is one universal feeling of mistrust of Louis Napoleon.' It is useless to go into the cause of this, or to try to show its injustice. He has enemies, of course, interested in spreading a hatred and mistrust of him, and there are parties in England who, for their own ends, foster this feeling of panic. The part for a wise man like the Emperor to perform

Richard Cobden : The International Man

is to do a striking act, which shall at once put his enemies in the wrong, and give those who, like myself, have taken the unpopular side in England an argument by which we can turn the tables on the panic-mongers. Nothing but a decided measure of Commercial Reform will suffice for this purpose."

A long and troublesome series of discussions was required, first, to drive an intelligent apprehension of the proposals into the head of M. Fould, the French Premier, who, though not averse to a modification of the existing prohibitive tariff, still clung to high duties as necessary to appease the manufacturing interests.

It was very difficult even to keep M. Fould up to this timid committal, or to get him to face definitely the proposal of a Commercial Treaty. "He saw great difficulties in the way. How, when, and where could a negotiation be carried on, and with whom? He was afraid that, if a meeting between himself, the Minister of Commerce, M. Rouher, and myself were to take place, it could not be kept a secret; that at present they had concealed even from M. Walenski, the Foreign Minister, the fact of any conversation having taken place between the Emperor and themselves and me." "The droll part of these interviews, besides the timidity of the people, is that here is a Government having so little faith or confidence in one another, that some of its members tie me down, a perfect stranger, to secrecy as against their most elevated colleagues." [1]

On a short visit to London he saw Mr. Gladstone, who was whole-heartedly with him in the matter, and Lord Palmerston, whose mind was again obsessed by stories of French aggressive intentions.

It is, indeed, doubtful whether his laborious pleadings

[1] "Life," ii. 253.

The French Treaty

in Paris with French Ministers would have reached success had not the French Minister in London, M. de Persigny, taken up the matter with real zeal and understanding. For even after M. Rouher had prepared his plan of a Commercial Treaty, the mind of the Emperor still remained undecided. At last M. de Persigny seems to have turned the balance by playing upon the fears of Napoleon, and representing war as possible unless some measures were taken to avert the profound distrust of the English public.

But, even when the Emperor's assent was won, the battle had to be fought in detail over the concrete proposals in the treaty. Here, again, it was a question of courage rather than of economic or political principle. The central contention turned upon the height of the proposed tariff, or, putting the same matter in another way, the extent of the French concession to possible English competition.

"Referring to the details in his intended tariff, he said the duties would range from 10 to 30 per cent. I pointed out the excessive rate of the latter figure, that the maximum ought not to exceed 20 per cent.; that it would defeat his object in every way if he went as high as 30 per cent.; that it would fail as an economical measure, whilst in a political point of view it would be unsuccessful, inasmuch as the people of England would regard it as prohibition in another form."[1]

Long after the Emperor was supposed to be converted and had given formal assent, his mind was liable to relapse before the protectionist attacks, now reinforced by M. Magne, the new Finance Minister who had replaced M. Rouher. Cobden had to wrestle anew with the influence of this man upon the

[1] "Life," ii. 258.

Emperor's mind, and he laboured under the disadvantage that all the earlier negotiations were unofficial. For not until the last days of the year was Lord John Russell induced to give Cobden the official position demanded for any effective action. Even then the project was far from safe. For the French protectionists and their ministerial friends had many devices for shelving it. One was to tack on to it as an integral part a political treaty of alliance. Another was the Emperor's demand for the submission of the Commercial Treaty to the Legislature, though he himself had informed Cobden of the irreconcilable objections of that body. Then came the demand for an "Inquiry" into the desirability of abolishing the prohibitive system, an inquiry actually held. At last the Emperor made an open committal of his intention to ratify the treaty in a letter to the *Moniteur*. This letter aroused intense anger among the ironmasters, cotton-spinners and other protectionists, and the danger was continuous, until the actual signature of the treaty on January 29, 1860.

The following passage from a letter written to his friend M. Arles Dufour gives a vivid picture of the most precarious stage of this great affair.

"PARIS, *January* 27, 1860.

"I had fully expected to leave Paris without fail to-morrow for Lyons, but a telegraphic despatch from London has again detained me. There are some little verbal alterations to be made in the treaty which has been returned. And we are to meet Messrs. Baroche and Rouher this afternoon to agree to them.

"There is nothing which will affect the conclusion of the *affaire*, which will be effected, and the ratifications exchanged, before next Friday. The prohibition-

The French Treaty

ists have made a great mistake in resorting to such violent language. They only prove their own impotence, for, as they cannot follow up their big words with big deeds, they only make themselves ridiculous. Nobody will pity them. They are gone back to their mills and factories, and as everything goes on much as before, they will learn for the first time that they are not all France and that the world can go on pleasantly even *when they* are not satisfied. They have been spoilt children so long, with every caprice gratified, at the expense of other people, and even sometimes of themselves, that I dare say it is very difficult for them to bear this contradiction, but it will do them good notwithstanding."

But the signature of the treaty by the Emperor was very far from a completion of the transaction. For in the first place it had to run the gauntlet of criticism in the House of Commons, where strong suspicions were aroused against any treaty of French origin on the part of the Francophobe faction whose passions were being freshly fed by the intrigues of Napoleon in the affairs of Italy and the Zurich treaty between France and Austria for the rearrangement of Italy.

Cobden himself took a private hand in an attempted adjustment of the situation by means of a long conversation (January 30th) with Prince Metternich, the Austrian Ambassador at Paris. The sympathies of Lord Palmerston and Lord John Russell were strongly with Italy, and, as the months of 1860 passed by, a powerful backing of public resentment gathered against the Franco-Austrian intrigues which went to endanger Cobden's treaty. Nor was that the only danger. Among free-traders there was a vociferous section that objected on grounds of principle to commercial treaties

Richard Cobden : The International Man

as a violation of the pure gospel of economic freedom. The measure had to steer its course between these opposed tides of criticism. Fortunately this task was committed to the able hands of Mr. Gladstone, who, in his exposition of the treaty (February 10th), paid the following well-merited tribute to its creator :—

"Rare is the privilege of any man who, having fourteen years ago rendered to his country one signal and splendid service, now again within the same brief span of life, decorated neither by rank nor title, bearing no mark to distinguish him from the people whom he serves, has been permitted again to perform a great and memorable service to his country." The measure emerged triumphantly from its ordeal in the Commons. "Nothing was given to France which was of any value to us. On the other hand, nothing was received from France except a measure by which that country conferred a benefit upon itself. At a small loss of revenue we had gained a great extension of trade."[1] Such was the compact and successful presentation of the case by Gladstone.

But there still remained a vast amount of anxious toil for Cobden before the treaty was got into an operative shape. In fact, the treaty itself was little better than a sketch, the detailed provisions of which had yet to be filled in by a Supplementary Convention provided for in one of the Articles of the treaty. Over these details a fierce battle had to be fought in order to prevent the French protectionists maintaining the duties up to the 30 per cent. standard which the treaty made permissible, instead of reducing them towards the 10 per cent. for which Cobden had been arguing.

Cobden himself took command of the English Commission, confident in the strength of the evidence he

[1] "Life," ii. 289.

The French Treaty

could produce and in the support of M. Rouher and the Emperor. The work, which began in April and lasted until November, was of a most arduous nature, taxing his industry, astuteness and temper to the utmost. The main matter of discussion was the comparative costs of production of the British and French products liable to be brought into competition in the several trades. Cobden and his colleagues had first to prepare evidence and witnesses to prove in each particular that the French Commissioners ought to be content with a lower duty than that which was demanded by the French manufacturing interests. "The strain of the conflict and its preparation, both in Cobden and his colleagues, was very great. The discussions at the Foreign Office usually lasted from two until six o'clock, when they went to dine. Later in the evening came laborious interviews with commercial experts from England, who brought tables, returns, extracts from ledgers. Commercial friends at home were apt to be impatient, and Cobden was obliged to write long letters of encouragement and exhortation. In the morning, after two or three hours devoted to correspondence and preparation for these interviews, soon after eleven Cobden proceeded to the offices of the English Commissioners in the Rue de l'Université, where his colleagues had already arranged the matter acquired in the previous evening. This they examined and discussed and prepared for the meeting at two o'clock, when the encounter was once more opened."[1]

During the whole of this delicate but tedious business Cobden was harassed by the growing strain of the political situation. The French and British Governments accused one another of increasing their armed preparations, either upon grounds of unjust suspicion

[1] "Life," ii. 295.

Richard Cobden : The International Man

or with aggressive intentions. The annexation of Savoy had seemed to us the first step in a larger career of imperialist aggression, which, according to the information given by M. de Girardin to Cobden, included an extension of the French frontier to the Rhine and a pacific annexation of Belgium.

On the other hand, Prince Napoleon, the ablest survivor of his family, in conversation with Cobden in June, imputed the bad relations between the two countries mainly to our vacillating foreign policy and our constant increase of arms. It was during this conversation that Prince Napoleon made the interesting suggestion which Cobden thus records in his Diary:—

"He then said he was about to mention a delicate matter, and he suggested that I ought to be appointed Ambassador to France; that that would do more than anything besides to cement the good relations between the two countries. As this was said with a good deal of emphasis, and appeared to be the communication he had in view when he sent for me, I replied with equal emphasis, 'Impossible! You really do not understand us in England!' I then explained exactly my position towards Lord Cowley: that I had been from the first only an interloper in his domain; that he had acted with great magnanimity in tolerating my intrusion; that a man of narrow mind would have resented it, and either have given up his part altogether to me or have resisted my encroachment on his functions. I remarked that Lord Cowley had frankly owned that I had superior knowledge to himself on questions of a commercial or economical character, and that, considering how much they had been my study, it was not derogatory to him to grant me precedence in my own speciality. I begged him to say no more upon the subject."

The French Treaty

As the summer advanced Cobden's plans were more and more disturbed by the English proposals for fresh military expenditure, which, as he urged, "completely falsified my promises to the Emperor." Fanned by the fire-eaters of the Press, the panic spread through the nation and was shared by all the men who counted in the Government, excepting Gladstone, who, keeping in close personal touch with Cobden, was able to bring closely informed eloquence to bear in his pacific speeches. Even Palmerston, who until the winter of 1859 had been a supporter of the Emperor, succumbed to the prevailing passion and came to the conclusion that "at the bottom of his heart there rankles a deep and inextinguishable desire to humble and punish England."

On July 10th Cobden addressed to Palmerston a long letter of remonstrance and argument of which the following are the most salient passages:—

"The extraordinary military and warlike displays of the last few months in England have tended to diminish the hopes which were at first entertained in connection with the treaty. And this state of discouragement in the public mind has been increased by the rumour that it is the intention of the Government to propose a large increase to our permanent defences." "It is on this point that I am more immediately led to address you. It seems to me that the two questions are intimately connected; and I venture to suggest that, in fairness to the public and to Parliament, as well as to the Government itself, the results of our negotiations here should be known, before the country is pledged to a further large outlay for defensive armaments." "Should the treaty prove as unsatisfactory in its details as is predicted by those who are urging us to an increase of our warlike preparations, I shall have nothing to say in opposition to such a policy. But if, as I expect, the French Government should take but a single step from their prohibition system to a tariff more liberal than that of the Zollverein or the United States, then I think the public mind in Europe will undergo a considerable change as to the prospects of peace with our great neighbour, and it is doubtful whether the country, on the very eve of such a change, will subject itself to increased burdens in anticipation of a rupture with its new customer. All I desire is that it should be allowed a choice when in possession of a full knowledge of these circumstances." " In the important discussions on the details of the French tariff (and it is wholly a question of details) I shall be placed in a very disadvantageous position, and shall find myself deprived of those arguments with which I most successfully urged the adoption of the Free Trade policy, if in the meantime the present Government commits itself, and what is still more important in the sight of France, if it be allowed to commit the Free Trade and popular party in England, to a permanent attitude of hostility and mistrust."

Palmerston remained unconvinced, and a fortnight later introduced his proposals for increased armaments in a speech directly offensive in its allusions to danger from France. It had a most injurious effect on French opinion. Cobden wrote in his Diary that " People speak of it as an indication that our Court and aristocracy are inclined to renew the attitude of 1792, by forming another coalition in opposition to France. They say that the inspiration of our policy in arming and fortifying comes from Berlin and Brussels through the British Court." This was the view of Prince Napoleon, and M. Rouher, Cobden's stoutest political aid in carrying through the Treaty, was not less outspoken in his condemnation of Palmerston's speech.

The French Treaty

"He characterized the policy of our Cabinet as a pitiful truckling to the popular passions of the moment, for the sole purpose of securing a majority in Parliament, in disregard of the interests of commerce and civilization and the higher duties of statesmanship."

But while the political value of the treaty was thus grievously impaired, the instrument itself was brought to completion, though not without further impediments and delays. Cobden thus comments in his Diary upon the obstructive attitude:—

"This Convention was ready for signature, so far as the negotiation *here* was concerned, on the 18th September, and the delay which had taken place is attributable to our Foreign Office, to their habitual procrastination, the desire to meddle, and I fear also to the willingness on the part of some of the officials in that department to find fault with *my* performance. My position is that of a poacher and their feeling towards me is akin to that of a gamekeeper towards a trespasser in quest of game. I am afraid, too, that the majority of the Cabinet is not very eager for my complete success here. The tone of our Court is very hostile to the French Emperor, and in the present nearly balanced state of political parties the Court has great influence. There is an instinctive feeling on the part of our aristocratic politicians that, if the Treaty should prove successful and result in a largely increased trade between France and England, it would produce a state of feeling which might lead to a mutual reduction of armaments, and thus cut down the expenditure for our warlike services in which our aristocratic system flourishes."

.   .   .   .   .   .

At last the second Supplementary Convention, completing the treaty, was signed on November 16th, and

Richard Cobden : The International Man

Cobden was set free for a much-needed holiday. He left in December, with his wife and eldest daughter, for Algiers, where he remained until the following May.

The proposal, raised in certain friendly political quarters, to vote him a sum of money for his services at Paris, was peremptorily stopped by Cobden in its initial stage, and he was equally firm in refusing Palmerston's offer to make him a Baronet or a Privy Councillor. In his letter of refusal to Palmerston he says :—

"With respect to the particular occasion for which it is proposed to confer on me this distinction, I may say that it would not be agreeable to me to accept a recompense in any form for my recent labours in Paris. The only reward I desire is to live to witness an improvement in the relations of the two great neighbouring nations which have been brought into more intimate connection by the Treaty of Commerce."

It is hardly necessary here to dwell upon the great importance of Cobden's treaty, not only for the commerce of this country and for the improved political relations with France, but for its contribution to the wider policy of free commercial intercourse throughout the world. The purists of Free Trade who objected to any commercial treaty, as binding our national fiscal policy and buying favours by favours, were mistaken in their objections. England did not, by the French treaty, give any special favour to French products entering this country. England maintained no differential duties and the reduction or abandonment of our import duties upon agreed classes of goods extended automatically to every other nation besides France. France, on her part, took the treaty as the model for a number of similar trade treaties extended within the next five years to cover Belgium, the German Zollverein,

The French Treaty

Italy, Scandinavia, Austria and Switzerland. Thus was erected and applied the principle of most-favoured nation's treatment, by which every arrangement to reduce a tariff with one country has a liberating effect far wider than its immediate area of application and helps to strengthen the bonds of international commercial co-operation.

. . . . .

Cobden's absorption upon this laborious task and his long absence from Parliament and from close contact with affairs at home naturally reduced the volume of his correspondence with Mr. Richards and other friends. But the letters written this year show that he was still following with zest the affairs of China and India, and that from Paris he kept a guiding hand upon the agitation against increased armaments which his friends in England were organizing.

"*June* 16, 1860.

" I observe what Lord John said about China matters. But I am not without hopes yet that Lord Elgin will reach his destination in time to prevent a renewal of the war. He has a common interest with the Government in putting an end to the expense which is the great rock ahead for Gladstone. Lord E. never ought to have returned before the ratifications were exchanged and left the matter in the hands of his brother, who is evidently a commonplace person with just those contentious attributes which led him to be constantly seizing the small ends of things, the only ends he was competent to handle. This conduct of Lord E., by the way, is an illustration of the aristocratic system under which we are ruled and which is practically an irresponsible regime. If he had been an employee of this or the United States Government, he could not have done so with impunity. But being a lord he is invulnerable. Apart from this he is not to be blamed for his proceedings in China, which were conducted with temper and moderation.

"Apropos of this subject, I have been in correspondence with some persons at Manchester in the Chamber of Commerce, and urging them to take the question of China politics into their hands. I believe the Lancashire people, who are more interested than any one besides in the trade with China, are not in favour of a warlike policy. They are afraid that it may have the effect of throwing the whole empire into confusion. I wrote a letter to one of my friends, who put the substance of it into the *Manchester Examiner* with the signature of 'A London Merchant,' and it will be also in the *Morning Star*, I expect, to-day or Monday. I am following this up, and hope to identify the Manchester people with a peace policy from the point of view of their own interests. The last correspondence between the China Government and Mr. Bruce places us more in the wrong than ever. How our conduct must puzzle the Chinese! They must regard us as a people without moral sense, common sense, or any logical faculties. Some great retribution must befall us in the East to vindicate the justice of God's government. My only astonishment is that we have been allowed to run riot so long.

"Here I am immersed in the details of the French tariff, a tedious task and slow, but one which could not be avoided. I am more than ever satisfied that the result will be a great reality, and not the sham which your rifle-club heroes are predicting. The state of the public mind is so suspicious in England regarding everything French, and especially everything which the Emperor's Government meddles with, that not one person in a hundred believes that I am doing anything better than subjecting myself to the tricky devices of a gang of unscrupulous

The French Treaty

swindlers, and that nothing satisfactory can result from my labours. It is almost incredible that so many people still allow themselves to be influenced by their belief in *The Times*, though that paper never believes in itself for three days together. By the way, what can be the motive of that journal in so systematically and with such transparent dishonesty attacking the treaty, and refusing to wait till the work in which we are engaged is completed, but passing judgment in anticipation? It cannot be to please its readers of the mercantile and manufacturing classes, for they desire to be quiet and wait at all events to see if any good can be got from the treaty. It seems as if that journal had sworn to pull down the Emperor or to embroil the countries in the attempt. What is their motive? Are they under sinister influences or are they satanic enough to do their vile work for the mere love of mischief?

"Can it be possible that the Government is looking with favour to the plan of expending £14,000,000 for fortifications in addition to the thirty millions already voted for armaments? I cannot bring myself to believe it. Having now been nearly nine months in France, mixing with everybody, having access to all information and knowing what is doing by the Government, I declare to you that I am only the more lost in amazement at the cry of invasion which is still potent enough to draw millions of money at any moment from the pockets of the people. Most solemnly do I assure you that a delusion more gigantic, or a hoax more successful, was never practised on the public mind since the days of Titus Oates, and including the feats of that immortal impostor. There is not one fact to warrant the belief that the Emperor or the French people desire to draw on themselves the greatest of calamities, a war with England; there are thousands of facts spread over ten years to prove that he wishes to be at peace with us. If forced to a choice, he would prefer a war with the whole Continent to a war with England. In the one he might conquer, in the other he knows he could have nothing but suffering for his people without the power to strike a blow in return. It is a thing so monstrous from my present point of view that I hardly have patience to discuss it.

"I trust our friends in Parliament will refuse to be identified with anything so monstrous. And indeed I will not believe that the Government really contemplates proposing such a waste of public money.

"Give me a few years for the operation of my treaty, and I will make it very difficult for diplomatists or anonymous journalists to set the two nations at work cutting each other's throats. My only fear is that they who do not like this prospect will destroy my work before it can produce its good fruits."

"*August* 10, 1860.

"I send by this day's courier from the Embassy a copy of the pamphlet to which you refer. It is now published for sale avowedly under the auspices of the Government here. Could it be translated? It strikes me that taking into account, *on both sides*, the forces by land and sea, at home and abroad, regular and voluntary, there are more British than French being drilled to arms at this moment. We are certainly spending from five to six millions more than the French on our Army and Navy. Yet we turn up the whites of our eyes and thank Heaven we are not a warlike or military nation as the other nations of the Continent! There is, I fear, as you say, no direct and immediate cure for the madness that has come over the people of England. But what concerns me is the danger of this state of things leading to another great European war. I don't like the gathering of crowned heads, and

The French Treaty

the tone of feeling towards France. In Germany and Switzerland the newspapers are as bad as our own. There are sometimes half a dozen of the German journals seized at the French frontiers in a day for outrageous articles against the Emperor. Unfortunately, too, there is among the Liberal Prussian party a growing idea that a war with France is the best solution of their internal German difficulty, which is at the bottom of much of their restlessness upon foreign questions. The Germans are yearning for a more perfect union, which is impeded by the pretensions of their small kings and dukes. The Prussian Liberals have an idea that a war with France would get rid of them all. If they feel sure that they can reckon on England in case of a rupture with France, they will not long be without an occasion for a quarrel. In fact, all this preparation and menace on the part of other countries will make it the more difficult for the French Emperor to put up with an affront from any quarter. It is easy to bear hard words from an unarmed man, but even a look may convey an intolerable insult from one who is threatening you with a loaded pistol. It is the same with nations. The real difficulty and danger is that France and England and other countries are gradually assuming such an attitude of armed defiance that they may some day be placed in such a predicament that war or humiliation to one or the other may be inevitable. Hitherto the French Government have scarcely taken a step to increase their armaments. In respect of their Navy they have really done nothing. But if Germany and England continue their course France must of necessity follow.

"The great evil we have to contend with in England is that the people are really misled and are under the impression that France is meditating an attack on them. The *Government* takes advantage of this to lay on heavy and unnecessary taxes for armaments which naturally increase the irritation. How is this to be met? The Government alone could speak with authority and disabuse the public mind, but that is not their cue. Unfortunately the people will not believe anybody else, and least of all you and me. I have sometimes thought that if I were free I would pay a visit to the editors of the leading newspapers in the provinces and show them quietly how they had been imposed upon.

"But perhaps, after all, what I am now doing here, and which must in two months more be brought to a close, is, as you say, the best and only way of really reaching the roots of the evil. I hope when the new French tariff is published it will be so complete a revolution in the French commercial system as to convince the English public they have been under a great delusion with respect to the policy of the Emperor. I am afraid that my friend Henry Ashworth was right when he said, 'Get the two nations into debt with each other, and the ledger will do more than the Bible to keep them at peace'! It is lamentable enough that there should be so much truth in this sentiment."

"*November* 13, 1860.

"Do not take a step about armaments until I have the opportunity of seeing you. I mean a direct step, such as a meeting of the friends of peace on the subject. I shall have something to say to you and our friends upon the subject when we meet.

"Observe the tone which *The Times* takes upon the treaty. I am glad of this, for it will infallibly sink it in the estimation of the commercial classes.

"If I were on the spot, I should suggest an article or a letter in the *Star* putting the conduct of *The Times*, in thus, by its opposition to the treaty, braving

The French Treaty

the proof of facts and the universal approbation of the manufacturing districts, on a choice of hypotheses. Either it must be a desperate game to prevent the paper duty from being abolished and thus being itself swallowed up by the cheap Press. To do which Gladstone and his financial policy, of which the treaty is the cornerstone, must be discredited.

"Or it must be, as some people have long believed, itself in some way in the hands or under the influence of the Orleans party, and is doing its best to prevent that consolidation of peace between the two countries, arising out of the success of the treaty, which that party dread because they believe that it would strengthen the Buonaparte dynasty. There is, of course, a collateral aim in view. *The Times* knows that the only way of keeping up our present enormous expenditure is by maintaining the hostile attitude between France and England, and that the moment this expenditure slackens the paper duty goes. There is nothing but an overpowering motive, such as is to be found in one of these alternatives, which can account for this paper persisting in going, on a question of commercial interest, in the teeth of the unanimous feeling of the mercantile and manufacturing classes. Can you pen a letter to the *Star* in this sense?

"Mr. Hargreaves, in a letter which I recently got from him, said that the *Telegraph* accused *The Times* of wishing to keep up the expenditure in order to prevent the repeal of the paper duty. If this, which I believe is the true view of the case, could be made apparent to all the cheap Press, it would give you the best possible assistance in promoting the reduction of armaments. It is therefore desirable that this view should be well expounded in the *Star*."

Richard Cobden : The International Man

"*December* 31, 1860.

"I will not dwell on the beautiful climate here (Algiers), where we sit all day with our windows open, and now as I write, at nine o'clock in the morning, my wife has just closed the venetian blinds because the sun is too hot, and where we are eating green peas and ripe strawberries; if I dwelt on this, it might make you dissatisfied with your snow and frost, and so I will go to business.

"I wish you would write a paper or two on our commercial relations with China, to be printed in the first place in the *Star* and then published in a pamphlet form, and I should like it done before the meeting of Parliament. The point I wish to see developed is this, what has been the increase of our trade since we began 'opening up' China by the Opium War in 1840, and what has been the increase of our expenditure, civil and military, in that country? The statistics of the trade might be furnished for you through some house engaged in that quarter and who sympathizes with our views. Or I am sure my last colleague of the Paris Commission, Mr. Mallet, of the Board of Trade, or our intelligent Secretary, Mr. Lock, of that department, would help you to put your fingers on the official tables in the Blue books. As to the trade direct with the Chinese, it resolves itself into the quantity of tea and silk we take from them, and the quantity of manufacture we send direct, and the quantity of opium which is purchased by our manufacturers in India and sent to China as a remittance. There is also some specie. If you can contrive to interest some intelligent merchant, he would help you. White, M.P. for Brighton, is acquainted with the Shanghai trade. He lived there six years.

The French Treaty

"As respects the expenditure in China. There is first the amount which our wars cost in excess of the indemnities extorted. This is not very easily arrived at. But the increase of the *current* annual expenditure, beyond what we spent before we began to bring armies and navies to aid our commerce in China, may be more easily ascertained. I think Sir W. Molesworth, in one of his great 'Colonies' speeches alluded to the growth of this expenditure. Montgomery Martin also, I think, in his huge pamphlet, gives some facts. If there has been no Parliamentary return of the expenditure on 'works' at Hong-Kong, the amount could with a little trouble be picked out of the annual estimates. Did not Lord Ellenborough move for a return in the House of Lords last year of the warlike expenditure in China? The fact is, as you have often observed, that, when once the amount of force on the coast of China has been raised by a war, it never comes back on the return of peace to what it was before. This will be most strikingly the case at present, for we have thrown that country into a state of anarchy by our violence and injustice.

"If you can present a dry debtor and creditor account now of the profit and loss of our wicked outrages in that country, I think the public mind is in a state to listen, and your facts shall certainly be reproduced in Parliament. Let me hear if I can be of further use. The postage to this place is the same as to France."

A few other passages from letters of this period, addressed to other friends, may be conveniently given here.

To J. Schwann, Esq.

"*July* 6, 1860.

"I must say I have heard with sorrow (not unmixed, I will own, with indignant surprise) that there are men

Richard Cobden : The International Man

in Yorkshire and Lancashire, who cheered me on at public meetings whilst advocating arbitration and non-intervention, who now profess to disapprove of the course I took, because, forsooth, I refused to surrender those principles to the exigencies of a political party. They know little of my character if they think me capable of pursuing a course which would sacrifice for any such consideration my long-cherished convictions. If they want a man who will put on and off his principles at the bidding of Treasury whippers-in, they must look out for another and more pleasant representative."

.   .   .   .   .

This is a convenient place to insert a few extracts from Cobden's letters to his intimate friend, M. Arles Dufour, written during the years 1861–2 and bearing mostly upon Anglo-French relations.

To M. Arles Dufour.

"ALGIERS, *January* 19, 1861.

"I observe what you say about the abstinence from all allusion to the treaty in Palmerston's speech. It was certainly significant. I suspected from the first that the majority of our Cabinet were not much in love with my undertaking in Paris. Our aristocracy and Court have sharp instincts where their own interests are concerned, and they feel probably in some doubt whether they may not be obliged to abandon their tone of irritation and mistrust towards France when the trading and manufacturing classes have a good market there; and then what will become of the pretence for our enormous armaments which are maintained on the plea of being necessary to protect us against the hostile designs of your Emperor?

The French Treaty

"You are quite right, it is lamentable to see our vigorous communities under the influence of these old men verging on fourscore years. As for Brougham, it is painful to see him, in his eagerness to be heard on every topic of the day, forgetting what he said in his better days. For instance, he has lately written a letter to an American in which he rebuked him for his violent anti-slavery doctrines and for his disregard of the rights of the slave-owners. Some clever critic has extracted a passage from one of his own speeches against slavery made thirty years since, in which he denies the right of property in *man*, and has published it in juxtaposition with an extract from his recent letter. It is a pity the friends of the old man cannot withdraw him from public life, and thus prevent him from tarnishing the lustre of his own past fame."

To Mr. W. Hargreaves.

"PARIS, *May* 7, 1860.

"I am not very proud of the spectacle presented by our merchants, brokers and M.P.'s in their ovations to the pugilist Sayers. This comes from the brutal instincts having been so sedulously cultivated by our wars in the Crimea and especially in India and China. I have always dreaded that our national character would undergo deterioration (as did that of Greece and Rome) by our contact with Asia. With another war or two in India and China the English people would have an appetite for bull fights, if not for gladiators."

"PARIS, *August* 4, 1860.

"The English people in Parliament have undertaken to be responsible for governing one hundred and fifty millions of people, despotically, in India. They have adopted the principle of a military despotism, and I have no faith in such an undertaking being anything but a calamity and a curse to the people of England. Ultimately, of course, Nature will assert the supremacy of her laws, and the white skins will withdraw to their own latitudes, leaving the Hindoos to the enjoyment of the climate to which their complexion is suited. In the meantime we shall suffer all kinds of trouble, loss, and disgrace. Every year will witness an increased drain of men and money to meet the loss entailed on us. In the meantime, too, an artificial expansion of our exports growing out of Government expenditure in India, will delude us as to the value of our 'possessions' in the East, and the pride of territorial greatness will prevent our loosening our hold on them. Is it not just possible that we may become corrupted at home by the reaction of arbitrary political maxims in the East upon our domestic politics, just as Greece and Rome were demoralized by their contact with Asia? But I am wandering into the regions of the remote future. It is, however, from an abiding conviction in my mind that we have entered on an impossible and hopeless career in India, that I can never bring my mind to take an interest in the details of its government."

APPENDIX TO CHAPTER X

Cobden's attachment to France and his French friends was an exceedingly important influence in his life. A typical Englishman in most respects, he was attracted by that quality of the intelligence which is peculiarly French, lucidity and the reasonableness with which it is associated. Cobden had thought out for himself a clear, consistent body of political and economic thought. Though no pedantic exponent of this

Appendix to Chapter X

system among his countrymen, who have little liking for logic and less for its application to practical affairs, Cobden was sufficient of a rationalist to believe that social progress could and should be guided by clear, consistent principles. He was well aware that these principles were very imperfectly grasped by those who had worked with him most earnestly for the liberation of trade in this country, and that even those who clearly comprehended them as economic principles had little realization of their wider application for breaking down the barriers of nationalism and establishing the solidarity of mankind.

Now, among the group of distinguished Frenchmen who gathered round him as a champion of Free Trade in the late forties, he found just this quality of thought and this enthusiasm for peace and internationalism in which most of his Manchester friends were lacking. The most brilliant exponent of the sheer logic of Free Trade in this or any other country was Frédéric Bastiat, a scholar and country gentleman, who, brooding long in seclusion over political theories, discovered in 1845 that a powerful body of Englishmen were engaged in trying to put his reasoning into practice. Coming over to this country, he spent some time studying the work of the League and formed a personal attachment to Cobden, whose presentation of the issue came nearest to his own. From that time on he remained a close friend and correspondent of Cobden. His book " Cobden et la Ligue" spread the gospel most effectively in France, and his "Sophismes Economiques" remains the sharpest and most humorous exposure of protectionist fallacies. A speculative mind, Bastiat saw all the implications of Free Trade in the development of a sound foreign policy based on peace, economy, colonial emancipation and anti-imperialism. His friendly relations with Cobden were maintained until his death in 1850. But, as he himself recognized, he was not fitted for political agitation, and the active leadership of the group of men who from this time forth struggled to hold up the banner of internationalism in an intensely nationalistic people fell to other hands.

The most important of these was M. Michel Chevalier, a distinguished member of the little band who in the thirties attached themselves to the principles of Saint-Simon, an early speculator upon socialism, and one who had applied himself with special zeal

Richard Cobden : The International Man

to the promotion of international union by improved communications and commerce. It was he who was chiefly instrumental in inducing Cobden to undertake the onerous and delicate negotiations which led to the French Treaty. Lord Morley describes how a speech of John Bright's in the Session of 1857, proposing an approach to the French Emperor upon the question of Free Trade, fired the mind of Chevalier, who wrote to Cobden on the subject and, visiting this country in the summer of that year, urged him to undertake the conversion of the Emperor. Chevalier was one of the little knot of ardent reformers with whom Cobden kept in closest personal touch during his residence in Paris.

Other members of the group were M. Paillottet, one of Cobden's most active correspondents, though unfortunately the letters passing between them have been lost; Frédéric Passy, who survived well into this century, one of the most ardent advocates of peace and internationalism; M. de Molinari, one of the founders of the *Journal des Economistes* and a leading writer upon economic questions; and M. Emile de Girardin, at whose house Cobden met Prince Napoleon in January 1860, and with whom he kept up a close friendship afterwards. To M. de Girardin we owe the famous eulogy in the Introduction of the volume published in August 1865 in Paris to the memory of Cobden by his French admirers.

"Nommer Christophe Colomb, c'est nommer le nouveau monde; nommer Richard Cobden, c'est nommer le monde économique. Rien ne manque à la justesse de ce rapprochement, car Robert Peel doit à Richard Cobden sa célébrité, comme Améric Vespuce a dû la sienne à Christophe Colomb.

"Le monde économique : c'est le monde transformé; c'est la paix succédant à la guerre; c'est la science détrônant la force; c'est l'esprit de réciprocité chassant l'esprit de rivalité; c'est la liberté des échanges abaissant de toutes parts la hauteur des barrières; c'est l'unité de lois et d'usages, de monnaies, de poids et de mesures, simplifiant tous les rapports de peuples entre eux; c'est la neutralité universelle des mers; c'est l'abolition de l'esclavage et du servage sur tous les points du globe; c'est la rédemption définitive de l'homme par le travail, mais stimulé par l'épargne et fécondé par le crédit.

"A l'entier accomplissement de cette bienfaisante transforma-

Appendix to Chapter X

tion, il ne manque plus que le Souverain qui mettra judicieusement sa gloire à récolter ce que Richard Cobden a mis laborieusement toute sa vie à semer."

The greater portion of the memorial volume consists of an eloquent account of Cobden's character and influence as a worker for international friendship, and in particular for the establishment of friendly relations between his own country and France. I quote one illuminating passage : " Richard Cobden était anglais, fier et heureux d'être, admirateur de sa patrie et de l'ensemble de ses institutions, mais non aveuglément et sans réserve. Adversaire, en général, du monopole et du privilège, et ami chaud de l'égalité, il ne nourissait aucun sentiment amer contre l'aristocratie de son pays ; sa belle-âme si bienveillante repoussait instinctivement le fiel. Mais tout en restant anglais sur ses habitudes et ses affections, il croyait fermement qu'ici bas l'homme a deux patries, la communauté où il a vu le jour, et la terre, patrimonie commun du genre humain. C'était entendre le patriotisme à la grande manière du Cicéron qui est si bien d'accord avec la philosophie moderne, je pourrais dire avec le génie du Christianisme. Le sentiment cosmopolite n'était pas chez lui a qu'il est chez d'autres si souvent, un signe d'indifférence, une forme policée de l'égoïsme. C'était une sympathie forte et agissante, l'amour de l'humanité, une sorte de religion. A ses yeux les haines nationales étaient un contre-sens et une duperie, un débris d'un temps passée où le travail était dédaigné et flétri, et où l'exploitation du faible par le fort était au dedans la base du gouvernement des Etats, au dehors le but et la règle de leur politique ; un débris que dans certains pays au moins, les classes dominantes s'efforçaient de conserver pour leur avantage propre et pour le maintien de leur ascendant. L'hostilité systématique entre l'Angleterre et la France lui semblait une aberration où l'absurde allait jusqu'à l'odieux. Il pensait que si, au lieu de se jalouser dans les quatre parties du monde, ces deux puissances vivaient en bonne harmonie et, tout en gardant leur indépendance et leur originalité, concertaient volontiers leurs démarches dans l'intérêt commun et pour le bien général, elles arriveraient au plus haut degré d'autorité, et rápandraient, ne fût-ce que par la contagion d'l'example, les bienfaits de toute espèce sur la genre humain, dans l'ordre moral comme dans l'ordre matérial. Il goutait fort l'esprit français, il en avait eu lui-même des traits frappants. Il appréciait nos

Richard Cobden : The International Man

institutions et nos usages beaucoup plus que ne le font la plus part de ses compatriotes auxquelles il semble que, livre de leur type, il n'y a point de salut, de grandeur, que, sais-je, d'élégance et de grace, et au gré duquels la tyrannie et l'abaissement de la dignité humaine commencent là ou cesse leur manière de comprendre et de pratiquer la liberté. L'égalité politique et sociale de la France excitait son admiration ; en un mot, il aimerait la France. Il la connaissait bien, il l'avait etudiée avec une sagacité et une pénétration qui n'etaient pas les moindres de ses facultés."

But the appreciation of the greatness of Richard Cobden in France was not confined to the circle of his private friends or even to his fellow-workers in the cause of Free Trade and Peace. When the news of his death came there was evinced in every public quarter a desire to honour his memory. At the meeting of the Corps Législatif next day M. de Forcade la Roquette, its Vice-President, described the event not only as a calamity for England but as "a source of mourning for France and for humanity." The Emperor addressed the following letter to Mr. Charles Cobden :—

"Monsieur, j'ai pris un grand part au malheur qui a frappé votre famille ; car M. R. Cobden avait toujours montré pour la France une grande sympathie, et son influence sur ses compatriotes ne pouvait que contribuer à resserrer les liens qui unissent l'Angleterre et la France. Je vous prie d'être auprès de sa veuve l'interprète de mes sérieux regrets et de recevoir l'assurance de mes sentiments de haute estime."

Jerome Napoleon, who had been closely associated with Cobden in the Commission for the Exhibition of 1861, wrote in terms of the keenest admiration and esteem to Mrs. Cobden, and the Foreign Minister made an eloquent eulogy in a dispatch to the French Minister at London. The French Press, both in Paris and the provinces, contained a number of striking testimonies to Cobden's international services. Important articles appeared in the *Revue Contemporaine*, from the pen of E. Lavasseur, in the *Economiste Français* by M. Jules Duval, and in many other magazines. The Political Economy Society, which in 1846 had given a banquet in honour of Cobden's work for Free Trade, consecrated to his memory a special meeting on April 5th, at which the President, M. Hippolyte Passy, MM. Chevalier, Joseph Garnier, Foucher de Carel, and Bénard made orations in honour

Appendix to Chapter X

of a great worker for humanity. I will quote the concluding words of the President's address : " La vie de Cobden a été un grand et tutélaire enseignement ; elle a montré tout ce que peuvent l'énergie du caractère, la rectitude de l'esprit, la hauteur du sens moral dans les temps où nous vivons. Cobden a fait pour l'apaisement des haines internationales, pour l'extinction des rivalités jalouses qui tout de fois ont armé les peuples contre les autres, pour les intérêts fondamentaux de l'humanité, plus que n'a fait aucun homme d'Etat auquel a appartenu jusqu'ici le gouvernement des nations. Cobden n'est plus, mais ses œuvres subsistent et l'avenir les respectera : car de jour en jour en apparaissent plus distinctement la sagesse et l'utilité."

CHAPTER XI

CORRESPONDENCE, 1861-4

AFTER his arduous labours at Paris were brought to a successful end, Cobden spent the winter and the early spring of the next year (1861) in a much-needed holiday and rest at Algiers, returning to England in the middle of May. By that time the cloud of unpopularity in which his opposition to the Russian War had surrounded him was entirely dissipated, and business men and politicians recognized the important services which he had rendered in securing the Commercial Treaty with France. A large meeting at Rochdale on June 26th proclaimed the enthusiasm of commercial Lancashire, and on July 17th the Freedom of the City of London was presented to him at a great gathering in the Mansion House. In a speech vindicating the principles of the treaty and reciting its advantages, one passage deserves quotation as illustrating the view persistently maintained by Cobden that the palpable gains of free commerce must in the nature of things prevail. " You may ask me whether I think other nations will follow in the footsteps of France and England. I frankly avow to you I am not much concerned about that question. Whatever England and France unite to do, whether it be a policy of war or peace, they will assuredly draw the whole civilized world within the circle of their influence. Any other nation which

Correspondence, 1861-4

should attempt to hold aloof from the policy which England and France have now frankly embraced would find themselves so far behind in the race for civilization and wealth that their own self-love, if no other motive existed, would induce them to follow the example we have set."

From Algiers he kept up a large correspondence with Mr. Richard and other friends. His early letters to the former were chiefly concerned with the strain of the Anglo-French relations, which, though less tense than they had been, were still serious. The competition in armaments was at once cause and effect of the mutual ill-feeling and suspicions, each side representing its new preparations as a defensive reply to some aggressive movement of the other. As early as February 4, 1861, we find him proposing a memorial in favour of a convention between the two Governments for the limitation of armaments, and urging Mr. Richard to look up the question of comparative naval expenditure. No sooner had he got settled in England again than he began to make preparations for an argued statement of the whole armament and international issue, which took fuller shape in the last of his long pamphlets, published early in the following year under the title of "The Three Panics." This proved to be an exceedingly laborious task, requiring close research, not only into Hansard but into various official and other statistical documents extending over a long period of years. Much of this detailed work was done by Mr. Richard and other assistants whom he procured, and a great many of Cobden's letters during the period relate to their co-operation in this task. The armament question, however, important as it was, belonged to the wider issue of a constructive policy of international law for

Richard Cobden : The International Man

the protection of commerce in time of war, the nature of which was well set forth by him in a letter to Mr. Ashworth in the April of the following year (1862).

In 1856 the American Government, invited by the Paris Congress to abandon privateering, had made the important counter-proposal to Europe to exempt private property at sea from capture, both by privateering and armed Government ships. This offer was well received by France, Russia and other maritime Powers, but found no encouragement in Great Britain. The American Government for several years pressed various proposals for reform of maritime law, including one communicated to the House of Commons, on the very eve of the outbreak of the Civil War, in which they pressed for a revision of the right of blockade, urging that "the only case in which a blockade ought to be permitted was when a land army was besieging a fortified place and a fleet was employed to blockade it on the other side ; but that any attempt to intercept trade by blockade, or to blockade places which were commercial ports, was an abuse of the right which ought not to be permitted."[1] Lord Russell, in reply, took the stand which has been consistently maintained by our Government and extended up to the present day, viz. "that the system of commercial blockades is essential to the maintenance of our naval supremacy." That argument Cobden set himself to destroy, by applying tests of reason and experience. He first dwelt upon the fact that, more than any other great nation, we are dependent not only for prosperity but for subsistence upon large over-seas supplies of foods and materials. He next pointed out how these considerations practically compelled us to rebut our own theory of

[1] "Political Writings," ii. 383.

commercial blockade, even so far as to permit by licences the entrance of foods of enemy origin into our own ports during war-time. This occurred during both the French and the Russian wars. He then proceeded to show how unjust and intolerable such a blockade policy was for neutrals, and how inconsistent with the Free Trade policy to which we were committed. "Free Trade, in the widest definition of the term, means only the division of labour, by which the productive powers of the whole earth are brought into mutual co-operation. If this scheme of universal dependence is to be liable to sudden dislocation whenever two Governments choose to go to war, it converts a manufacturing industry, such as ours, into a lottery, in which the lives and fortunes of multitudes of men are at stake." He summarizes the reforms that are required in three propositions:—

> "(1) The exemption of private property from capture at sea during war, by armed vessels of every kind.
> "(2) Blockades to be restricted to naval arsenals, and to towns besieged at the same time on land, with the exception of articles contraband of war.
> "(3) The merchant ships of neutrals on the high seas to be inviolable to the visitation of alien Government ships in time of war as in time of peace. These reforms we regard as the necessary corollary of the repeal of the navigation laws, the abolition of the corn laws, and the abandonment of our colonial monopoly."

The outbreak of the war between the Northern and Southern States of the American Union in the early summer of 1861 gave renewed importance to these and other related questions. The blockade came

Richard Cobden : The International Man

soon to have a particular importance in its bearing upon Lancashire trade, and several of Cobden's letters in the summer dwell upon that aspect of the case. As early as July we find him urging pressure on his friend Charles Sumner, Chairman of the Foreign Relations Committee of the Senate, for a reconsideration of the blockade policy.

As the months passed by, the American War came to occupy an increasing part of his attention. At first he was disposed to sympathize with the Southern case, partly on the right of secession, partly also because the Southerners were the Free Traders of America. But, as the slavery issue emerged more clearly and the cause of the great democratic experiment for which the Republic stood became so plainly implicated in the struggle, partly also influenced by the precepts and example of his friend Bright, he soon definitely ranged himself upon the side of the North. We find him in December taking an active part in the formation of a Committee for the foundation of an Arbitration Society and for the application of the principle to the American War.

Before discussing the fuller part he was drawn to take in these momentous matters, it may be well here to print some of the 1861 letters to Mr. Richard, indicative of his labours in this year and the depth of his thought and feelings as the American conflict began to open out.

"*February* 4, 1861.

"A week ago I wrote to Mr. S. Morley suggesting that an Address to the Queen should be signed in the City urging the desirableness of the Governments of France and England coming to some understanding to limit their naval armaments. I recommended a very mildly worded memorial which scarcely any person could object to sign. The main object to be aimed at is to bring such a pressure of public opinion on the Governments as shall induce them to break ground on the disarmament question. When once they have accepted the responsibility of the task of trying to do something, they will be obliged to show grounds for failure. This would totally reverse the present attitude of the parties. Each would have to resort to facts and figures to prove the other in the wrong; and to justify itself each would try to parade its own moderation. You will see at once how much the public would gain from such an exposure and controversy. I have written to Paris to sound a friend, a banker there, on the propriety of getting signatures to a similar memorial to the Emperor. But England is so immeasurably superior in her naval armaments (we have a personnel of eighty-four thousand in our service to thirty-one thousand in France) that we ought to make the first advance.

"In my letter to Mr. Morley I said that it was of the utmost importance that the Address should emanate from the 'bankers, merchants and others of the City,' and not from the Peace Society or the 'Manchester School.' But if he could induce a few such men as Baring, Rothschild, Huth, etc., to lead off, your friends in the City, who are so active and disinterested, could do much afterwards to fill up the list.

"You will recollect that there was an Address to the Emperor signed by the City magnates some years ago. I think Mr. Hall, of Tower Hill, took an active part in that movement. There was also a Mr. Christy in it, a rather excitable person living in Kent. It requires energetic people to follow up successfully such a project. I rely on your friends, if necessary, giving their hearty co-operation.

Richard Cobden : The International Man

"There were two quotations which we often used from the speeches of Lord Aberdeen and Sir Robert Peel. The one from the latter was to the effect that so great was the danger from the immense growth of these standing armaments that he hoped the Government would put some check to the evil, and if not, that the people would. Lord Aberdeen's remark was to the effect that he doubted the truth of the maxim that to prepare for war was the best way to preserve peace ; that, on the contrary, when nations had made great preparations for war they were apt to feel anxious to test their efficiency. How would it do to print these extracts and distribute them in the City ? Along with the quotation from Sir R. Peel might be given the expenditure for our armaments when it was spoken, and the amount spent *now*.

"Whatever you do will, I am sure, be guided by your never-failing prudence and judgment.

"It strikes me that there never was a time when there was such a chance of such an Address being signed by men of all parties in all parts of the kingdom as at present, when the country is startled at the dilemma in which the backbone of our national industry may be placed at any moment by events over which we have not the slightest control in the Cotton Slave States of America."

"*March* 1, 1861.

" I have had a letter from Mr. W. S. Lindsay, M.P., who is, or was, at Paris assisting in arranging a treaty of navigation, informing me that the Minister of Marine, who has thrown open every detail to him, has convinced him that the English Government and people have been acting under a great delusion respecting the naval armaments of France. Chevalier writes to me by the same post giving me the same news. He acted as interpreter, and says the Minister proved to L. that all that had been said about the great preparations in France was 'humbug.' Lindsay tells me that he had written a long letter to Lord Clarence Paget, to be shown to Lord Palmerston, in which he urged the former to come to Paris for a couple of days to investigate the matter for himself, and offering on the part of the Minister of Marine the most complete explanation of every detail of their naval armaments. Lindsay told Lord C. P. that he ought not to take another step in moving the Navy Estimates until he had accepted this invitation, and he adds in his letter to me that if the British Government will not take a straightforward course on this question, he will obtain the consent of the French Government to make a full exposure in the House.

"I am inclined to hope that good will come of this. It will be the first step towards an understanding on the subject of limiting the armaments of the two countries—when one of the Ministers invites another to a conference of this kind. It will not, however, be an easy task to retrace our steps. So many people have gone wrong that it will be a severe test of their self-love to admit themselves in error. I have never heard anything about the memorial which I sent to Mr. Morley."

"*April* 7, 1861.

"Your kind letter has followed me to this place, where I have come in the course of a little excursion into the province of Algiers. The country is most beautiful and the climate at this season very delightful. There is a great future for the African shores of the Mediterranean which two thousand years ago were

Richard Cobden : The International Man

covered with splendid cities. Yesterday I visited a little village standing in the midst of the ruins of an ancient seaport. It is not an exaggeration to say that for several square miles outside of the walls of the old city the ground was so thickly covered with empty *stone* coffins which had been disinterred, and the fragments of tombs, that it was with great difficulty I could thread my way among them. But what struck me most in the remains of this old seat of commerce was the enormous extent of remains of private habitations, which presented themselves not only within the old walls but for miles outside over the country, in the form of large and well-dressed stones, proving that the population generally were living in substantial buildings. When walking over the ruins of Athens, Alexandria, Rome, etc., I have often asked where the *people* lived, for whilst you everywhere see the gigantic remains of temples, circuses, and arches of triumph, you see nothing to lead you to suppose that the bulk of the people inhabited such large houses as those in this neighbourhood. Perhaps the reason may be that this was a port and not the seat of government. The place to which I allude is called Tipasa.

"I am very much obliged by your kindly thinking of me. You must not suppose that I am afraid of being brought into contact with the Peace Society. I honour your efforts too much, and have too great a mistrust of the motives of all who decry them to be averse to exchange compliments with your body. But, as you have consulted me, I must candidly avow that the greatest trouble I have on my hands is the meeting and replying to friendly demonstrations from public bodies, and you will really oblige me by not at the present moment adding to the number. On my return home I shall have a battle to fight to escape from dinners and addresses. Every refusal I make to these invitations adds to my difficulty and indeed to the inconsistency of accepting your offer. Let it lay over for the present.

"You would have seen a letter and enclosure I sent for your perusal through Mr. Morley. Really, this conduct on the part of Lord Palmerston, in stating so broadly and repeatedly facts which I knew to be groundless respecting the French armaments, was quite incomprehensible until I read his speech on the Afghan dispatches, which offers a key to the whole mystery. No doubt he will be able to say in a few years, if he should remain so long on the scene, that what he said about the French Navy was uttered merely to accomplish some other good object. And as this is a principle tolerated and indeed approved by the majority of Parliament, there is nothing more to be said about it —except that as such ethics are not yet recognized in Westminster Hall or the Old Bailey, we may hope that they will not for ever remain the standard of Parliamentary morality. But in the meantime it must be confessed we are little better than a nation of political mountebanks fairly led by a pantaloon."

"*April* 17, 1861.

"I wish you would take up the question of the French and English navies as discussed in the House of late, with a view to urge on the public the desirability and the practicability of *now* coming to some understanding with the French Government to put some limit on their naval armaments. This is a most excellent time. *All parties agree that no more wooden line-of-battle ships are to be built.* Those in existence will soon decay, and if not replaced there will be a gradual end of this description of ship, which was

Richard Cobden : The International Man

formerly considered the main test of maritime power. As yet the iron-sided invention has not taken their place. England and France are just beginning the race of folly in these novelties, and there is no reason why it may not grow quite as large and costly as the old force. But America, Russia, and the other Powers have not yet taken the first step. Now then is the time for common sense to interfere. Let England and France only set a limit to their iron-cased ships, the rest of our gigantic waste will disappear with time. Urge this in a letter or two to the *Star*, in order to prepare public opinion for a movement, and if you can get up a public meeting *afterwards*, with Mr. S. Morley in the chair, and secure a few speakers not of the Peace Society to lead off, *and you to come in at the end*, and taking the precaution beforehand to secure such an attendance as will fill the room at the City of London Tavern, it could not fail to do good."

"*July* 12, 1861.

"If the American Civil War goes on, and all the ports of the South remain blockaded after the new cotton crop is ready—a state of things one can hardly realize and yet from which it is difficult to see an escape—then all parties will be very sick of blockades. As a peace must come some day, it has struck me that perhaps it might be made the occasion for extending the provisions of the Treaty of Paris beyond the mere abolition of privateering, and including the terms stipulated for by Mr. Marcy and even going beyond and putting an end to blockades. There is no doubt that *we*, as the greatest manufacturers, merchants, shipowners and carriers, have the largest interest at stake in this question, and if we were not governed by a feudal class which is always looking to the interests of the 'services,' and which does not like to part with the barbarous usages of war, we should have been the first to agree to put down the robbery of private individuals at sea by armed *Government* ships, as well as to abolish blockades.

"How different would have been the state of feeling now in Lancashire if, instead of seeing the ports blockaded from which the cotton comes, there had been no interruption to the trade of the South. And this might have been the case if the English Government had favoured the views of the Democratic party in the States. This ought now to be made known to the English public.

"If you are writing to Sumner, you might ask him to keep his eye on the question of blockades in the future terms of pacification. English opinion will be keenly alive to our *national* interest in this question, as apart from the interest of the Admiralty and Horse Guards, after we have seen the peril to our cotton trade arising from the blockade of the South."

"*August* 17, 1861.

" I had an idea of writing a pamphlet giving a running history of the Anglo-French armaments, with extracts from speeches since 1844—when the game of beggar my neighbour began. But I don't know whether I shall have the courage to begin it. I get discouraged as to the effect of reason and argument and facts in deciding the policy of the country. We are a very illogical people, with brute combativeness which is always ready for a quarrel and which can be excited at the will of a governing class that has subsisted for centuries upon this failing in John Bull's character.

"Is it not vain to expect any honest attempt to put a limit to our expenditure so long as Palmerston rules and Gladstone, whilst protesting against the waste, lends his eloquent genius to its perpetuation? I am convinced that we should save three or four millions a year by the return of the Tories to office—which is an event that cannot be distant. Palmerston is fouling the Whig nest, and preparing to hand over the reins to the Tories.

"As respects the Americans, we can do nothing but wait the effect of taxation and suffering on the combatants. I am told the Washington Government have become more moderate in their temper to Foreign Powers since the unhappy affair of Bull's Run. It remains to be seen how the people will relish the new taxes. They have been reckoning on borrowing in Europe, in which I suspect they will be disappointed.

"I really don't see how you can operate directly on the French question. Perhaps the great development of trade that is going on between the two countries is the best peace-maker that could have been devised. I still think it would be a good thing if the British people could be enlightened as to the social and political state of France. However, that project will keep. Meantime enjoy yourself, and lay up a stock of health for another campaign."

"*September* 11, 1861.

"I hope there is no truth in the rumour that our Government will acknowledge the Southern Confederacy. I have great faith in their stupidity and ignorance, and still more in their false and selfish predilections in all cases where liberty and the true interests of the millions are concerned, but can hardly believe them bad enough for this."

Correspondence, 1861-4

"*October* 16, 1861.

"I am still busy reading back in *Hansard* and other repositories the sayings of our alarmists. It is a curious history. It shows what a monomaniac or an interested partisan endowed with obstinacy can do, to run over the career of Napier in this line; how his laughable exaggerations and absurdity of this year got a somewhat willing hearing the year after, and became the policy of the Government the third year. In fact, our armaments have been really dictated by such people as old Attwood, who chooses to go mad with Urquhart about Russia, and as Napier or Horsman, whose judgments would have been utterly repudiated by sensible men on a matter of private business. These men have created a sort of senseless panic which has been taken advantage of by the governing class. I have just got from Paris an account of the yearly expenditure for the French Navy, and of the number of men borne in their navy each year, from 1835 to the present time. Nothing can be more clear than that the whole charge against the present Government of having surpassed their predecessors in their naval preparations is groundless. It is a fact that during the whole twenty-five years our Navy was never so disproportionately large, as compared with that of France, as in 1860, when Palmerston raised the cry of alarm and brought forward his project for fortifications. I have written to Gladstone to this effect. He has nothing to say to contradict, and yet, sad to say, he continues to minister to such a state of affairs! There ought, in the interest of conscientious men, to be another verse added to our Litany, and in addition to praying the good Lord to deliver us from 'battle and murder and sudden death' we ought to pray to be preserved from the temptations of the post of a Cabinet Minister."

Richard Cobden : The International Man

"*October* 19, 1861.

" It is quite evident that I must publish my pamphlet with a retrospect of our panics and follies for the last twenty years. Looking to Collier's speech at Plymouth, and other similar performances, it is quite evident that there is to be another 'revival' of the invasion mania this autumn. We were told that the volunteers would set this topic to rest. But the ghost is not laid. How are we to account for this inveterate propensity to be deluded and excited about an imaginary foe? Is it the inordinate pugnacity of our people? It really amounts to a disease or a mania. I doubt sometimes whether a war is not the only sedative that can cure it."

"*October* 26, 1861.

"A few days ago I sent the accompanying 'Memorandum' to Lord Palmerston with a request that he will bring it under the notice of the members of his Cabinet. I have forwarded a translation to M. de Persigny, begging him to bring it under the notice of the Emperor. I send it confidentially for your perusal. It is only fair that it should in the first place be kept a secret. If nothing be done, I will publish it before Parliament meets. I have had no answer from P. He would like to put it in the fire or give it to the volunteers to light their pipes with it. But Disraeli's speech, the coming collapse of trade, and the resolution come to at the close of the Session to stop the line-of-battle ships, give a little practical weight to it at this moment. Still, I don't expect anything to come from it."

"*December* 7, 1861.

"I have written very strongly to Sumner urging the Government at Washington to take old General Scott's hint, and go further—to propose to raise the blockade

Correspondence, 1861-4

on condition that the system of blockades and all the rest of the belligerent rights be abandoned by Europe. Whether this can be done I know not. But I am convinced that the indefinite maintenance of the blockade, with little or no progress in the Civil War on the side of the North, will lead to an intervention of some sort in the coming year. I have written to the same effect to General Scott."

"*December* 8, 1861.

"It is enough to make one forswear one's kind, let his beard grow, and retire to a cave, to witness the sudden madness that can seize so many people! I remember when I was at the Peace Congress meeting at Edinburgh, in the winter of 1863, saying in my speech that if a person had left England for a voyage round the globe in the spring of that year, he would have left the public just apparently worked up in a frenzy which rendered a war with France inevitable. And on his return to England, if he had not seen a newspaper in his absence, he would have been startled to find the French and English fleets broadside to each other in Besika Bay, but instead of the collision which he would expect to witness he would have been still more amazed to learn that the two countries were going to fight as allies against Russia.

"So now, before I can put my extracts together to show up the frenzy again with France, here we are for rushing into war with America, totally forgetting all that we were saying a few months since of the danger from France.

"'A mad world, my masters!'"

"*December* 11, 1861.

"Don't let the conduct of this incorrigible old dodger annoy you. It is exactly what I expected. This American affair might seem to be playing his cards for him beautifully. But I am not sure he will not over-play his game. There will be no war on this legal question. Make yourself quite easy on the point. The object of all this bustle is to justify the maintenance of the present expenditure. But we will try to spoil the game. What a case these men who now clamour for war against America give us against their outcry against France!"

"December 18, 1861.

" By all means make any use you please of my name on the Committee for Arbitration.

" Though the object should be at present to urge arbitration in the American difficulty, yet I think it would be well to form a permanent Society for the sole object of applying the resolution of the Paris Congress in favour of arbitration to all cases of misunderstanding as they may arise. There should be an advertisement and an invitation to co-operate as soon as possible, to give people an opportunity of combining their movements.

" I received the enclosed discouraging note from Baines, and have written to encourage him. It is deplorable to see how the rich and influential people must always be led by the poor and illiterate. From the time of the Apostles it has always been so. I advise Baines to let a meeting of working men be called.

" I am writing to Brighton to advise them there to form a permanent committee after the meeting.

" The Unitarian leaders in Leeds never can be got into action. Directly there is anything to do they begin hair-splitting."

"December 18, 1861.

" The accounts I get are very warlike, and yet I cannot believe in war. But would it not be well to turn all your efforts to an agitation in favour of arbitration?

Correspondence, 1861-4

"Bright says he is sure that there is no town where a public meeting would not vote for arbitration, and I dare say he is right. No time should be lost. The clubs and cliques about Pall Mall are very warlike. It is desirable that if there be more sense in the country it should display itself."

. . . . . .

The shock of the American Civil War continued to be the great disturbing factor in European politics. Its economic influence was chiefly due to the blockade of the Southern ports, which cut off the cotton supplies of Lancashire and brought unemployment and poverty to its inhabitants. But two naval incidents caused intense political feeling and came near to causing a severance of pacific relations between the British and American Governments. The first was the affair of the *Trent*. Two Commissioners, Mason and Slidell, despatched to Paris and London by the Southern Confederacy, were seized on November 8, 1861, by a federal warship when on board a British mail-boat sailing for Havana, and were taken away as prisoners. The British Government immediately demanded their release and an apology, and before an answer was possible ordered a brigade of Guards to Canada. This impetuous action brought us to the brink of war, only averted by the interposition of the Queen and the Prince Consort, who got Palmerston to accept as an adequate redress the release of the prisoners and a statement from the United States Minister in London to the effect that the action of Captain Wilkes in seizing the Commissioners was without the authority of the United States Government. So the trouble blew over.

In June another untoward incident took place, the blame of which fell upon our Government—the sailing from Liverpool of the *Alabama*, a vessel built at Birkenhead for the Confederate Government. The reply of our

Richard Cobden : The International Man

Government, that due vigilance had been taken to prevent the escape of the *Alabama* as soon as her true character was known, was not accepted as satisfactory by the American Government, and was not in fact true, as later evidence showed. For the next two years the vessel, largely manned by British sailors, played havoc with Federal trade, and the tension caused by the refusal of the demand for compensation made towards the close of 1861 by the American Government lasted for several years and threatened more than ever to lead us into war.

In another part of the American Continent we were also for a time embroiled in serious trouble. The civil war which broke out in Mexico in 1861 had brought in the Governments of France, Spain and England, which despatched a joint expedition for the protection of their subjects and the enforcement of the payment of bonds held by their subjects. England and Spain withdrew from the expedition in May 1862, having obtained satisfaction from President Juarez, but France, having ulterior imperialistic objects, persisted, and embarked upon the scheme of conquest which ended a few years later with the execution of the Emperor Maximilian, the French nominee to the throne. The United States, absorbed in their domestic trouble, refused all part in the Mexican imbroglio, but the intrusion of European forces upon their Continent, in violation of the Monroe Doctrine, served to exasperate their people against the European Governments.

Cobden's view of this enterprise is conveyed in the following passage from a letter of October 1863 to M. Arles Dufour :—

"Park Hill, Streatham, *October* 23, 1863.

"The world's affairs seem to be getting into a considerable confusion. Shakespeare somewhere says, 'The world is out of joint, oh cruel spite! That ever I was born to put it right.' Now there seem to be many busy people who are eager, without being born to it, to engage in the task of putting the world to rights. There is our little Foreign Minister with his pen, and your ruler with his sword. And yet they do not seem to meet with very encouraging success. What could have possessed your Emperor when he engaged in the task of resuscitating Mexico? 'The Latin Race'! Why, the majority of Mexicans are half-breeds—a mixture of negroes, red Indians, and Spaniards. I remember returning from New York to England, having for my companions in 1835 two very intelligent men, one a Swiss, the other a Scotchman, who had been living seven years in the interior of Mexico purchasing cochineal. Their description of the state of ignorance, of demoralization, and utter extinction of moral sense in that country was most appalling, and they wound up their narrative of the character of the people by the observation, 'We have been living seven years in a community where there is not one human virtue extant.' Why should your Government, or any Government *not responsible for this state of the Mexican people*, take on themselves the responsibility of redeeming them from their degradation? That is surely the work of the Almighty, and not of your Zouaves. When Prince Napoleon was in England last year I told him that people in England were comparing the expedition to Mexico to the invitation of Spain from Bayonne by his uncle.

"Depend on it, *we* shall not take a part in a war against Russia for Poland. All classes are opposed to it. There is a very serious obstacle to our going to war which may not have occurred to many people yet, but which would have come home to us all if a war with Russia were imminent. We have to face the certainty of having ships fitted out by the Americans to prey on our commerce in retaliation for our *Alabamas*. The Americans are waiting to offer their services to any country with which we shall be at war."

This diversion of political interest to Mexican affairs to some extent cut across Cobden's intention of mobilizing his political and intellectual forces for a general assault upon Palmerston's European policy. His important pamphlet " The Three Panics " was near completion at the beginning of the year, but he hesitated to launch it upon the public in the critical situation which the *Trent* affair brought about. Eventually he decided in favour of publication, and it appeared towards the close of April. A detailed and closely documented narrative of the panics which had seized both Governments and people in 1848, 1853 and 1862, it was his fullest formal indictment of the statesman whom he regarded as the most dangerous rogue of the age. Cobden was a good deal disappointed with its early reception. In truth, its very virtue of thoroughness repelled many minds which most needed its instructive revelation. Nevertheless it performed a serviceable work in preparing English Liberalism for the return to sanity which followed the disappearance of Lord Palmerston and ushered in the temperate epoch of Gladstone and Bright.

But his immediate political energy was by no means exhausted by the production of " The Three Panics " and the perpetual controversy against the competition with France in armaments, which he waged with unusual vigour this year in the House of Commons. The improvement of International Law in relation to sea commerce during war had taken strong root in his mind some years before, as one of the essential safe-

Correspondence, 1861-4

guards of civilization. The events of the American War gave special urgency to this reform. In letters to the Press and to political friends he is tireless in pursuance of his educative work, blocked in the House by the obstinate fallacy that we, as the possessors of the most powerful navy, are gainers by maintaining the full belligerent rights stretched to the widest limits which precedent can yield. There are many references to the subject in his correspondence with Mr. Richard. But as a prefatory note I will print portions of two other letters of this year, already published in the "Life." [1]

To M. Chevalier.

"*August* 7, 1862.

"Our Government, as you know, is constantly declaring that *we* have the greatest interest in maintaining the old system of belligerent rights. Lord Russell considers that we must possess the right of blockade as a most valuable privilege for ourselves on some future occasion, and you will see that almost the very last words uttered by Lord Palmerston at the close of the Session were to assert the great interest England had in maintaining these old belligerent rights. In fact, we are governed by men whose ideas have made no progress since 1808—nay, they cling to the ideas of the Middle Ages."

"*October* 25, 1862.

"England cannot take a step with decency or consistency, to put an end to the blockade, until our Government is prepared to give us their adhesion to the *principle* of the abolition of commercial blockades for the future. This our antiquated Palmerstons and Russells are not prepared to do. They have a sincere faith in the efficacy of commercial blockades as a

[1] Vol. ii. pp. 400-2.

belligerent weapon against our enemies. They are ignorant that it is a two-edged sword, which cuts the hand that wields it—when that hand is England's—more than the object which it strikes. Lords Palmerston and Russell feel bound to acquiesce in the blockade, and even to find excuses for it, because they wish to preserve the right for us of blockading some other Power.

"I am against any act of violence to put an end to the war. We shall not thereby obtain cotton, nor should we. coerce the North. We should only intensify the animosity between the two sections. But I should be glad to see an appeal made by all Europe to the North to put an end to the blockade of the South against legitimate commerce, on the ground of humanity, accompanied with the offer of making the abolition of commercial blockades the principle of International Law for the future. But this, I repeat, our Government will not agree to at present. We have a battle to fight against our own ruling class in England to accomplish that reform. I am by no means so sure as Gladstone that the South will ever be a nation. It depends on the 'Great West.' If Ohio, Michigan, Illinois, Indiana, Iowa, Wisconsin and Minnesota sustain the President's anti-slavery proclamation, there will be no peace which will leave the mouth of the Mississippi in the hands of an independent Power."

To Mr. Richard.

"*January* 30, 1862.

"We will talk over the subject of the 'Arbitration Committee' when we meet. I shall be in Town at the opening of the Session.

"I have got nearly to the end of my pamphlet; but now what is to be done with it? Before I had time to finish the story of the last invasion panic, here we are led on by *The Times* and *Saturday Review* for a war in the other hemisphere! It is just the same tale over again as in 1852-3, when we were caught with the Russian War in the midst of the second panic. I had better perhaps keep the MS. until we see what course the American question takes. If we get thick into that—which I suppose will be Palmerston's game to divert attention from other matters—nobody would read anything about the French panics—what say you?"

"*February* 2, 1862.

"I think your Society wrong. With a French army ravaging Mexico, without a shadow of justification, and indeed in violation of the professed purpose for which, in conjunction with Spain and England, the expedition was undertaken, and with an army occupying Rome in violation of all principles of self-government, you are surely not justified in assuming the French Government to have any objects in common with your Society. Unless you go to condemn or protest against these acts, you are surely open to the charge of condoning them—in making a display of confidence in their author. I intreat you not, at all events, to send a deputation.

"I still adhere to the opinion that our Government will not commit us to a war about Schleswig—I have reason to know that they are fully alive at headquarters to the danger of exposing our commerce to reprisals from Yankee 'Lairds,' if we become belligerents with any other Power. After the fatal example we have afforded to the tremendous amount of injury which half a dozen swift steamers can inflict upon a whole mercantile marine, I do not see how we can ever go to war again unless in defence of our own shores. We must give up the 'Balance of Power' for the future."

Richard Cobden : The International Man

"*February* 2, 1862.

"I return the Bond with thanks. The explanation you give of the object of the intervention alters the view of the question as respects the rights and duty of the Government to interfere. If our bondholders have been robbed of money in transition by what is called a Government we certainly have a right to redress, if it can be had.

"I agree with you in every word you say about the motives for publishing my pamphlet. It is just brought to an end. You never saw such an exposure, and old P. the radiant figure for twenty years! But then I shall be just the same Ishmaelite I was after the Free Trade victory in 1847. *Then* I might have set up for a genteel politician, and everybody was disposed to tolerate me.

"Now I am in the same position after the treaty. Everybody again is tending to tolerance and favour. But when this pamphlet comes out—how I shall be baited in the House and the Press! However, I have the rogues on the hip, and there is not one of the chief offenders — Pam, Pakington, Clarence Paget, Horsman, etc., that I cannot fire a reserve shot into if they open on me in the House. I only keep the MS. until I go to Town and see that at the opening of the Session there is no American event to *stun* the public ear. It is to be translated and brought out in Paris at the same time. How had I better manage for printing and publishing it in London?"

"*Wednesday, February.*

"I will certainly say something outside the programme of the factions, but whether it should be an attack on the old and ghastly phantom of the Balance of Power, or an argument for pure and simple non-intervention remains to be seen. I should like a little conversation with you on this very point. It is an unpopular part to take, but I am inclined to show up that spirit of braggadocio in the Press and in higher places which threatens and blusters without measuring our powers to fulfil our menaces, or rather our impotency to do so, and which spirit is really accountable for what those same parties call our present humiliation."

"*April* 16, 1862.

"The founders of your Society ought to have added a serpent to their device of a dove. The wisdom of the one is as necessary in this world, even in good works, as the innocence of the other. I think you have relied too much on your harmlessness.

"I would say nothing about 'peace' or 'war' and I would put the International Law *first*. And I would in defining the objects keep as much as possible to a dry formula and not prejudge the matter with epithets. I don't say that mine may not be mended, but I would have it as dry and unlike a Peace Society programme as possible."

"*April* 18, 1862.

"I did not mean to discourage you, and you mistake me if you suppose I meant to say you should do nothing. What I meant was that you should approach your work strategically.

"Some of the best services you have rendered to the cause of Peace have been through the instrumentality of men who did not start from your point of view or even perhaps seek your objects. Such, for instance, was the case with Lord Clarendon, whom you and Sturge incited to move in the arbitration clause, and such

Richard Cobden : The International Man

was the case when you disinterred the resolution of the Paris Congress during the French affair and got the religious bodies to take up that ground. I have sometimes regretted that the Americans did not hang fire a little and propose arbitration, that we might have had an agitation in favour of that mode of settling the *Trent* affair.

"I shall be glad to talk the matter over when I return to Town. Such men as Chevalier will come at the opening of the Exhibition and remain some time; others will come later. We had better discuss the subject with such men as he—in which direction alone we can hope to enlarge our circle."

"*April* 26, 1862.

"I am not surprised that the papers hang fire in noticing the pamphlet. The *facts* can't be refuted, and to acknowledge them is in general an act of self-condemnation with our writers and politicians. When you come to look back over the last twelve years, what a contemptible clique of eccentricities that party has been which did not give way at any time to these war maniacs! How can you expect ninety-nine one-hundredths now to confess that the 1 per cent. alone have kept their senses? We Peace men must moderate our triumph; it will only endure through a period of commercial depression. If there had been no Civil War in America, and the French treaty had come at the top on the great flood-tide of prosperity, we should have now been more bumptious than ever and the fortifications would have gone on."

"*May* 26, 1862.

"There is an apparent intention on the part of the Opposition to play the game of economy and retrenchment. The one great indispensable and desirable preliminary step to any diminution of the armaments is to get rid of the present Prime Minister. But this is very difficult, for the Tories prefer him to their own leader—a precious illustration of the way in which the so-called Liberal Party allow themselves to be befooled!

"Have you been paying any attention to the proceedings in China? There is a small Blue book lately presented containing, among other despatches, one from Lord Russell authorizing the naval commanders to defend the Treaty Ports, which I think opens the doors to a war in all parts of China. I have lately been in the way of conversing with Baron Gros and Mr. Ward, the American and French plenipotentiaries, and they seem to be of one opinion as to the impolicy of our proceedings, to say nothing of their injustice. Mr. Ward says we shall have to take the whole country on our hands, like India. It is just possible that we may bring on ourselves a retribution from the East by our persistent course of violence and injustice; and God help us if it is to be commensurate with our deserts!"

"*July* 15, 1862.

"I really think the old sinner has got rather the worst of the last week's contest. But I hope for other occasions before the Session closes for putting a mark on him by which the Liberals may know him better. It is desirable that he should be labelled with his true character, so as to prevent him as much as possible from playing the successful demagogue during the recess.

"By all means try to raise a protest against this China business. We are plunging into a sea of blood

Richard Cobden : The International Man

and guilt there for which we may bring down on ourselves a *fatal* retribution. It is, I fear, too late to arrest the mad career of our Government. But it is not too late to protest."

"*September* 15, 1862.

"I have been some weeks among the mountains of Scotland, and have derived great advantage to my health. Indeed, one must be very unreasonable not to improve under the influence of pure air, mountain scenery, and kind welcome from friends. I hope you have taken your usual tour to Wales.

"I try to forget politics and Palmerston during my holiday, and rarely see the London Press. But the bloody telegrams from America meet my eye in the local penny papers, and haunt me everywhere. The future of that horrible contest seems to me more shrouded in gloom every day. It appears to be more than ever probable that it will end in the North half ruining itself in the process of wholly ruining the South, rather than agree to allow another independent State to be established on the American Continent."

"*October* 15, 1862.

"I made up my mind during the Crimean War that if ever I lived in the time of another great war of a similar kind, between England and another Power, I would not as a public man open my mouth on the subject, so convinced am I that appeals to reason, conscience or interest, have no force whatever on parties engaged in war, and that exhaustion on one or both sides can alone bring a contest of physical force to an end. Such being my view with regard to a war in which our own country is engaged, it is still more strongly applicable to the case of a foreign country

Correspondence, 1861-4

Unless compelled incidentally to allude to it, I shall not say a syllable in public upon the subject of this horrible American War. I need hardly add that I would walk barefoot to the end of the earth if by so doing I could put an end to the sanguinary struggle. I am as much as ever in the dark as to the prospects of the contending parties. But it still seems to me that if the North choose to endure the burden of the war, it can ruin the South by only half ruining itself. It is a question of endurance and of time.

"I am not likely to be in London before the close of the Exhibition, and therefore shall not be able to take a part in any demonstration in favour of peace. But if a declaration in favour of reduction of armaments could be made under the auspices of new men it would be a good step."

"*December* 5, 1862.

"Be assured that if I can help to shelve this old dodger I shall do it as an act of piety to Heaven and of charity to man—for he is the evil genius of our generation. He has hitherto had such a run of luck that it has not been easy to try to bring him seriously to account. But the Lancashire trouble is very unfortunate for him. He would have had two or three foreign clap-traps ready for the meeting of Parliament to divert public attention from home affairs if we had continued prosperous, but now the scent lies so close in the cotton districts that a red herring in Greece or Montenegro will not answer his purpose. Lord Derby's serious personal implication in the cotton trouble is not without its significance. It may lead his party into the path of retrenchment. If the Tories will outbid the Whigs in reduction of expenditure even in a small matter, the victory is theirs."

Richard Cobden : The International Man

"*December* 18, 1862.

"There is a point to discriminate upon in memorializing the Government. It is quite proper to raise a protest against the equipping of ships for belligerent purposes. Not only should the Government be called on to observe good faith in the matter by preventing such a violation of the law of nations, but you should denounce in very strong language any house of business calling itself respectable which built ships for such vile purposes as privateering knowing what they are intended for, and risking a war with a friendly Power for the sake of their own mercenary gains.

"But you *can't* interfere with the trade in ordinary articles of commerce such as powder, shot, etc., in time of war any more than in time of peace; it is, in fact, quite impracticable. I admit there is some difficulty in the discrimination in such matters to which I have referred above, but I will direct your attention to an American document in which that Government gives its ideas of the law of the case."

"*December* 21, 1862.

"You will find in the American President's Message, in the *Annual Register* for 1855, page 289 ('History'), the law laid down as the Americans interpret it respecting the rights and duties of neutrals. Last spring Mr. Adams, the American Minister, was complaining to me very strongly that our Government did not interfere to prevent the shipments of arms and ammunition which were known to be intended for the Confederates, although they were ostensibly being sent to Nassau. He told me he had been to Lord Russell to complain of this at the request of Mr. Seward. I told him that his Government seemed to be unaware of the principle laid down by themselves, and I sent him an extract from the President's Message, to which I now refer you, and I begged him to forward it to Mr. Seward. The fact is, the Republican or Whig party now in power in the United States hardly know the principles of the *Democratic* party who have for the last fifty years generally ruled America. That party, with their one sole blemish of having 'held the candle to the devil' in winking at slavery for the sake of the Southern Alliance, has been identified with the greatest and soundest principles of the Union.

"I also reminded Mr. Adams that the North had been purchasing arms and ammunition in England to a far greater extent than the South. If you intend to send a memorial to Government, it should, I think, be confined to the one point of urging them to enforce the law of nations, and to insist on the observance of the Queen's Proclamation by preventing ships-of-war from being built for the Confederates. By the way, I rather think that the Queen's Proclamation goes farther than to forbid the fitting out of vessels. I believe we profess to prevent the sale of arms and ammunition, which the Americans do not.

"After all, it is impossible practically to prevent a foreign Government from obtaining ships suited for war purposes in this country. They may be bought off our lines of steamboat traffic. When I was in Scotland I heard, I know not how truly, that Mason, the Confederate envoy, had purchased swift steamers to the value of £70,000 in the Clyde. The true remedy is to keep out of war, or, if that be not practicable, to adopt such reforms in the rules of war as shall put an end to such wanton destruction of property as that which is going on by the *Alabama*."

Richard Cobden : The International Man

Though Cobden had much to say on the American Civil War, his thoughts were chiefly communicated to Bright, Paulton and other friends in this country and to Sumner in Washington. The preserved correspondence with Mr. Richard contains only a few passing allusions to the American events of 1863. Nor are these letters occupied with the new trouble of Schleswig-Holstein, that most recondite of foreign issues of which Lord Palmerston was recorded to have said that three men in Europe had alone grasped its meaning, one of whom (the Prince Consort) was dead, another (a Dane) was mad, while he, the third, had forgotten it. It is sufficient here to remind readers that the disturbance in 1862 of the 1852 *modus vivendi* by the Powers, first by Frederick VII of Denmark in the political incorporation of Schleswig, and next by Prussia in the forcible occupation of Holstein, brought this country in the summer of 1863 to the brink of war. Palmerston was once more the firebrand. On the last day of the Session he made the statement that "if any violent attempt were made to overthrow the right and interfere with the independence of Denmark, those who made the attempt would find in the result that it would not be Denmark alone with which they would have to contend." If he could have carried with him the French Emperor, this would have meant war. But Napoleon was not prepared to come in, save on a basis of French annexation and a general European war. Palmerston was apparently prepared to go on alone, and only the determined deletion by the Queen of certain language inscribed in the Queen's Speech at the opening of the 1864 Session averted the conflict.

The resolution, moved by Roebuck on June 30th, in favour of a recognition of the Southern Confederacy,

Correspondence, 1861-4

failed of support, and was withdrawn. But public opinion in high quarters still favoured the view that the South would establish its independence, although the tide of war was now turning in favour of the North. The lesson of the *Alabama*, however, had been learned, and no more vessels were permitted to go out from our ports for Confederate use, while the endeavours of the Confederate envoys in Europe to induce this country to support Napoleon in his proposed mediation between the belligerents entirely failed.

Towards the end of the year Cobden's attention was once more drawn to a new outrage in the Far East. This time, not China but Japan was the victim. As a reprisal for the killing of a Mr. Richardson, our Admiral in the China Sea, exceeding, as usual, the instructions from home, proceeded to destroy the Japanese city of Kagosima, containing a hundred thousand inhabitants.

The latest letters of that year are largely concerned with a fierce controversy with the Editor of *The Times*, which the latter had provoked by false accusations against Cobden of appealing to working-class revolutionary passion. These letters I do not here reproduce, as the matter to which they refer is fully set forth in Lord Morley's "Life," and is not closely germane to the special purpose of this volume.

"*January* 4, 1863.

"It is perfectly true that the course Palmerston took in the House in his fortification speech on July 23, 1860, was calculated to thwart my labours in Paris, as I have stated at p. 116 of 'The Three Panics.' But I have not stated the more weighty fact that he made this speech and took the course he did in spite of my urgent private appeal to him a fortnight before to let me finish my work before he moved in the matter.

Richard Cobden : The International Man

Baines of Leeds knew all this. And some of the other Yorkshire M.P.s know how I was thwarted by that old man. But they continued their allegiance to him, and the *Mercury* has since that time again and again defended him against my attack. Yet Yorkshire has been saved from the fate of Lancashire by the treaty! What can one do for people who have so little self-respect? The negroes have shown themselves better able to discriminate between their friends and enemies! A few baronetcies, a timely invitation or two to the Queen's ball, and our commercial and manufacturing M.P.s, with few exceptions, are prepared to enlist in the ranks of the governing class, and forget that they represent a new civilization which wants its own leaders, and to whom a far higher rank might be assigned in the world's estimation than that of a feudal effete aristocracy."

"September 20, 1863.

"I send by post a speech I made on the Foreign Enlistment Act. It was with great difficulty I could get a hearing for it, so overwhelming was the feeling of the House the other way. The other speech, made in a morning sitting to a score or two of members, went more into the argument—as I was not subject to interruptions. It was delivered a week before the close of the Session, and the report, *copied from the 'Star,'* appeared in *The Times* the Monday prior to the Prorogation. I have since corrected it for *Hansard*, but do not know whether it has yet been published.

"There is something revoltingly base about the mode in which our organs of opinions and the Government of this country alter and adapt their conduct to foreign Powers according to their strength or weakness. Lord Robert Cecil said, rather smartly, that our Foreign Office had a tariff of manners for other countries, regulated according to their power. He might have added that we have a different manner for the same Power, according as it may for the moment be weak or strong. It is only because the North has had great successes since July that the British Lion is becoming so lamb-like towards it.

"It is truly an awful reverse for our Peace principles to see the Federation principle no safeguard against war, in its most gigantic proportion, spreading over the fairest part of the New World! It is useless to argue against the continuance of hostilities after they have once broken out. You might as well reason with mad dogs as with communities engaged in the work of slaughter. It is only the exhaustion of one or both parties that can bring war to an end. I still hope that negro slavery will receive its death-blow in North America, and though few men would have agreed beforehand to purchase emancipation at such a price, it will be a consolation to witness the triumph of right at the hands of belligerents, neither of whom two years ago would have voted for such a consummation. There is an obstinate tendency for the right to get its own, even in spite of the powers and authorities of the world."

"*November* 2, 1863.

"I am much obliged by your kindness in sending me the papers upon Japan. Horrible as the idea may seem to you, I could not help a momentary feeling of satisfaction that the Japanese had shown so much courage, and so deadly an aim, in their resistance to our attack! It is the only way in which our 'service' in the East can be restrained from outrages and conquests, the consequence of which, if God rules this world on

Richard Cobden : The International Man

principles of retributive justice, must be far heavier on us as a nation than the instant punishment of the aggressors. For, observe, that our commanders in the East, confident in their strength, always exceed their instructions. Observe, for instance, Lord John Russell, in his dispatch of instructions to Colonel Neale, merely suggests that the Admiral may 'shell the prince's (Satsuma's) residence' and 'seize or detain' his steam-vessels. Straightway Admiral Kuper proceeds to *burn* the prince's steamers, and to reduce to a heap of ruins Kagosima, an inoffensive city of a hundred thousand or more inhabitants. I cannot see by the dispatches that our fleet succeeded in destroying or silencing the Japanese forts. They were armed with 13-inch guns or mortars, and, judging by the number of killed and wounded on our side, I should say it was a drawn battle. And I venture to say, with shame, that this evidence of courage and resources will do more than any appeals to our justice in making us respect the rights of that people in future. I foresee a new element in the future relations of Europe with the Eastern world that may endanger our filibustering policy in that region. The most powerful weapons of war are becoming every day more and more articles of private manufacture and commercial dealings. There are companies for making Whitworth's guns—and of course the United States has become a great arms manufactory. All kinds of warlike stores are finding their way to China and Japan, and by and by those nations will have arms equal to our own. Then with their vast population and remote distance, it may not be in our power to indulge in bloodshed and rapine at so cheap a rate. If the maxim *Si vis pacem para bellum* be a peace-preserver, according to the theory of our fire-eaters, why should it not apply to the East?

Correspondence, 1861-4

"I have been lately reading some articles in successive numbers of the *Revue aes Deux Mondes* on Japan, by a traveller in that country, and when I think of the peace, order, happiness, and civility to well-conducted foreigners which generally prevail in that country, it does make my blood boil to think of the outrages we are committing and provoking in that country: for there is no doubt that even the murder of Mr. Richardson was almost invited by a violation of the established uses of the country.

"If you will help to prepare me, I should really be disposed to bring on the whole question of our policy in the East and test it by an appeal to the principles of justice, as well as national self-interest."

"*November* 7, 1863.

"Whenever you can pay us a visit we shall be most happy to see you.

"I sat down to write to Gladstone about the Japan outrage, but I preferred to send it to the public. He can find such good reasons for not *acting* up to the dictates of abstract justice that I find him a very unsatisfactory Judge of Appeal.

"I suppose Sir Rutherford Alcock's book could be had cheap at second-hand from Mudie's. I have not read it through, but I had some talk with him, and he said the treaty with the Japanese was entered into by them *with the Americans*, under the alarm that if they waited till Lord Elgin came from his triumphant violence in China he would subject them to worse terms. When you come, I will trouble you to bring your copy of the correspondence. I know precisely the course which ought to be taken in Japan, and which should have been pursued in China. We should adopt the plan which the rude common sense of our ancestors reverted

Richard Cobden : The International Man

to in the time of the Plantagenets. Then, the merchants of the Hanse Towns (the 'Esterlings,' and hence the word *sterling*), who came to London to trade in our raw products in exchange for their manufactures, lived under a distinct code of laws and were exempt from the jurisdiction of our Admiralty Courts, on condition that they lived apart and did not mingle with the natives. They were located in a walled-in place called the 'Steelyard' near the river, and which still bears the name. This is the only way in which collisions can be avoided, and in which trade can be carried on with these Eastern people with profit to the English people, as distinct from the few filibustering British residents in the East to whom wars and confusion are often profitable. If I bring on the question, this is the policy I shall try to enforce.

"You are quite right in absolutely restricting your memoir of Sturge to one moderately sized volume.

"By the way, I observed that that most vain and inaccurate old man, Brougham, took credit to himself at Edinburgh for having abolished the negro apprenticeship. Now, I remember a very graphic description which he gave me in a conversation at his house in Grafton Street of Sturge's conduct in the matter, and which he adduced as an illustration of our friend's indomitable energy. He told me of Sturge coming to him, whilst he was, I believe, still Lord Chancellor, to arraign the conduct of the masters in the West Indies for oppressing the apprentices; how he (Brougham) laughed him to scorn, deriding him in this fashion for coming to him to propose that he should abolish the apprenticeship: 'Why, you old woman, Joseph Sturge, to dream that you can revive the anti-slavery feeling and raise an agitation to put an end to the apprenticeship'; how the quiet Quaker met him with this reply:

Correspondence, 1861-4

'Lord Brougham, if thou hadst a ward in Chancery who was apprenticed, and his master was violating the terms of his indenture, what wouldst thou do?' Now he (Lord B.) felt this as a home-thrust, and he replied, 'Why, I should require good proof, Joseph Sturge, before I did anything'; how our friend rejoined, 'Then I must supply thee with proof'; how he packed up his portmanteau and quietly embarked for the West Indies, made a tour of the Islands, collected the necessary evidence of the oppression that was being practised on the negro apprentices by their masters, the planters; how he returned to England, and commenced an agitation throughout the country to abolish the apprenticeship, to accomplish which it was necessary to reorganize all the old anti-slavery societies which had been dissolved or had laid down their arms happy to be relieved from their long and arduous labours; how he brought them again into the field and accomplished his objects. This was the narrative of Lord Brougham, and well do I remember the very words in which, in conclusion, he assigned the whole merit to our friend—'Joseph Sturge,' said he, 'won the game off his own bat.'"

"*November* 11, 1863.

"I do not see *The Times* here, and should like to have the copy containing Buxton's letter about Japan. From letters that reach me from men of the different parties, I suspect that the national conscience is a little moved. Looking back to the time of Clive and down to our day, cruel and remorseless as our policy in the East has been, I do not believe there is any one outrage to compare in magnitude with that of Kagosima. And this I hope you will say in your memorial to the Queen.

"I very much doubt the policy of your stirring in the Congress question at *present*. You cannot feel

Richard Cobden : The International Man

confidence in the object of the Emperor, whose Mexican expedition has paralysed him morally and materially to a serious extent. Besides, he alludes but obscurely to the reduction of armaments. My advice is to wait. If our Government agree to a Congress, which the *Morning Post* would seem to lead one to expect, then there would indeed be a grand occasion for the Peace Society to come out in all its strength on the armament question. Then you must be prepared with some well-founded statistics of the *growing* character of the *peace* establishments, and with citations from Peel and others to place you on practical ground. But if you stir previously to our Government agreeing, you put yourselves in the position of backing the Emperor, which *I* should not at present like to do.

"Apropos of that anecdote of Brougham and Sturge, I could swear to the main incidents, and I remember well how Brougham brandished a poker as he said, 'Joseph Sturge won that game off his own bat.' But it is more than twenty years ago, and I should like to be sure that the details are correctly remembered, but this you can tell me. For instance, was Brougham Lord Chancellor when the apprenticeship was abolished ? If not, the colloquy must have merely been different to this extent : Sturge must have asked him what he *would* have done in the case of an apprentice who was a ward in Chancery when he was Lord Chancellor ?

"By the way, I have heard those who listened to Brougham's speech on that question say it surpassed any of his previous efforts."

"*November* 19, 1863.

"Many thanks for the Parliamentary Papers, and the extract from *The Times* of Buxton's letter. By the way, do you see that in the *Star* there is an announcement of his intention to bring on the Kagosima affair on the meeting of Parliament? He gives the terms of his notice, which is unusual and uncalled for. It absolves the Foreign Office, by alleging that the Admiral did not act according to instructions. I have suspected Buxton of sometimes playing the part of 'buffer' to the Whig Ministry. This propensity to prefer aristocratic party convenience to principle runs in the blood of the Buxtons. I have no doubt the Government will try to shelter Kuper under the plea of *accident*. No other defence will, I think, carry the House. I have had a very wide response to my letter from men of all parties in every part of the country. I hope it will be the turning-point in our Eastern policy. The bravery of the Japanese and their mechanical ingenuity and progressive character will be their best security against injustice. I am glad you are going to write a summary of our doings in Japan.

"Do you happen to have access to the *Lancet*? There was an account of a visit which the Queen paid to the Military Hospital of Netley about six months since in that paper, with a vivid picture of the Indian invalids. I should like to be able to lay my hand on it. There is a new field altogether untouched to explore and expose, in the cost of life, health, and morality of our Oriental occupations. It would be found that the cost in life and sickness is equal to a couple of Battles of Waterloo yearly. I remember the late George Combe relating to me a conversation he had had with M'Culloch ('Commercial Dictionary'), who was expatiating on the national loss, vitally and financially, which our Indian possessions entailed on us; and on his (Combe's) suggesting that he (M'C.) should give publicity to his views, the latter replied, 'That will never do, for if I did the public would not believe me, or read anything I said on any other subject.'"

Richard Cobden : The International Man

"*November* 21, 1863.

" What you say about the demand actually made for compensation for the murder of Mr. Richardson from the Japanese Government increases the enormity of our wickedness. It is so outrageous that it may perhaps serve the cause of justice by creating a revulsion in public feeling. One of the advantages to be gained by the fall of the present Government, and the return of the Tories to power, would be the opening it would offer to the latter for a complete change in our filibustering policy in the East, in which they have not been the guilty party. Nothing serious can be done in this or any other direction, in the way of reform, whilst the present old joker is at the head of affairs."

"*December* 30, 1863.

" Can you get me Carlyle's address ? I don't find it in the Court Guide. His name is *Thomas*, is it not ?

" Be cautious how you endorse the Emperor. His views and purposes are not ours—at least not at present. Give him the Rhine boundary, and I believe he would go for a general disarmament. But there is something *to do* before that is effected.

" Is it certain that these wild and visionary Teutons may not, after all, put Europe in flames ? They are mad about Schleswig, and it is just out of such a foolish fanatical outbreak that a man like L. N., who is always as cool as a cucumber, will make his winning game. If Germany precipitates itself on Denmark, there will be something come of it on the Rhine, Danube, and Mincio. And so completely will the sympathies of England and Europe be on the other side that it is not easy to say what may not come of it.

" At the same time, apropos of the Congress, I have

always been of opinion that England would be the last Power to wish to see a reduction of armaments."

. . . .

Cobden's general view of the situation at the close of 1863 is well conveyed in the following letter to his French friend, M. Arles Dufour :—

"MIDHURST, *December* 6, 1863.

"When I spoke to my constituents at Rochdale on the evening of the 24th, I knew that our Government had determined not to attend the Congress. Yet I took the opportunity of saying that, as the Emperor's programme contained an allusion to the Emperor's armaments, I could not agree in opposing him. At the same time, I said I had but little faith in a Congress for any other purpose. This is my real opinion. It is indeed consistent with my principle of non-intervention, for I have no faith in the power of other nations to put down the coils of a civil war in any particular State. The only plan is to leave them to settle their own quarrels.

"Then as regards Mexico, you ought to be thankful that somebody even at Rochdale tells the Emperor the truth about his most unwise expedition to that country. If he remains there until the North has subdued the South, *which is only a question of time*, he will either have to go to war with that powerful nation with all his iron-clad batteries ready to move to Vera Cruz, or he will be subjected to great humiliation in being obliged to leave the country at the instance of the Government of Washington. The expedition to Mexico is, under the circumstances, an insult to the United States. How would Frenchmen like the Americans to come and set up a Republic in Belgium without consulting *them*?

"As to M. Guéroult's threats of a general war, I attach little importance to them. Some people talk as if

Richard Cobden : The International Man

mankind naturally gravitated towards war. Now I see very good and sufficient obstacles in our days to the Powers of Europe entering on a general war. The imagination, particularly of a Frenchman, may easily make such a state of things, but the poetical flight of such writers as M. Guéroult will have to be brought to the test of M. Fould's prosaic figures of arithmetic. The nations of Europe, so far from being able to commence a general campaign, will find themselves during the next year puzzled to sustain the burdens of their peace establishments.

" We are only now beginning to feel the effects of the cotton famine. You will remember that two years ago you and I used to speak of the terrible convulsion which would follow from the sudden cutting off of the supply of American cotton. People have been pooh-poohing the cotton industry ever since, and saying that its importance has been overrated. The truth is that the very strength of that industry, so far as England is concerned, has enabled it to bear up so well under the trial.

" But the diversion of specie to pay fifty or sixty millions sterling more than the ordinary price for cotton next year threatens all the money markets with panic and confusion, will bring Governments to look for their wicked waste of the floating capitals of the world, and give them other employment than in carrying out M. Guéroult's imaginary war."

. . . . .

The last year of Cobden's political activity (1864) was remarkable not only for the pressure of foreign affairs upon the popular interest of our country, but as marking the close of the era of Palmerstonian Jingoism. Writing on May 10th to Mr. T. B. Potter, Cobden remarked that " nothing except foreign politics seems to occupy

Correspondence, 1861-4

the attention of the people, Press, or Parliament." He wrote in a regretful tone, for foreign politics had always carried the menace of intervention, with militarism in the background. The romantic figure of Garibaldi, who visited this country in the spring, had roused a wild enthusiasm among all classes, which the Government, who had here no definite axe to grind, found very inconvenient. A champion of national liberties, a first-rate fighting man, an enemy of the Papacy, as he was deemed, he presented just the combination of qualities for the rôle of hero. But when the populace began to recognize in him the exemplar of the modern democratic revolutionist, and had made arrangements for a series of receptions in the great Northern cities, the Government took alarm and whisked him off to Caprera in a ducal yacht.

But the really critical event of the year was the failure of Lord Palmerston and Lord John Russell to bring their country into conflict with Prussia over the Schleswig-Holstein question. Two passages from the last of Cobden's speeches addressed in November to his Rochdale constituents give the best summary of the episode as he saw it.

"In 1852, by the mischievous activity of our Foreign Office, seven diplomatists were brought round a green table in London to settle the destinies of a million of people in the two provinces of Schleswig and Holstein, without the slightest reference to the wants and wishes or the tendencies and interests of that people. The preamble of the treaty, which was there and then agreed to, states that what these seven diplomatists were going to do was to maintain the integrity of the Danish monarchy and to sustain the Balance of Power in Europe. Kings, emperors, princes were represented at that meeting, but the people had not the slightest voice or right in the matter. They settled the treaty, the object of which was to draw closer the bonds between these two provinces and Denmark. The tendency of the great majority of the people of those provinces—about a million of them altogether—was altogether in the direction of Germany. From that time to this year the treaty was followed by constant agitation and discord ; two wars have sprung out of it, and it has ended in the treaty being torn to pieces by two of the Governments who were prominent parties to the treaty."

Then, turning to immediate issues of this year, the proposed intervention in behalf of Denmark, he proceeds : " The newspapers that were in the interest of the Government were harping in favour of war to the last moment in large leading articles. Some announced the very number of the regiments, the names of the colonels, the names of the ships, and the commanders that would be sent to fight this battle for Denmark. In the House of Commons there was a general opinion that there was a great struggle going on in the Cabinet as to whether we should declare war against Germany. At the end of June the Prime Minister announced that he was going to produce the protocols and to state the decision of the Government upon the question. He gave a week's notice of this intention, and then I witnessed what has convinced me that we have achieved a revolution in our foreign policy. The whippers-in—you know what I mean—were taking soundings of the inclinations of members of the House of Commons. And then came up from the country such a manifestation of opinion against war that day after day during that eventful week member after member from the largest constituencies went to those who acted for the Government in Parliament and told them distinctly that they would not allow war upon any such matters

Correspondence, 1861-4

as Schleswig and Holstein. There came surging up from all the great seats and centres of manufacturing and commercial activity one unanimous veto against war for the matter of Schleswig and Holstein."

Cobden was not aware of the powerful pressure from the Throne which co-operated with this public opinion, or he might have been less confident in imputing to this latter influence the sole or chief determination of our governmental action. But no doubt the experience of the American Civil War and the recent memories of the Crimean folly had a marked effect in a pacific direction, while the rising economic prosperity of the country disinclined the middle classes from participation in the proposed foreign enterprise.

"The manufacturing and commercial interests of this country were in a state of almost unparalleled expansion. They had entered into vast engagements, expecting that they would be realized and fulfilled in time of peace; both capitalists and labourers felt that, if war had arisen just then, it would have produced enormous calamities, such as no nation ought ever to bring upon itself, unless in defence of its vital interest and honour."

The pretext given by Palmerston for the abandonment of Denmark, whose resistance he had stimulated by definite promises of aid, was the unwillingness of France and Russia to support his action. But none the less the War party felt the humiliation of their failure, and Cobden was justified in holding that his policy of non-intervention had triumphed. In his speech on Disraeli's Vote of Censure moved on July 5th he pressed home once more the relation between peace and free commerce.

The other important foreign issue which occupied his voice and pen in this year was the persistent brutality of our Far Eastern policy, the latest example of which

Richard Cobden : The International Man

had been the wanton attack upon Kagosima. On May 31st Cobden moved a resolution urging that the policy of non-intervention which we now professed to observe in Europe and America should be observed in our relations with the yellow peoples. Experience of the last few years was bringing home to him with ever-growing clearness of perception that our Asiatic policy in particular was directed by the push for markets more than by any other motive.

Such were the matters which chiefly occupied Cobden in the correspondence with Mr. Richard during 1864 which is given below. His important American correspondence is given in another chapter.

"*January* 28, 1864.

"I am sorry to say that I have not the slightest hope that the House will disapprove the Kagosima affair. Members have not forgotten the result of the vote in favour of my motion condemnatory of the Canton bombardment, when the constituencies repudiated the decision of Parliament, rejected at the polls the men who had supported me, and thus virtually gave Palmerston *carte blanche* to do as he pleased for the rest of his life in the East. The Opposition will not give him another opportunity of appealing to the British Lion. The stream does not rise above the level of its source. Nor will the House be better than the middle class of this country which creates it, and which has virtually declared, 'On us and our children lie the responsibility for our unrighteous deeds in the East!'

"It looks as though Palmerston was bent on involving us in the Danish quarrel. I have written to Gibson and Gladstone pointing out to them what the consequences will be if, by entering on a war with any maritime Power, we give the American 'Lairds' an

Correspondence, 1861-4

opportunity of supplying a belligerent with *Alabamas* to prey on our commerce, which they will certainly do. I can hardly bring myself to believe in such infatuation. But sometimes, when observing the spirit which pervades so large a part of even our mercantile and manufacturing classes—a spirit of arrogant pride and self-sufficiency—I am almost inclined to resign myself with cynical complacency to some national disaster or check as the only possible cure for our national vices."

"*February* 7, 1864.

"What a ridiculous mess our Foreign Office has got into! And yet it was for the 'foreign policy' of the Government that we were asked to condone all the shortcomings at home! We are a most heavy-witted, dull people, but I should think we must wake up sooner or later to the ridiculously absurd position in which we are placed by all this tall talk and fruitless Blue-bookism. It may, and must, I should say, bring us to the honest ground of non-intervention, for nobody will believe that our Government ever means to do anything but talk.

"I have no doubt it was the fear of American *Alabamas* that really kept us from committing ourselves to an act of hostility. We can no longer *localize* a war. It is an open question whether Laird has not been a great peace-maker by giving this fearful example of the injury that half a dozen swift steamers would inflict on our commerce. Depend on it, there is a complete revolution in our foreign policy to arise out of those Birkenhead doings."

"*February* 10, 1864.

"I am not sorry that I have been absent from Buxton's motion. But I wish to have an hour in the House

Richard Cobden : The International Man

upon the whole question of our relations with these Oriental peoples, and have no doubt there will be an opportunity in connection with the larger question of China. The *expense* of coercing China and Japan will, owing to the immense distance and to their gradual adoption of European arms and discipline, be constantly increasing. The unhealthiness of China is another terrible evil. Apropos of arms, I was told yesterday by a partner in the Whitworth house that the Chinese Government offered for the Whitworth rifled guns in Captain Sherrard Osborn's vessels, which are now returning, weight for weight in silver.

"*February* 12, 1864.

"What a wretched figure the mere Whigs and shabby Liberals cut on Buxton's motion! If the Tories had been in power, not one of the men of the stamp of Bass and Beale of Derby would have voted as they did. It is a sad feature in our popular constituencies that they have for the last ten years been falling into the way of returning some rich capitalist or contractor—a man past the middle age, of no political antecedents, and whose only ambition in going to Parliament is social position. The whole scope of the motives on both sides is of the lowest kind. The constituents offer the seat as a complimentary tribute to a rich man of the neighbourhood, and he accepts it that his wife may go to the Queen's ball! I wish you Dissenters would break in upon this state of things and supply some higher tests for party divisions. Has your letter been printed in a pamphlet form?

"But, to return to China and Japan, I wish for an opportunity of bringing on the whole question of our *commercial* relations, showing the relation of cost of armaments to the extent of trade, and showing how greatly the one increases beyond the other, and to advocate the principle of restricting rather than increasing the number of points of contact. I think the present discussions are leading up to the questions which I wish to bring on."

"*February* 17, 1864.

"You must especially refer to Kinnaird in your *Herald*. It is the only way to bring such humbugs to book. He voted against my motion in 1857 on the Canton massacre. You will see that he tried to speak the very last in the debate, but could not be heard. Sidney Herbert, in his speech in favour of my motion referred to Kinnaird and claimed his vote, but as usual the little fellow went with the Government. You must really take him in hand. You heard of Bright's remark on him. He (Bright) was talking to a member in the lobby as Kinnaird passed, and Bright remarked, 'There's a little fellow that will vote for any amount of slaughter on Evangelical principles.'"

"*July* 14, 1864.

"I am glad you approve what I said in the debate last week. The latter part of my speech, by the way, contained arguments of your own, quoted almost textually from the *Herald*. The week's wrangle will undoubtedly do good. Did you observe the speeches of Lord Stanley and Gathorne Hardy? You and I could endorse every word. The latter is a very rising man, and will be in the front rank of his party. There are parts of his speech, where he speaks of the power England may possess if she will assume a neutral ground, especially valuable. For myself, I never had so many private adhesions to my views as I did from men on both sides after speaking last Tuesday. Bright could not trust himself to speak. He was afraid of attacking the Ministry so strongly as to make it impossible for us to vote for them. Our Foreign Office and its diplomacy have had a shake. Two or three old men removed from the arena will leave the old dispensation without a defender."

"*November* 10, 1864.

"At my coming meeting with my constituents I must say something to clench the revolution in our foreign policy which I shall assume was effected in the last Session of Parliament. Indeed, I should like much to have an hour on the question alone. There is much to be done before we bring the great political parties to an honest recognition of the *principle* of non-intervention. They will not like to bury the red-herring."

"*November* 13, 1864.

"You are quite right in your idea of bringing out a résumé of past progress in the doctrines of the Peace Party. By showing how far you have been right in times gone by, you will exalt your authority in future controversy.

"By the way, I look on Mr. Laird as the greatest contributor to the success of non-intervention principles. The doings of the *Alabama* have alarmed not only our shipowners, but every statesman who can look beyond the horizon of Foreign Office maxims. I defy us to go to war for any of the old European issues, the Balance of Power, the Eastern Question, or any dynastic or territorial question whatever, and I shall say so at Rochdale. Our national life is more involved in countries out of Europe than on the Continent. The 'Equilibrium of Europe' was a phrase of some significance when the whole civilized world was in Europe. It has lost its meaning now."

CHAPTER XII

THE CIVIL WAR AND THE SUMNER LETTERS

BRIEF reference has been made in the foregoing chapters to incidents in the American Civil War which touched this country and to the attitude taken by Cobden both upon these matters and upon the wider issues of the conflict. But fortunately there survives a fuller and more continuous record of Cobden's opinions and sentiments regarding this great struggle, in the series of letters written during this period to his American friend, Charles Sumner, one of the most brilliant and influential men in the public life of America in the mid-century, who had formed a close attachment to Cobden as far back as the late forties. Though their personal acquaintance was confined to a few very brief visits, their political principles and enthusiasm had so much in common that they were able to communicate with one another across the Atlantic in a tone of close mutual confidence. Sumner was born and bred in Boston during a time when that city and the State of Massachusetts were enriched with a number of men of unusual eminence in intellectual life, some of whom devoted their energies to the new political causes which were coming up so rapidly in the forties and the fifties. Sumner was among the most Radical of these in his thought and sympathies, and his striking personal appearance, conjoined with unrivalled powers of oratory, made him a leader in every cause to which he attached himself. The Peace and Anti-Slavery movements claimed his adhesion from the early forties, when, as a young law graduate from Harvard, he launched in 1845 his first great oration to his fellow-citizens in Tremont Hall upon " The True Grandeur of Nations." Sumner stood on the policy of war and peace in exactly the same position as Cobden. He was not a non-resister or a "peace at any price" man. When the war broke out in his own country, he gave stout and consistent support to the Northern cause, recognizing a case in which an appeal to force, for the defence of higher principles than life itself, was necessary. These higher principles were individual freedom, violated by the institution of slavery, and the Constitution of the Union, menaced by secession. When the slave issue first took sharp political shape in the demand of the slave-holding States for an extension of the institution to the new territories wrested from Mexico, Sumner joined the Free Soil Party, and was one of its most powerful leaders. Later on, when in 1851 the issue forced the main body of the " Democrats " (afterwards " Republicans ") to combine with the " Free Soilers," in order to keep Massachusetts from capture by the " Whigs," Sumner was elected a Senator, and from this time, right through the stormy period of the Civil War and reconstruction up to 1873, he stood out as one of the most powerful voices of American Liberalism. His earliest known correspondence with Cobden is in 1848 and 1849. Of two letters of Cobden dated in these years, the first deals with the question of reduction of armaments in time of war, the second opens a remarkable speculation regarding the probable future union of the United States and Canada.

When the Civil War broke out Sumner held the important position of Chairman of the Senate Com-

The Civil War and the Sumner Letters

mittee on Foreign Affairs. Cobden, recognizing the value of this position in its influence upon American policy, set himself from November 1851 onwards to maintain a regular interchange of views with Sumner upon the several critical issues in which this country and France were involved by the events of the American struggle. With especial earnestness did Cobden strive to inform Sumner of the real state of public opinion in this country and to correct the exceedingly erroneous notion that our nation as a whole was sympathetic with the slave-owners and secessionists. As for himself, he frankly admits he would not have gone to war even for emancipation; and at the opening of the struggle his instinctive abhorrence of bloodshed made him, as we have seen, hesitate a little before casting his sympathy with the Northern appeal to force. But when clear as to the balance of the moral issues in favour of the North, he never swerved, and did more than any other Englishman, save Bright, to correct the mistakes of fact and judgment which confused the issue in this country at the outset, and to give sound counsel upon the sharp concrete cases which more than once brought us near to the breaking-point with the Federal Government.

When war broke out the more vocable section of our nation not merely declared its sympathy with, but put its money on, the South. The aristocracy and gentry of England, in taking this view, felt that in some measure they were standing by "their order." The "certain condescension in foreigners" which Lowell detected in England carried some measure of active dislike against Yankees, who were regarded as upstarts and whose manners, caricatured by Dickens and other satirists, were judged from their least worthy representatives. The deep human significance of the slave issue was skilfully obscured in influential

Richard Cobden : The International Man

British circles by Southern appeals to sentiments of constitutional right, and even in higher commercial circles there was a disposition to look upon the troubles of pushful American traders with a spice of malicious satisfaction. Most of our influential newspapers, headed by *The Times*, were openly pro-Southerner, and the general opinion that spread throughout the North represented the British people as hostile to the Union, and even as likely to intervene in some way favourable to the South, should a convenient opportunity arise. This kept in existence a dangerously sensitive atmosphere towards England in the Northern States, and the knowledge that active intrigues were going forward both in Paris and in London for intervention when the war showed signs of turning against the South, seemed to give powerful confirmation to the worst interpretation of British sentiments.

The grave episode of the seizure of the two Southern Commissioners on the *Trent*, the despatch of the Southern raider, the *Alabama*, from an English port, the ill-fated expedition to Mexico, in which this country took part with France and Spain for the alleged protection of their subjects, and above all the havoc inflicted upon British trade by the blockade of New Orleans and other Southern ports, afforded plenty of inflammable material.

These letters to Sumner form a triumphant vindication of the charge sometimes brought against Cobden by those who know little of the real spirit of the man, viz. that he was a disparager of his own country. In arguing these points of international policy and law with Sumner, he never fails to protest against the highhandedness and disregard for precedent to which a Government fighting for its existence is always prone. His strictures upon the grave irregularity of the *Trent* affair, his exposition of the sufferings imposed upon the

The Civil War and the Sumner Letters

people of Lancashire by the severities of the blockade, his pressure of the distinction to be drawn between the fitting out of privateers and the trade in munitions, will satisfy the severest tests of patriotism. Nowhere did Cobden fail at this grave juncture in supporting what history has recognized as the legitimate interests of his country. The whole correspondence may be cited as the supreme example of that moderation and fair-mindedness which throughout his career were his distinctive qualities. For English readers, his judicious analysis of the changes which public opinion in this country underwent regarding the merits of the struggle and the prospects of the issue is even to-day of great value. On the other hand, his strong insistence on the service rendered by our people and our Government in rejecting the French proposals for intervention must have exercised an exceedingly valuable influence in allaying the mistrust of our policy sown early in the war by the foolish utterances of some of our prominent public men. The consistent support rendered by Cobden and Bright to the Northern cause, and the evidence they adduced to show that the democracy of Britain was heart and soul with the Union, went far to help establish those better relations which from that time to this have existed between the two great English-speaking nations.

The collection of letters from which the following selection is made is in the possession of the College Library of Harvard. Most of them have been reprinted in the *American Historical Review*, and many extracts have appeared in Rhodes's "History of the United States." A number of passages are given in Lord Morley's "Life." But the full body of this valuable material (excluding only certain letters and passages of a purely personal or transitory interest) is set forth here for the first time in a continuous form.

Richard Cobden : the International Man

"*March* 9, 1848.

"I beg you to accept my thanks for your kindness in forwarding me a copy of your eloquent appeal in behalf of peace. It will probably be in my power to profit by your facts in dealing with the subject of our armaments in my place in Parliament. If so, I shall make free use of your materials without scruple. Whilst travelling on the Continent, I found one universal feeling of discontent amongst intelligent men at the enormous expenditure everywhere incurred for standing armaments; and, Utopian as the idea may appear to the men of routine, such as are our statesmen and diplomatists, I do not think it would be difficult for any one of the large Powers of Europe to persuade the rest to enter upon a career of gradual and partial disarmament. The difficulty has been to find a Government sincerely bent upon such a humane and enlightened policy. The truth is that hitherto the Governments of Europe have maintained their armies in times of peace almost as much for the purpose of defending themselves against their people as their neighbours. But after the proofs which have been given lately in Italy and France that soldiers can no longer be relied upon in time of need by despotic sovereigns or arbitrary ministers, it is probable, I should hope, that we may soon see a change of system; for surely Governments will begin to calculate the cost of these useless armed retainers, whose maintenance causes disaffection to the overtaxed people and tends, in fact, to produce the very rebellion which they were intended to prevent, but which now, it is found, they will not suppress. This is at least a great lesson for kings and princes, and is perhaps the only sure gain from the *last* French Revolution: for with the highest admiration for the forbearance of the Parisian populace and the energy of the Provisional Government,

The Civil War and the Sumner Letters

I must confess that I do not feel sanguine about the success of a Republic in France. Time will show."

"*November* 7, 1849.

"You will have seen that we have been trying to lead this wicked *Old* World into a new and hitherto unknown path. You have too much practical knowledge to require to be told by me that our Peace Congress and public meetings are but the faint glimmerings of a new light which is dawning upon the nations, and that we do not deceive ourselves with the belief that we are yet near to that perfect day when they shall learn war no more. And yet I think the last two years (for which I have been co-operating directly in the Peace agitation) have produced visible results. The first fruits of a discussion upon great principles are to be found in the altered tone of your opponents. In the Peace controversy we have brought the sneerers into serious debate. They have been compelled to take up their position. In doing so they have ceded their old ground. They tell us that the vast armaments of Europe are not now maintained for purposes of external warfare, but to maintain order at home. This is a damaging admission, for it converts the army into a *gendarmerie*, and robs it of its chivalry. It moreover tends to identify it with tyranny and despotism, and the people, which sooner or later is stronger than the Government, will yearn for the opportunity to put down the tyrants and their tools, both together. There is henceforth no popularity for armies in Europe. For the present, the soldier is the executive, throughout the Continent. How long this will last, or how it is to be altered, no one can tell. But it is not a rash prophecy to say it cannot endure for ever. The financial crisis which hangs over the Governments warns them that they are in only a provisional state. Whether it will end in

Richard Cobden : The International Man

the demoralization of the armies from irregular pay, or in Governments joining the people to get rid of a tyranny insupportable to both, or in a civil war between different parties in the army and rival generals, nobody can tell. In all probability Europe must suffer convulsions and revolutions, of which those of last year were but the feeble skirmishings, before the present system passes away. You may have observed that the Peace Party has resolved to do its best to 'stop the supplies' of the Governments, by commencing a moral crusade against the system of foreign loans. In proportion as we succeed in this, we shall drive the bankrupt rulers back upon their own subjects for the pecuniary means necessary for their own subjection. This plan will do more than anything besides to hasten the financial crisis which must precede any essential change. I have said that our opponents admit that there is no disposition on the part of the European nations to enter upon wars of conquest or aggression. Conquest of territory offers no prospect of increased power to any Government. On the contrary, half the Powers of Europe are at this moment suffering internal throes from the acquisition of fresh territory, with disaffected races, at the great 'settlement' (!) of 1815. For one of the peculiar features of the day is the assumption, on the part of the peoples, of a right to a choice of their rulers and of their countrymen. Hence the struggle of nationalities; hence the demand of Venice, Lombardy, Hungary, Poland, Germany, etc., to be left to rule themselves according to their several likings. Race, religion, language, traditions, etc., are becoming bonds of union, and not the parchment title-deeds of sovereigns. These instincts may be thwarted for the day, but they are too deeply rooted in nature and in usefulness not to prevail in the end. I look with less interest to these struggles of races to live apart, for

The Civil War and the Sumner Letters

what they want to undo than for what they will prevent being done in future. They will warn rulers that henceforth the acquisition of fresh territory, by force of arms, will only bring embarrassments and civil war, instead of that increased strength which, in ancient times, when people were passed like flocks of sheep from one king to another, always accompanied the incorporation of new territorial conquests. This is the secret of the admitted doctrine that we shall have no more wars of conquest or ambition. In this respect you are differently situated, having vast tracts of unpeopled territory to temper that cupidity which, in respect of landed property, always disposes individuals and nations, however rich in acres, to desire more.

"This brings me to the subject of Canada, to which you refer in your letters. I agree with you that Nature has decided that Canada and the United States must become one, for all purposes of free intercommunication. Whether they also shall be united in the same Federal Government must depend upon the two parties to the union. I can assure you that there will be no repetition of the policy of 1776 on our part, to prevent our North American Colonies from pursuing their interests in their own way. If the people of Canada are tolerably unanimous in wishing to sever the very slight thread which now binds them to this country, I see no reason why, if good faith and ordinary temper be observed, it should not be done amicably. I think it would be far more likely to be accomplished peaceably if the subject of annexation were left as a distinct question. I am quite sure that *we* should be gainers, to the amount of about a million sterling annually, if our North American colonists would set up in life for themselves and maintain their own establishments, and I see no reason to doubt that they might be also gainers by being thrown upon their own resources. The less your countrymen mingle in the controversy the better. It will only be an additional obstacle in the path of those in this country who see the ultimate necessity of a separation, but who have still some ignorance and prejudice to contend against, which, if used as political capital by designing politicians, may complicate seriously a very difficult piece of statesmanship. It is for you, and such as you, who love peace, to guide your countrymen aright in this matter. You have made the most noble contributions of any modern writer to the cause of peace, and, as a public man, I hope you will exert all your influence to induce Americans to hold a dignified attitude, and observe a 'masterly inactivity,' in the controversy which is rapidly advancing to a solution between the Mother Country and her American Colonies."

Two letters with a more personal bearing follow. Then opens the important series dealing with issues of the Civil War.

"June 16, 1856.

"I am tempted to write to express to you the feelings of sympathy and indignation with which, in common with everybody on this side of the Atlantic, I have heard of the dastardly and brutal attack made upon you.[1] These feelings are not unmingled with dismay at perceiving that there are parties and communities in your country who seem to give a deliberate sanction through the Press to the use of the bludgeon as a mode of replying to the arguments of a political

[1] After a powerful speech in the Senate on the Kansas pro-slavery question, Mr. Sumner was violently assaulted in the Senate house by a South Carolina Congress man named Brooks, who struck a series of blows from behind with a cudgel, rendering him unconscious.

opponent. Why, there is nothing so bad as this in Austria or Italy! Freedom of debate is the very breath of representative government, and if you cannot preserve that right, not merely against the encroachments of the Executive, but the terrorism of a ruffianly party in your own ranks, your boasted liberty will become a very vulgar and degrading despotism in the eyes of other nations. But I do not for a moment doubt that the unmistakable expression of public opinion will put down at once and for ever this attempt at the worst of all usurpations, that of the cudgel and revolver. Let me entreat you not under any amount of provocation to so far forget your self-respect as to descend to the use of the weapons of your assailants. You have given far too many proofs of moral heroism to require that you should assert the possession of that very vulgar attribute of physical courage which we all share with the lower animals, though to an inferior degree than some of them. For the rest, your political opponents (they who identify themselves with your assailant) have by this act done more than you could have ever accomplished to convince the world of the hopelessness of their cause. Heaven has evidently given them over to that madness which heralds the fall of parties more than of individuals."

"*May* 1, 1860.

"I cannot help looking with some interest to your coming election, though I confess I cannot feel all the sympathy I could wish for your party—as I suppose I must call the Republicans. Your probable candidate, Mr. Seward, did not please me, when I was in America, with a speech in which he declared himself opposed to the policy of *building railroads*

Richard Cobden : The International Man

with foreign iron over your own coal and iron beds. I suppose this was merely intended for Mr. Bunkum in Pennsylvania, but I don't like it any better for that. I must own that this gentleman did not make so great a mark on society in England as some of your other distinguished visitors have done. Remember me to your colleague Mr. Wilson, and, if you can talk to Southern men, do the same to Mr. Mason, Mr. Benjamin, and Mr. Hunter."

"*February* 28, 1861.

" The conduct of the South has disgusted everybody. I do not mean their desire to disunite—*that* they may have a right to do, and it may be for the interest of all parties. But they have shown a measure of passionate haste and unreasoning arrogance which has astonished and alienated all lookers-on. They have gone about the work of dissolving the Union with less gravity or forethought than a firm of intelligent drapers or grocers would think necessary in case of a dissolution of partnership."

"*November* 27, 1861.

"I say not one word about your troubles. *Cui bono?* I made a vow during the Crimean War that if ever another war broke out between England and any other Power I would not utter a word with a view of shortening its duration, for reason and argument are lost in the clash of armed men, whose struggle can only be concluded by the exhaustion of one or both parties. Did it ever occur to you in reading our history how utterly unavailing was the eloquence of Chatham and Burke to stay our war with the American Colonies, and how completely the efforts of Fox and his friends were thrown away in attempting to put a

The Civil War and the Sumner Letters

stop to the War of the French Revolution? You need not, however, doubt how much I sympathize with the North. My respect and admiration for your *free* States is so great that I have regretted you did not let the vile incubus of slavery slip off your back. And yet I confess the almost insuperable difficulty of making two nations of the United States. The geographical obstacles alone seem insurmountable.

"My object in writing to you is with a view to the future rather than the present. The maritime law of nations requires alteration, and I hope the result of this war will be to lead to the abolition of blockades, as well as to make private property as safe against capture by armed vessels on sea as it is by armed regiments on land.

"Upon this subject there has been some correspondence between your late Government and Mr. Mason, your representative at Paris, which I should like to see. If you will be good enough to refer to *Hansard*, February 18, 1861, p. 496, you will see that Lord John Russell refers to a despatch written by General Cass to Mr. Mason at Paris, and read to him (Lord John) by Mr. Dallas. I have tried both at the London and Paris Embassies to obtain a sight of this despatch, but it is against their instructions to allow it to be seen. I shall be obliged if you will let me have a copy, or at least know the purport of this despatch.

"PS. Since writing the accompanying, we have the news of the capture of Mason and Slidell in our packet-vessel. You may be right in point of law, though perhaps, in technical strictness, the lawyers may pick a hole. *But I am satisfied you are wrong in point of policy.* There is an impression, *I know*, in high quarters here that Mr. Seward wishes to quarrel with this country. This seems absurd enough. I confess I have as little confidence in him as I have in Lord Palmerston. Both will consult *Bunkum* for the moment, without much regard, I fear, for the future. You must not lose sight of this view of the relations of the two countries. Formerly England feared a war with the United States as much from the dependence on your cotton as from a dread of your power. *Now* the popular opinion (however erroneous) is that a war would give us cotton. And we, of course, consider your power weakened by your Civil War. I speak as a friend of peace and not as a partisan of my own country in wishing you to bear this in mind. If Mr. Seward relies on the Irish *element*, he may be misled, as others have been.

"Now with regard to our conduct towards your nation—I mean our conduct as a government and people—I do not think it has been such as to warrant any resentment on your side. Considering our vital stake, we have borne the blockade with more temper and moderation than I should have expected. As for the Press, let the London *Times* and the *New York Herald* pair off, and the account is balanced. We have nothing so bad as to be paired against your Petersburg Minister's speeches and letters since he came to Europe, of which there has been no official disavowal on your part."

"*November* 29, 1861.

"I am induced to write another letter from London, where I have come for a day or two, owing to the turn the question of the seizure of Mason and Slidell seems to be taking. I hear that the Law Officers of the Crown have decided that you are not within the law in what has been done. I leave your lawyers to answer ours. The question of legality, in matters of

The Civil War and the Sumner Letters

international law, has never been very easily settled. However, the only danger to the peace of the two countries is in the *temper* which may grow out of this very trivial incident. The Press will as usual try to envenom the affair. It is for us, and all who care for the interests of humanity, to do our utmost to thwart these mischief-makers. You may reckon on Bright, myself and all our friends being alert and active in this good work, and we reckon on the co-operation of yourself and all who sympathize with you. Though I said in my other letter that I shall never care to utter a word about the merits of a war after it has begun, I do not less feel it my duty to try to prevent hostilities occurring.

"Let me here remark that I cannot understand how you should have thought it worth your while at Washington to have reopened this question of the right of search, by claiming to exercise it in a doubtful case and a doubtful manner, under circumstances which could be of so little advantage, and to have incurred the risk of greater disadvantages. The capture of Mason and Slidell can have little effect in discouraging the South, compared with the indirect encouragement and hope it may hold out to them of embroiling your Government with England. I am speaking with reference to the *policy* and leaving out of sight the law of the case. But in the latter view, we are rather unprepared to find you exercising in a strained manner the right of search, inasmuch as you have been supposed to be always the opponents of the practice, I was under the impression that our Government was told pretty plainly at the outbreak of the Crimean War that it would be risking the peace of this country with yours if we claimed the right of search in the open sea. I am not in the position to know how far this was the case. Can you tell me if there be any documents on the subject? If it were so, we should, of course, all unite in holding you to your own doctrine."

"*December* 3, 1861.

"I wrote you two letters by the last mail. This steamer will take out a report of Bright's speech [1] and my letter of excuse for not being able to attend. You will see that we stand in the breach, as usual, to stem the tide of passion. But you know that *we* don't represent all England at such a moment. For myself, I may say that never were people so willing to listen and so desirous of agreeing with me. My Paris labours have opened such a trade with France as almost to compensate the manufacturing districts for the loss of your market. But still, on this Peace question, I am somewhat in your position in the matter of slavery: people tolerate my 'crotchet,' and then go their way.

"If you take the trouble to read my letter to the Mayor of Rochdale you will observe that I try to turn the tide by showing that your country offered to relay these absurd maritime laws, and that *we* were the obstacle. Nothing is so calculated to cool the temper of the public as this diversion. And I again beg you to send me copies of any documents or despatches which have not been made public in this country. For instance, on what did President Pierce found his statement, in his Message, that Russia and France were favourable to the plan put forth by Mr. Marcy for exempting private property from capture by all armed vessels? Were there any despatches? But especially I wish for a copy of the despatch from General Cass to Mr. Mason referred to by Lord John Russell in the House on February 18th

---

[1] Bright's great speech at Rochdale in July 1861, espousing the cause of the North and denouncing slavery.

last. Was there any despatch from Mr. Mason in reply to this, stating the views of the French Government, and any from Mr. Dallas giving an account of what passed between him and Lord John when he read this despatch to him? *And will you ascertain for me from Mr. Dallas whether he left a copy of this despatch with Lord Russell?* Now, pray hunt up every document of this kind for me. A friend writes to me to-day from London to remind me that there was an important correspondence between Mr. Webster and Lord Ashburton, after the Boundary Treaty, in which the former proposes to abolish the right of search, which is declined by Lord A. in the name of our Government. I can, of course, obtain this last correspondence here.

"We are in much suspense as to what your Government will do. Some of my friends predict one of two courses: either that you will offer to restore matters to the *status quo*, on the agreement that the question shall be decided in an Admiralty Court of the United States, or that you will offer to take the benefit of that declaration at the Congress of Paris in favour of Arbitration.

"Now, having premised so much, I shall add a few words of unreserved remark on the 'situation.' I write to you, of course, in confidence; and I write to you what I would not write to any other American—nay, what it would be perhaps improper for any other Englishman than myself to utter to any other American but yourself. But we are, I think, both more of Christians and Cosmopolitans than British or Yankee.

"You will see a new feature in this disagreeable matter in the ardour with which the French Press takes up the cry against you. Some of the papers most eager to push us to extremities are those which are conducted by parties who are supposed to be in the confidence

Richard Cobden : The International Man

of the Emperor. Spending as I did eighteen months in France, and always in close communication with the Emperor's ablest advisers, and frequently having very free audiences with himself, I came to the conclusion that *the corner-stone of his policy was friendship with England.* He has studied his uncle's life with the view of profiting by his errors as well as his example, and he knows that the first Napoleon always lamented in his exile that he could not have been at peace with England. To preserve this friendship, Louis Napoleon has borne with equanimity attacks from our Press and public men, armed defiance from our successive Governments, and insults of every kind towards himself personally, such as have not in the worst of times been bandied between the Press and 'tribunes' of England and the United States. To preserve this friendship, I believe he would submit to anything short of such a humiliation for France as would emperil his dynasty. It is to preserve this friendship that he has sought our alliance in the Crimea, in China, and in Mexico. And if I were asked what were the motives which led him to agree to the Treaty of Commerce with me, I should say that they were nine-tenths political, rather than politico-economical, with a view to cement the alliance with this country. *I leave you to make an application of these facts to your present situation.* It was because I knew the inner policy of the French Government that I could not see without mortification and disgust the shallow antics of some of your official representatives in Paris, at that most lamentable public meeting where individuals, *accredited by your Government*, invited the Emperor to join you against England to avenge Waterloo and St. Helena ! These proceedings, not having led to the recall or official rebuke of the parties, have done more harm in this country than all

The Civil War and the Sumner Letters

the ravings of your *Herald*. There are three things which have given our Tory Press a great advantage in exciting animosity against you. First, Mr. Seward's speech in the Far West in allusion to the annexation of Canada. This, coming from the candidate for the Presidency and the future Prime Minister, had a significance for Englishmen which *you* can appreciate. Second, Mr. Seward's circular holding out a threat to those who recognized the rebels, and speaking with a somewhat bombastic confidence in the future of your country, which were in bad taste, and not complimentary, under your terrible circumstances, to the intellect of the writer or those whom he addressed.

"I think I told you in my last that I felt satisfied with the tone of forbearance in this country respecting your blockade. Hardly a paper or public man has hinted at such a measure as breaking the blockade until this *Trent* affair. Last August, Mr. Sandford from Brussels called on me in London, and asked me my private opinion whether I thought the blockade would be borne, and I told him that though I should be found to the last on the side of legality, cost what it might, I hoped the endurance of Europe would not be put to the test. I must at the same time remark that there is a universal impression that a war with the North would give us the cotton—to which I have alluded in a contrary sense in my letter to Rochdale. From all that I hear from France, the trade of that country is dreadfully damaged, and *I feel convinced the Emperor would be supported by his people if he were to enter into alliance with England to abolish the blockade and recognize the South*. The French are inconvenienced in many ways by your blockade, and especially in their relations with New Orleans, which are more important to them in *exports* than to us.

Richard Cobden : The International Man

"For ourselves in England, in spite of the bluster of *The Times*, the majority are anxious for peace. Do not overrate the power of *The Times*. Seven years ago it had a monopoly of publicity. Now its circulation is not perhaps one-tenth of the daily Press. *The Star* and *Manchester Examiner*, two admirable papers, circulate far more than *The Times*. But it cannot be denied that the great motives of hope and fear which kept us at peace and inclined the English Government always to recede in pinching controversies with you are gone. The English people have no sympathy with you on either side. You know how ignorant we are on the details of your history, geography, constitution, etc. There are two subjects on which we are unanimous and fanatical—*personal freedom and Free Trade*. These convictions are the result of fifty years of agitation and discussion. In your case we observe a mighty quarrel: on one side protectionists, on the other slave-owners. The protectionists say they do not seek to put down slavery. The slave-owners say they want Free Trade. Need you wonder at the confusion in John Bull's poor head? He gives it up! Leaves it to the Government. Which Government, by the way, is the most friendly to your Government, that could be found in England, for, although Palmerston is fond of hot water, he boasts that he never got us into a serious war. As for his colleagues, they are all sedate, peaceable men.

"God bless us. 'A mad world, my masters'!"

"*December* 6, 1861.

"Since writing my letter of yesterday's date I have read General Scott's admirable letter. It contains a passage to the following effect : 'I am sure that the President and people of the United States would be but too happy to let these men go free, unnatural

The Civil War and the Sumner Letters

and unpardonable as their offences have been, if by it they could emancipate the commerce of the world. Greatly as it would be to our disadvantage at this present crisis to surrender any of those maritime privileges of belligerents which are sanctioned by the law of nations, I feel that I take no responsibility in saying that the United States will be faithful to her traditional policy upon this subject, and to the spirit of her political institutions.'

"Upon this text I wish to say a few words, and I only regret that I could not present myself personally to talk the matter over with you. It appears to me that there is a great idea in his suggestion, worthy of the renowned sagacity of its author. If I were in the position of your Government, I would act upon it, and thus, by a great strategic movement, turn the flank of the European Powers, *especially of the governing class of England*. I would propose to let Mason and Slidell go free, and stipulate at the same time for a complete abandonment of the old code of maritime law as upheld by England and the European Powers. I would propose that private property at sea should be exempt from capture by armed Government ships. On this condition I would give in my adhesion to the abolition of privateering. I would propose that neutral merchant vessels in time of war, as in time of peace, should be exempt from search, visitation, or detention, by armed Government vessels, when on the ocean or high seas. I mean when beyond that distance from the shore which removes them from the jurisdiction of any maritime State.

"I would propose to abolish blockades of purely commercial ports, excepting for articles contraband of war.

"The first objection that might arise in your mind

to this programme is—it would relieve the South from the pressure of the blockade. *But is not the pressure becoming greater on the North?* Have you not the consciousness at Washington that this unnatural interruption of commerce will in less than six months from this time bring all Europe to your door demanding entrance? Recollect that the state of things will be wholly without a precedent for urgency and peril. It will be a question of the peace, and very existence, of many millions of people, and the supreme necessity of the case will sanctify in the opinion of the whole of Europe an intervention for which, you may be sure, an excuse will not be wanting. Ask yourselves deliberately what is the greatest danger that presents itself for the next six months, and you will be compelled to admit that it is the interference of Europe, driven by the necessities of a social and political crisis. Can you be sure that in one winter you can subdue the South? If not, when summer approaches, you must withdraw your armies from that coast, which will be pronounced by Europe a retreat. The South knows this, and knows that the great Powers of Europe are standing ready for an excuse to declare its independence. This encourages resistance.

"But assuming that you abolish the blockade, you retain the power of preventing the introduction of munitions of war. Such a blockade would require fewer ships, and it would relieve a part of your force for direct military operations. The South would get some gold. But it would not get cannon, or rifles, or powder, and the other munitions of war. It would be still in the same want of mechanical and industrial resources. It would, in fact, be in the same comparative barbarism as at present.

"In a word, all that the North wants is *time* to

The Civil War and the Sumner Letters

ensure its triumph over the South. *With time*, Slavery, if shut up within itself, will be its own destroyer. *And the only way in which you can have time is by abolishing the blockade.*

"You must know our political organization too well here in England to suppose that these propositions would be acceptable to our Government. We are, in ordinary times, *two* nations: a busy toiling multitude, and a governing 'class. The latter would be most averse to this revolution in maritime law, by which the pretence for vast armaments would be annihilated. The favourite plea when we vote the Navy Estimates is that they are necessary for the protection of commerce. It would be useless, therefore, for you to propose these changes through the channels of secret diplomacy. It must be done publicly. I have said that in ordinary quiet times we are ruled by a governing class. But when a sufficient motive is presented to induce the busy millions to exert their power, they can always bring the aristocracy into subjection to their will. Now, if it were publicly announced that you had made the above proposals to our Government, I will engage that our mercantile and manufacturing community will compel this Ministry, or some other, to accept them. Our Parliament will, I suppose, meet at the end of January, or certainly the beginning of February. Before that time your decision ought to be known, in order that our Chambers of Commerce and great trading bodies may have time to make their wishes known to the Government.

"Now, understand me, I have not considered myself speaking in the character of a foreigner, and therefore do not let my language seem to be a menace. I am a better American than many of the citizens you send to Europe to discredit their institutions. Recollect how immensely

Richard Cobden : The International Man

you would gain in moral power by leading old Europe in the path of civilization. You owe it to yourselves and us."

"*December* 12, 1861.

"I am afraid that we in England who are well-wishers to the North take a more accurate measure of the difficulties of your position than you who are in the heat of the turmoil can do—just as you took a more correct view of the Crimean War, and its utter uselessness, than the bulk of Englishmen did. We do not believe that the subjection of the South can be a *speedy* achievement. Nobody doubts the power of the North, ultimately, if it choose to make the sacrifice, to ruin the South, and even to occupy its chief places. But this will take a very long time, and the world will not look on, I believe, patient sufferers during the process. I am not justifying any interference on the part of Europe; but it is a fearful thing to have the whole civilized world undergoing privations and sufferings which they lay at the door of the North, thus making it the interest of their Governments to interfere with you. Recollect that your own Government has condemned blockades of purely commercial ports; the world has in truth outgrown them. During the Crimean War, whilst we blockaded Cronstadt with our ships, we connived at the importation of Russian tallow, hemp, flax, etc., overland through Prussia, our own manufacturers openly declaring that they must have those raw materials. *I do not believe there will ever be another blockade.* The state of modern society, where you have millions of labourers in Europe depending for the means of employment on the regular supply of raw materials brought from another continent, to say nothing of hundreds of millions of capital invested on the same dependence, will necessitate a change in the law of blockade and other belligerent rules. Our recent doctrines, on which you have also acted, with reference to China and Japan, denying them the right of shutting up themselves from the rest of the world, are symptoms of the same tendency of men's minds. I do not, I repeat, say that the rest of the world has the right to force you to raise your blockade. But I do think you ought to consider these tendencies of the world's opinion, and how much you are acting in opposition to the spirit of the age; and above all, in your present state, weigh well the danger of putting yourself in the dilemma of making all the world your enemies. The recognition of the independence of the South, and the forcing of the blockade, will come to be viewed, about next March, as a matter of life and death by many millions of people in Europe, and as a question of high political urgency by the most powerful Governments of the world. There is another fact to be borne in mind. We, in England, have ready a fleet surpassing in destructive force any naval armament the world ever saw, exceeding greatly the British Navy in the great French War in 1810. *This force has been got up under false pretences.* There is always a desire on the part of Governments to use such armaments by way of proving that they were necessary. *France* was the pretence, and now we have plenty of people who would be content to see this fleet turned against *you*. Coming from me, who have resolutely opposed this armament, this will not be considered a menace.

"Have you considered how easy it will be to find a flaw in your blockade? In the Declaration of Paris in 1856, Art. 4, it is said : 'Blockades, in order to be binding, must be effective; that is to say, maintained by a force sufficient really to prevent access to the *coast of the enemy.*' How very easy it will be to prove that along your thousands of miles of coast *access* is possible.

Richard Cobden : The International Man

"Now a word upon the military view of the matter. Do you believe that the privation of comforts and luxuries ever brought a people to subjection ? Where have you an instance ? Look at your own shoeless people during our blockade of your coasts in 1780 ; did they feel more inclined to submit because their garments were in rags ? On the contrary, it becomes the more a point of honour not to yield. Even in the blockade of a garrisoned town, it would be considered disgraceful to yield for anything short of *starvation*—unless the garrison were stormed, or reduced by artillery and regular siege operations. Now, I need not tell you how impossible it is to starve the South. They have food enough, and as they are diminishing the production of cotton, they will next year have a superabundance of corn, beef, pork, rice, sugar, whisky and tobacco. Did a people ever yield to a blockade that possessed these necessaries, because they were deprived of tea, wine and coffee ? Would it not be unmanly to think of it ?

"Is there not another side to this blockade ? Does it not, in a certain sense, aid the other party ? So long as all foreign trade is cut off it gives an excuse to those who are in debt not to pay (and who in the South is not in debt ?). Nobody can press for payment even from those who are able to pay, so long as the blockade furnishes a patriotic excuse for suspending all payments. Everybody is therefore relieved from pressure. Meantime the blockade increases the bitterness against the North. But, above all, does it not encourage the South to hope for foreign interference ? Then, the negroes being withdrawn from the cultivation of cotton makes labour more available for defensive works. And the whites, having no profitable occupation, turn out to fight. These are points worth your consideration.

"There appear to me only two ways in which you can

The Civil War and the Sumner Letters

expect to subdue the South: either by great military operations in the field, or by a sort of armed truce by which you refuse to acknowledge the South, but take your own time to wear out your adversary, leaving it to slavery to do its work for you. But either of these courses must take a long time. As for your expeditions along the coast, you must withdraw the Northern troops next summer, or they will share the fate of our Walcheren Expedition. The South know this, and of course reckon on it. The great Napoleon, in his correspondence with his brother Joseph, seems to treat with contempt these coasting expeditions. If you are to rely on great operations in the field, it is, of course, desirable that you should not be hurried forward from the necessity of doing something to meet the impatience of foreign Powers. You are thus liable to be tempted to precipitate measures.

"By raising the blockade, except for articles contraband of war, you get rid of all pressure from abroad, and the tone of public feeling in Europe would naturally become favourable to the North. *It is the suffering and misery that your blockade is bringing on the masses in Europe that turns men against you.* How can you hope to have a blessing on your cause from those on whom you are inflicting such misery?

"As respects the question of smuggling goods through Southern ports into the North, your only remedy is to put on duties *strictly for revenue* in the North—duties, I mean, from 10 to 20 per cent. If you cannot do this —if your Congress will have 'Protection' for the North and war with the South, God help your people that have two such burdens to bear. Your finances will soon be on a par with those of Austria. And all this for a mere chimera! For it is demonstrable that New England and Pennsylvania would be more prosperous with moderate revenue duties.

Richard Cobden : The International Man

"*The Times* and its yelping imitators are still doing their worst, but there is a powerful moderate party. I hope you will offer promptly to arbitrate the question. There is one point on which *you must absolutely define your platform. You must acknowledge the South as belligerents to give you a standing ground on the 'Trent' affair.* Some of your newspapers argue that you have a right to carry off a *rebel* from an English vessel—which means that Austria might have seized Kossuth under similar circumstances. Were you to take such ground there would be war."

"*December* 19, 1861.

"Everybody tells me that war is inevitable, and yet I do not believe in war. But it must be admitted that there are things said and done on your side that make it very difficult for the advocates of peace on this side to keep the field. We can get over the sayings of your *Herald* that 'France will not and England *dare* not go to war.' Your *newspapers* will not drive us into war.

"But when grave men (or men that should be grave), holding the highest post in your cultivated State of Massachusetts, compliment Captain Wilkes for having given an affront to the British Lion, it makes it very hard for Bright and me to contend against the British Lion Party in this country. All I can say is that I hope you have taken Bright's advice and offered unconditional arbitration. With that offer publicly made, the friends of peace could prevent our fire-eaters from assaulting you, always providing that your public speakers do not put it out of our power to keep the peace.

"I was sorry to see a report of an anti-English speech by your colleague at New York. Honestly speaking, and with no blind patriotism to mislead me, I don't think the nation here behaved badly under the terrible evil of loss of trade and danger of starving under your

The Civil War and the Sumner Letters

blockade. Of course, all privileged classes and aristocracies hate your institutions—that is natural enough. But the mass of the people never went with the South.

"I am not pleased at your projects for sinking stones to block up ports! That is a barbarism. It is quite natural that, smarting as you do under an unprovoked aggression from the slave-owners, you should even be willing to smother them like hornets in their nest. But don't forget the outside world. And especially don't forget that the millions in Europe are more interested even than their princes in preserving the *future* commerce with the vast region of the Confederate States. Be assured that the civilized world will not acquiesce in a policy which looks to a permanent extinction of that commerce. All blockades must in their nature be temporary, and they will only bear the test of reason when, as stated by General Cass in his despatch to Mr. Mason to which I referred, they are in combination with great military operations. But if you are to remain yourselves besieged in Washington, whilst with your naval resources you are permanently destroying the navigation of the great arteries of commerce in the South, it will put you in the wrong with the whole world. By and by the European Governments, pushed on by the distress of their people, will begin to take a retrospect of the time you have been at war, and to estimate the progress you have made in *reoccupying* the country over which you claim authority—for *that* will be made the measure of your success. Then, if no progress can be shown, except in blockading and destroying ports, see what a temptation you are offering to the European Governments to acknowledge the independence of the South, by which they will neutralize the Mississippi, under that law of nations settled at Vienna which prohibits the interruption of the trade

Richard Cobden : The International Man

of a navigable river flowing through two or more independent States. Of course, all Europe would unite in enforcing this law if the South were acknowledged an independent State.

"I come back to the view I always hold, that your wisest course would be to raise the blockade yourselves, take high ground with Europe for a complete sweep of the old maritime code, and then take your own time to deal with the Slave States, either by fighting them at your leisure or by leaving the West to outgrow them or Slavery to undo them."

"*January* 23, 1862.

"It is perhaps well that you settled the matter by sending away the men at once. Consistently with your own principles you could not have justified their detention. But it is right you should know that there was a great reaction going on through this country against the diabolical tone of *The Times* and *Post* (I suspect stock-jobbing in these quarters). The cry of arbitration had been raised and responded to, and I was glad to see the religious people once more in the field in favour of peace. Be assured, if you had offered to refer the question to arbitration, there could not have been a meeting called in England that would not have endorsed it. The only question was whether we ought to be the first to offer arbitration. I mean this was the only doubt in the popular mind. As regards our Government, they were, of course, feeling the tendency of public opinion. A friend of mine in London, a little behind the scenes, wrote to me, 'They are busy at the Foreign Office hunting up precedents for arbitration very much against their will.' I write all this because I wish you to know that we are not so bad as appeared at first on the surface. There is now a new newspaper Press in the provinces, a daily penny Press, which has grown up since the removal of the stamp, and it presented a marked contrast for moderation with the Metropolitan *Times* and *Post*.

"Now I return to the old difficulty and danger of the blockade. Parliament will meet in a fortnight. I am very much afraid of the tone which will prevail there. There are strong symptoms that a powerful party will press on the Government the recognition of the independence of the South. There will be motives for this step which will not be avowed. Our aristocratic classes would in their hearts like to see your great Republic dismembered. You have been too prosperous to please them; and then it must be admitted you have not always borne your prosperity with too much meekness; and it is the latter fact that makes our official politicians rather happy at the prospect of your power being a little impaired. Your diplomacy has sometimes, as our politicians think, been a little too brusque and exacting. However, none of these motives for helping to break you asunder will be avowed. Some of our politicians will talk of humanity, and profess a desire to put an end to the war. This, however, with those who could gulp the Crimea and Solferino, will be indeed straining at a gnat after swallowing a camel.

"But I come back again to the one sole cause of all your danger—the blockade. This it is which alone will give any dangerous power to those who wish you ill. Whatever is done, it will give the vague impression to the public that something will arise out of it to assist in raising the blockade. And it is this common feeling of suffering and danger which will bring all Europe together (with perhaps the exception of Russia) on the question of the Southern blockade. If our Government were not pressed forward by this question of material interest, there never was a time when the doctrine of non-intervention was so strongly in the ascendant in our maxims of foreign policy as at present. Therefore, whatever you see in our debates or whatever you encounter in diplomacy, no matter what pretences may be put forward, be assured it is the blockade which is at the bottom of every movement of European politicians in the direction of your affairs. You must have expected this. It was not possible to cut off the sources of employment and subsistence from many millions of people, and the profitable use of hundreds of millions of capital, suddenly and without warning, without producing a terrible revulsion of feeling against you. I regret that your Foreign Secretary did not give a word of sympathy in this direction instead of threats. However, he had his hands full at home, and I am bound to say there is much in his correspondence of which a copy has been sent to me to inspire both admiration and respect.

"But the question recurs—what is to be done?

"If you really intend to prosecute the war to the end, about which I offer no opinion, and if it be likely to last *years*, then I say, a thousand times, devise some means of raising your blockade voluntarily, or it will bring all Europe on you—first to acknowledge the South, then to pick a quarrel with the blockade on the ground that it is ineffective, and to claim the Mississippi as a free river. There will be no chance for you to fight with England or France; it will be all Europe upon you, of which you have had a specimen in the case of the *Trent*.

"Were I in your situation, and bent on carrying on the war for *years*, I would throw open the Mississippi and some other ports at once for all commerce, exports and imports, except articles contraband of war. If you can occupy the ports of New Orleans, Mobile, etc., and open commerce through a Federal Custom-house, so

The Civil War and the Sumner Letters

much the better, but if not, open them to the Confederates. Then afterwards, if by military operations you were to take those places, and the Southern planters refused to send their produce, *you* of the North would not be to blame. As respects the fear of losing revenue in the North by smuggling, you can prevent it by laying on moderate revenue duties. No other duties ought to be thought of. Tell Mr. Chase from me that if any man or party in the North at this moment of his financial exigency wishes him for sectional and selfish purposes to swerve a hair from such a scale of duties as will bring the greatest amount of revenue at the customs, irrespective of protection, they are as great traitors as the Southerners, and not so open and courageous in their treason to the State. Now all experience proves that moderate duties, which neither impede commerce nor promote smuggling, are the most productive to the revenue. All the reflection I have been able to give the subject confirms me in the views I expressed in my former letter.

"Propose to Europe a clean sweep of the old maritime law of Vattell, Puffendorf & Co. Abolish blockades of commercial ports on the ground laid down in Cass's despatch which you sent. Get rid of the right of search in time of war as in time of peace. And make private property exempt from capture by armed vessels of every kind, whether Government vessels or privateers. And as an earnest of your policy offer to apply the doctrine in your present war. You would instantly gain France and all the continent of Europe to your side. You would enlist a party in England that can always control our governing class when there is a sufficient motive for action, and you would acquire such a moral position that no Power would dream of laying hands on you."

Richard Cobden : The International Man

"*February* 21, 1862.

"We have been in session for a fortnight, and I merely write you a few lines to give you my impression of the feeling among members. Nobody seems to have any faith in your being able to subdue the South into submission to the Federal Union. This is an honest view of almost every one I speak to. This is the view which Gladstone in his recent speech said people took who were still well-wishers to the North. There are two distinct questions in men's mind :

"(1) Are the people of the North in the right?

"(2) Can they succeed in restoring the integrity of the Union?

"To the first question I should say the overwhelming popular majority would answer in the affirmative. To the second, I should say the numbers would be in the negative.

"I hardly know anybody except our courageous friend Bright, who rather likes to fight a battle with the long odds against him, that thinks you can put down the 'rebellion.' It is important you should know this, for it enhances, I think, the merit of the strong desire on the part of those who are so sceptical to give you fair play. There is a universal opinion apparently everywhere here, both among the English and Americans, that your war will be brought to an end in two or three months. But how is this to be brought about? It certainly cannot be by conquest, and I see no door opening for compromise. If I meet Mason, he says the war can only end by the North leaving the South to itself. If I speak to a Northern man, he says it can only end by the South submitting to the Union! Where is then the issue? We look, of course, to your military operations, which in the next

The Civil War and the Sumner Letters

two months must decide matters, and it is useless to speculate about events so near at hand.

"Opinion in England is favourable to the North, in spite of *The Times* and its imps."

"*July* 11, 1862.

"It is a long time since I wrote to you. Indeed, to confess the truth, it is a painful task for me to keep up my correspondence with my American friends. But I have not been a less anxious observer of the events which have passed on your side. I shall now best serve the interests of humanity by telling you frankly the state and progress of opinion here. There is an all but unanimous belief that you *cannot* subject the South to the Union. Even they who are your partisans and advocates cannot see their way to any such issue. It is necessary that you should understand that this opinion is so widely and honestly entertained, because it is the key to the expression of views which might otherwise not be quite intelligible. Among some of the governing class in Europe the wish is father to this thought. But it is not so with the mass of the people. Nor is it so with our own Government entirely. I *know* that Gladstone would restore your Union to-morrow if he could, and yet he has steadily maintained from the first that, unless there is a strong Union sentiment, it is impossible that the South can be subdued. *Now* the belief is all but universal that there is no Union feeling in the South, and this is founded latterly upon the fact that no cotton comes from New Orleans. It is said that if the instinct of gain, with cotton at double its usual price, does not induce the people to sell, it is a proof beyond dispute that the political resentment is overwhelming and unconquerable.

Richard Cobden : The International Man

"I have precisely the same views with regard to a European intervention that I had last winter when I wrote to you. The action of the Governments has been put off, by two or three considerations, to the present time. It has been thought proper to wait the result of your spring campaign. Then there was a large stock of cotton in the hands of *rich* spinners and merchants, and they were interested in keeping out cotton. Moreover, we had great merchants who had over-speculated in cotton goods which were shipped to India and China, and they were glad of a rise in the raw material which enabled them to get out of their stocks. But all these motives for forbearance are now at an end. The merchants, manufacturers, spinners and operatives are all on the same footing, and they are all anxious to obtain raw cotton, and they will be all equally pressing on our Government the necessity of 'doing something.' What that 'something' is to be is more than I can pretend to say. I am, of course, as strongly convinced as ever that nothing but harm can possibly be done by interference of any kind. But where the welfare and the lives of millions of persons are at stake, you cannot present the alternative of a greater possible evil to deter a Government from attempting to remedy so vast a present danger. I feel quite convinced that, unless cotton comes in considerable quantities before the end of the year, the Governments of Europe will be knocking at your door. I do not pretend to say what form their representation will take. I expect it will be a joint action on the part of all the Governments interested—or rather a joint demonstration, for I do not believe that any violent action will be resorted to or contemplated. But you know what a moral demonstration means, with a vast material force behind it. And such a step would

The Civil War and the Sumner Letters

beyond all others encourage the South, and tend to decide them against any concession or compromise.

"Now, are you doing all you possibly can to allow the cotton to come out? I am afraid not. Your *Republican Party* are *mesquin* and narrow in their commercial policy. You must instruct your military commander at New Orleans to allow the sale or purchase of cotton by foreigners in the interior without asking any questions. When Mr. Thurlow Weed, who won all hearts, was here, he led us to expect that after the spring campaign was at an end, and the ports should be in the power of the Federals, there would be a supply, and he went so far in conversation as to say that your Government had no right to expect the European Powers to wait indefinitely for cotton. Now, depend on it, the world will not wait quietly for six months longer.

"Now, the course you should take, and the only one to avert trouble with Europe, is this: to place foreigners on precisely the same footing in the interior, as respects the trade of New Orleans, as that which they occupied before the war. I mean this: that if an Englishman comes to New Orleans with a cargo of goods, *other than contraband of war*, and pays duty on them at the custom-house, he should be allowed to exchange those goods for cotton in the interior without any inquiry as to whether he was dealing with rebels or loyalists. And the same rule should apply if he took sovereigns to make his purchases. Unless this rule is applied, the pretended opening of the ports is a delusion. If it be said that this will enable rebels to supply their wants, all I can urge in reply is that you will play the rebels' game far more effectually by keeping back the cotton than by allowing the South to sell it.

"Let me hear your views on this subject. But

Richard Cobden : The International Man

pray urge your Government to act as I advise. Parliament will be prorogued in a few weeks, and *it is during the recess that all the mischief is generally done in our foreign relations.*"

"*February* 13, 1863.

"If I have not written to you before, it is not because I have been indifferent to what is passing in your midst. I may say sincerely that my thoughts have run almost as much on American as English politics. But I could do you no service, and shrunk from occupying your overtaxed attention even for a moment. My object in now writing is to speak of a matter which has a practical bearing on your affairs.

"You know how much alarmed I was from the first lest our Government should interpose in your affairs. The disposition of our ruling class, and the necessities of our cotton trade, pointed to some act of intervention; and the indifference of the great mass of our population to your struggle, the object of which they did not foresee and understand, would have made intervention easy, and indeed popular, if you had been a weaker naval Power. This state of feeling existed up to the announcement of the President's emancipation policy. From that moment our old anti-slavery feeling began to arouse itself, and it has been gathering strength ever since. The great rush of the public to all the public meetings called on the subject shows how wide and deep the sympathy for personal freedom still is in the breasts of our people. I know nothing in my political experience so striking as a display of spontaneous public action as that of the vast gathering at Exeter Hall, when, without one attraction in the form of a popular orator, the vast building, its minor rooms and passages and the streets adjoining, were crowded with an enthusiastic audience.

The Civil War and the Sumner Letters

That meeting has had a powerful effect on our newspapers and politicians. It has closed the mouths of those who have been advocating the side of the South. And I now write to assure you that any unfriendly act on the part of our Government, no matter which of our aristocratic parties is in power, towards your cause, is not to be apprehended. If an attempt were made by the Government in any way to commit us to the South, a spirit would be instantly aroused which would drive that Government from power. This I suppose will be known and felt by the Southern agents in Europe, and if communicated to their Government must, I should think, operate as a great discouragement to them. For I *know* that those agents have been incessantly urging in every quarter where they could hope to influence the French and English Governments the absolute necessity of *recognition* as a means of putting an end to the war. Recognition of the South by England, whilst it bases itself on negro slavery, is an impossibility, unless, indeed, after the Federal Government has recognized the Confederates as a nation.

"So much for the influence which your emancipation policy has had on the public opinion of England. But judging from the tone of your Press in America it does not seem to have gained the support of your masses. About this, however, I do not feel competent to offer an opinion. Nor, to confess the truth, do I feel much satisfaction in treating of your politics at all. There appears to me great mismanagement, I had almost said incapacity, in the management of your affairs, and you seem to be hastening towards financial and economical evils in a manner which fills me with apprehension for the future.

"When I met Fremont in Paris two years ago, just as you commenced this terrible war, I remarked to him that the total abolition of slavery on your Northern Continent was the only issue which could justify the war to the civilized world. Every symptom seems to point to this result. But at what a price is the negro to be emancipated! I confess that, if *then* I had been the arbiter of his fate, I should have refused him freedom at the cost of so much white men's blood and women's tears. I do not, however, blame the North. The South fired the first shot, and on them righteously falls the malediction that 'they who take the sword shall perish by the sword.' And it seems not unlikely that after all the much-despised 'nigger,' and not the potentates and statesmen of Europe, will be the final arbitrator in this great struggle."

"April 2, 1863.

"On receipt of your letter I communicated privately with Lord Russell, urging him to be more than passive in enforcing the law respecting the building of ships for the Confederate Government. I especially referred to the circumstance that it was suspected that some ships pretended to be for the Chinese Government were really designed for that of Richmond, and I urged him to furnish Mr. Adams with the names of all the ships building for China and full particulars of where they were being built. This Lord R. tells me he had already done, and he seems to promise fairly. Our Government are perfectly well informed of all that is being done for the Chinese.

"Now, there are certain things which can be done and others which cannot be done by our Government. We are bound to do our best to prevent any ship-of-war being built for the Confederate Government, for a ship-of-war can only be used or owned legitimately by a Government. But with munitions of war the case

The Civil War and the Sumner Letters

is different. They were bought and sold by private merchants for the whole world, and it is not in the power of Governments to prevent it. Besides, your own Government have laid down repeatedly the doctrine that it is no part of the duty of Governments to interfere with such transactions, for which they are not in any way responsible. I was, therefore, very sorry that Mr. Adams had persisted in raising an objection to these transactions, in which, by the way, the North has been quite as much involved as the South. If you have read the debate in the House on the occasion when Mr. Forster brought on the subject last week, you will see how Sir Roundell Palmer, the Solicitor-General, and Mr. Laird, the shipbuilder, availed themselves of this opening to divert attention from the real question at issue—the building of warships—to the question of selling munitions of war, in which latter practice it was shown you in the North were the great participators.

"You must really keep the public mind right in America on this subject. Do not let it be supposed that you have any grievance against us for selling *munitions of war*. Confine the question to the building of ships, in which I hope we shall bring up a strong feeling on the right side here."

"*May* 2, 1863.

"Though I have no news beyond what you will get from the public channels, yet I think it well to write a few lines on the present aspect of affairs.

"I am in no fear whatever of any rupture between the two countries arising out of the blockade or the incendiary language of the politicians or the Press on both sides of the Atlantic—though these may help to precipitate matters on another issue. But the fitting out of privateers to prey on your commerce and to render

Richard Cobden : The International Man

valueless your mercantile tonnage is another and more serious matter. Great material interests are at stake, and unless this evil can be put down the most serious results may follow. Now, I have reason to know that our Government fully appreciates the gravity of this matter. Lord Russell, whatever may be the tone of his ill-mannered despatches, is sincerely alive to the necessity of putting an end to the equipping of ships-of-war in our harbours to be used against the Federal Government by the Confederates. He was *bona fide* in his desire to prevent the *Alabama* from leaving, but he was tricked, and was angry at the escape of that vessel. It is necessary your Government should know all this, and I hope public opinion in England will be so alive to the necessity of enforcing the law that there will be no more difficulty in the matter.

"If Lord Russell's despatches to Mr. Adams are not very civil, he may console himself with the knowledge that the Confederates are still worse treated. You will be amused at one of the intercepted despatches from Mr. Benjamin to Mr. Mason, in which the former lectures Lord Russell on his bad manners. This despatch has been presented to Parliament. By the way, in Harriet Martineau's 'Thirty Years' Peace,' the continuation of the 'Pictorial History of England,' she gives an anecdote of a conversation which an English traveller (known to be herself) had with Mr. Webster, when the latter complained of the want of manners on the part of the Whig diplomatists which gave an advantage to the Tories over their political rivals in their relations with foreign countries."

"*May* 22, 1863.

"I called on Lord Russell and read every word of your last long indictment against him and Lord Palmerston, to him. He was a little impatient under the treatment, but I got through every word. I did my best to improve on the text in half an hour's conversation.

"Public opinion is recovering its senses. John Bull, you know, has never before been a neutral when great naval operations have been carried on, and he does not take kindly to the task. But he is becoming gradually reconciled. He also now begins to understand that he has acted illegally in applauding those who furnished ships-of-war to prey on your commerce. It will not be *repeated*. I cannot too often deplore the bungling mismanagement on your side, which allowed the two distinct questions of selling munitions of war and the equipping of privateers to be mixed up together. It has confused the thick wits of our people, and made it difficult for those who were right on this side on the Foreign Enlistment Act to make the public understand the difference between what was and what was not a legal transaction. In fact, your Foreign Office played into the hands of our politicians by affording them the means of mystification. If a plain, simple, short and dignified reclamation had been at first made against the fitting out of ships-of-war, with a clear statement of the law, and a brief recital of what your Government had done under similar circumstances to us, it would have been impossible for our Government to have resisted it. But when you opened fire on us for not stopping the export of arms and munitions of war, you offered an easy victory to our lawyers, and gave them an opportunity of escaping in a cloud of dust from the real question at issue.

"Mr. Evarts is 'the right man in the right place.' He is an able international lawyer. Quite a match for any one here in his own special walk. His manners are quiet and impressive. He is mixing very much

Richard Cobden : The International Man

in our best society, and I hear him spoken of with great respect. He seems pleased with his reception."

"*August* 7, 1863.

"Let me congratulate you on the improved state of your prospects. So far as fighting goes, I think you have now little to fear from the Confederates. The danger is from the *politicians*. There are so many in the North hankering after the 'fleshpots of Egypt' that I shall not be surprised at an attempt to compromise with the South, and to take them back, 'institutions' and all! Though I would not have begun the war for the emancipation of the negroes, and though I cannot urge its continuance for that object, yet I have always felt that the only result which could justify the war was the manumission of every slave on the Northern Continent of America. To restore the old Union, slavery and all, will be to cover with shame the partisans of the North throughout the world, and justify the opponents of the war everywhere. It would leave the question still to be settled by a similar process of blood by another generation. However, I do not see how this compromise can be accomplished.

"You will have had reason to feel but little satisfied with us during the late Session. Had our Government and Parliament taken an enlightened view of the interest of the nation, they would have competed with each other in their eagerness to amend our Foreign Enlistment Act, in order to preserve intact, as far as depended on us, the neutrality code in which we above all nations are so deeply interested. I consider the whole system at an end. Nothing but the experience of a war in which we are belligerents and you are neutrals will open our eyes to a sense of the new situation in which we shall find ourselves.

The Civil War and the Sumner Letters

"Though we have given you such good ground of complaint on account of the cruisers which have left our ports, yet you must not forget that we have been the only obstacle to what would have been almost a European recognition of the South. Had England joined France, they would have been followed by probably every other State of Europe, with the exception of Russia. This is what the Confederate agents have been seeking to accomplish. They have pressed recognition on England and France with persistent energy from the first. I confess that their eagerness for European intervention in some shape has always given me a strong suspicion of their conscious weakness. But considering how much more we have suffered than other people from the blockade, this abstinence on our part from all diplomatic interference is certainly something to our credit, and this I attribute entirely to the honourable attitude assumed by our working population."

"*October* 8, 1863.

"The admiration which I feel for the masterly ability of your speech at the Cooper Institute cannot suppress a certain amount of resistance to it on the score of *policy*. I was, I confess, rather beset with the feeling of *Cui bono?* after reading your powerful indictments against England and France *together*. It should have been your policy to have kept them asunder. Besides, if all we hear be true, we are not so bad as our great neighbour. We have done very uncivil things, but never has our Executive been prepared to take part with the French in recognizing the South or in planting a thorn in your side in Mexico. Again, was it politic to array us in hostile attitudes just at the moment when the hopes of the South were mainly founded on the prospect of a rupture between yourselves and Europe? Instead of bringing an indictment jointly against France and

Richard Cobden : The International Man

England for their past misdeeds, would it not have been better to have shown, in the most favourable colours consistent with truth, the strength of the alliance between the masses in England, led by so much of the intellect and the moral and religious worth of the kingdom, and the Federals, and to have demonstrated the impossibility of the aristocracy, with all their hostility, drawing us into a war with each other? You were, I suspect, speaking under the impression that the iron-clad rams would be allowed to leave. I was sure, as I told Evarts and Forbes again and again, that those vessels would not be allowed to sail. The fact that they were armoured, turreted, and *beaked* constituted them armed vessels even under the most lax interpretation of our Enlistment Act.

"Your career seems to be again chequered with partial reverses. I suppose this will tend more than ever to draw the Federal authorities towards the employment of the African race in the war. For my part, I have always thought that the negroes who are the main cause and object of the war will play an important part in its final operations. In India the Sepoys have always done the chief part in our territorial conquests, although they are a very inferior race physically to the negroes. Whoever heard of a Hindoo offering to fight a picked Englishman in the prize-ring? He would hardly have a better chance than a woman. But we have had black men doing this in England. Tom Cribb had to fight a severe battle for the champion belt with the negro Molyneux. If this horrible war for the freedom of the slaves is to go on, I think in the interest it is to be of the negroes themselves all over the world desired that the black man should be found fighting his own battle. To this you will be brought, probably against the wish of a majority of the Federals."

The Civil War and the Sumner Letters

"*January* 7, 1864.

"You may be assured that I have watched with anxiety your proceedings and have rejoiced with you at every step of your progress. After Gettysburg and Vicksburg I have ceased to fear the result, and it has seemed only a question of time. That the leaders of the rebellion will 'die hard' I have no doubt. But cut off from all hopes from Europe, with the negro escaping and being drilled against them, and with the certainty that in another year or two the supply of their darling cotton will be made good for Lancashire from other parts of the world, there can surely be sufficient intelligence found among the *rank and file of the white population* in the South to see that Secession is a dream of their leaders which has been dispelled by the sad realities of experience, and that they will resign themselves to the inevitable result. But I suppose that the ignorance of the mass of the whites in the South is nearly on a par with that of their negroes. I hope to see a hundred thousand coloured men under arms before midsummer. Nothing will tend so much to raise the Africans in the social scale as to put muskets in their hands and drill them as soldiers. I travelled in Egypt in 1836. Mehemet Ali had destroyed the Mameluke Beys and dispersed their followers, and called in some French officers to drill his drab Fellahs, of whom there were sixty thousand under arms when I was there. I was told that previously the Arab had been treated like a dog by these few thousand Mamelukes, a white race from the Caucasus, who for hundreds of years, by constant importations, had ruled the country, and who alone were privileged to bear arms. But after the Arabs had been accustomed to mount guard and control the movements of even white men, their self-respect had so increased with the consciousness of power, that they were no longer exposed to the outrages and injuries of former times. It will be so with the coloured race with you. Let a few regiments of them be seen in New York, and depend on it they and their countrymen will no longer be exposed to the insults of their rivals, the Irish.

"You will soon begin to busy yourselves with the task of President-making. I hope you will re-elect Mr. Lincoln. He is rising in reputation in Europe, apart from the success of the North. He possesses great moral qualities, which in the long run tell more on the fortunes of the world in these days than mere intellect. I always thought his want of enlarged experience was a disadvantage to him. But he knows his own countrymen, evidently, and that is the main point. And being a stranger to the rest of the world, he has the less temptation to embark in foreign controversies or quarrels. Nothing shows his solid sense more than the pertinacity with which he avoids all outside complications. His truthful elevation of character, and his somewhat stolid placidity of nature, put it quite beyond the power of other Governments to fasten a quarrel on him, and inspire the fullest confidence in those who are committing themselves to the side of the North. I say all this on the assumption that he has irrevocably committed himself to 'abolition' as the result of the war. Any compromise on that question would cover your cause with eternal infamy, and render the sanguinary Civil War with which you have desolated the North and South useless butchery, and the greatest crime against humanity recorded in the world's annals. You know I would never have fired a shot for the freedom of the negro, because I believe that God in His own good time would have

The Civil War and the Sumner Letters

found a way of emancipating the slave at a less cruel cost to his master. But I remember saying to Colonel Fremont at Paris in the spring of 1861, just as the news of the attack on Sumter reached Europe, that nothing but the emancipation of every slave in the United States would justify your Civil War in the eyes of Europe and posterity. This is, of course, more than ever my opinion after witnessing the gigantic dimensions which your struggle has assumed.

" You will observe that European politics are assuming a somewhat anxious tone. Is it not strange to see those dreamy Teutons pushing matters to such extremes on the Schleswig-Holstein question? It seems as if that people were only able to work themselves into a fever of excitement on some subject of such an unintelligible character and such shadowy merits that nobody out of Germany can understand it! Whilst they bear with the most stolid apathy the most insulting oppression from their own Governments, they are in a frenzy of sympathy for the sufferings of the Schleswig-Holsteiners, who are living under a far freer government than themselves. There is perhaps more than meets the eye at the back of this popular excitement in Germany. The Liberal Party are humiliated and irritated at the malorganization of the Confederacy. They would like to make a real Union of the forty millions of Germans, but they have tried in vain. Now the idea has possessed itself of the minds of a portion of the patriot party that a foreign war, especially with France, would unite the whole race and enable them to get rid of their little princes and even kings, and become a great Teutonic Empire. It is a terrible fact that this idea should have found favour with sedate and learned men of the professor class. Should a shot be fired on the Eider, it will have its echoes on the

Richard Cobden : The International Man

Rhine, Danube, and the Mincio. It would be in the power of Napoleon to bring upon Germany the Hungarians, Italians, Poles and Scandinavians. I should think that Austria and Prussia will thrust aside the agitators and smaller States, if they can, and occupy the frontier with their own troops and preserve the peace at all hazards. If not, it will be because the German *people* are resolved on war, in which case, like all wars of *peoples*, it will be a bloody struggle."

"August 18, 1864.

"It is long since we exchanged a letter. I do not know whether I am your debtor in our epistolary ledger. But I, at all events, have to thank you for the printed papers you have from time to time forwarded me, and which I have read with much interest, and heartily congratulate you on every step you have gained in your struggle for human rights and freedom. Whatever may be the fate of the war, *your* triumph will be a permanent gain for humanity.

"Along with your partisans generally in this country, I am looking with deep and constant solicitude to the progress of your terrible struggle. There is, however, a constant struggle in my breast against my paramount abhorrence of war as a means of settling disputes, whether between nations or citizens of one country. If it were not for the interest which I feel in the fate of the slaves, and the hardly inferior interest in the removal of that stigma of slavery from your character as a free Christian community, I should turn with horror from the details of your battles, and wish only for peace on any terms. As it is, I cannot help asking myself whether it can be within the designs of a merciful God that even a good work should be accomplished at the cost of so much evil to the world.

The Civil War and the Sumner Letters

"I have been much disappointed with the result so far of the Virginia campaign. I suppose it has been inevitable. But we were told by those who ought to have been well informed that you were approaching Richmond with three armies, any one of which was able to cope with the rebels. Now, however, we see two of these armies disappear from the scene, and the third held in check by a portion of Lee's army, whilst he sends part of his forces to menace you within your own territory and even to threaten your capital. All this, of course, tends to confirm nine-tenths of our politicians here in their belief that the success of the North is impossible. For my own part, having never considered that the issue depended on fighting, but on the sapping and mining of the social evil of the South, I still look forward with unabated confidence to the triumph of the North.

"But I begin to speculate on the effects which the failure of Grant's campaign may have on your *politics*. Sometimes I speculate on the possibility of your imitating the course which political parties often follow here, and that your Democrats, who *appear* to be for peace, may come into power and carry out even more successfully than *your* party could do the policy of war and abolition of slavery. Like Peel in his course of Free Trade and Catholic Emancipation, they would have the advantage of being sure of the support of the honest advocates of the policy they adopted, even although they were nominally in the ranks of their political opponents. What I most dread is your falling into political confusion in the North. That would be a severe blow to the principle of self-government everywhere.

"I must not omit to mention that my friend Mr. Goldwin Smith, Professor of Modern History at the University of Oxford, goes out by the *Europa* for a

Richard Cobden : The International Man

visit to the States. He needs no personal introductions, and I have given him no letters. But I need not tell you that he deserves well of your country. He is one of the few men moving in his sphere who have given a hearty and most brilliant support to your cause."

"*January* 11, 1865.

"I agree with a remark in the concluding passage of your last letter—that you are fighting the battle of Liberalism in Europe as well as the battle of freedom in America. It is only necessary to observe who are your friends and who your opponents in the Old World to be satisfied that great principles are at stake in your terrible conflict. But it is not by victories in the field alone that you will help the cause of the masses in Europe. End when it may, the Civil War will, in the eyes of mankind, have conferred quite as much 'glory,' so far as mere fighting goes, on the South as on the North. It is in your superiority in other things that you can alone by your example elevate the Old World. I confess I am very jealous of your taking a course which seems to hold up our old doings as an excuse for your present shortcomings. Hence I was sorry to see your republication of the old indictment against us in your very able and learned pamphlet. My answer is that your only title to existence as a Republic is that you are supposed to be superior to what we were sixty years ago. Had you returned the *Florida* to Bahia without a moment's delay, cashiered the captain of the *Wachusetts*, and offered to pay for the support of the survivors who were dependent on those who were killed or drowned in that wicked outrage, your friends would have felt some inches taller here. *That* would have been the true answer to the taunts of our Tory Press, and not the disinterment of the misdeeds of our Tory

The Civil War and the Sumner Letters

Government to show that they did something almost as bad as the Federal commander.

"You see I am taking the liberty of ancient friendship with you; and whilst in the vein, let me ask, What is the meaning of the Bobadil strain in which the New York *Times* treats the Canadian question? We are accustomed to disregard the *Herald* as an Ishmaelite organ which represented no political party, and whose proprietor was a renegade Scotchman. But *The Times*, with Mr. Raymond at its head, was supposed to be something different. I confess, however, I never saw anything from Mr. Gordon Bennett's paper more calculated to weaken your good influence over this country than the article to which I refer. Are we henceforth to have two *New York Heralds* instead of one? But enough of this vein.

"I observe an attempt by *The Times* (London) correspondent at New York to make it appear that the American public are again beginning to apprehend European intervention in some form. I do not believe there is the remotest risk of anything of the kind. You will, I hope, have soon got possession of all the ports of entry in the South, and re-established your custom-houses; when that is done, I do not see how a collision of misunderstanding with a neutral maritime Power can possibly arise.

"I was much pleased with your speech on the Canadian difficulty in the Senate, where you spoke of avoiding all quarrels with other countries and devoting yourself to the one sole object of putting down the rebellion. I am not blind to the fact that very grave questions will stand over for adjustment between your country and ours. Some of them, such as the injury done to your *whole* shipping interest by the losses and destruction of a part, can hardly be settled by Governments. They

Richard Cobden : The International Man

will, I fear, invite future retaliation on our shipping by citizens of your country, if *we* should ever go to war. But all these questions must be postponed till your war is ended, and then probably the whole world may be ready for a thorough revolution in international maritime law. It will be for you to show the way.

"I wish I could see more intelligence in your midst on questions of finance and political economy. Your Congress seems to me just about on a level with the British Parliament in 1818, before Huskisson commenced his first reforms of our fiscal system, which were afterwards followed up by Peel and Gladstone. I have always considered it a great misfortune that the New Englanders, who have been the schoolmasters of the Union, should have thought themselves interested in the policy of 'Protection.' They have spread the heresy over the land. However, I have great faith in the intelligence of your people, *after they shall have been in the school of adversity*.

"I observe that your Secretary of the Navy calls for Government yards. As a rule, all heads of departments wish to become manufacturers. In this country they have contrived to inveigle us into all kinds of undertakings, and it has been found very unprofitable. We are now trying to make our Government resort to private enterprise for the supply of their wants. But it is very difficult to retrace our steps. I send you a couple of copies of a speech I made on this subject last year. Pray put them into the hands of parties taking an interest in the subject."

"*March* 5, 1865.

"I feel it a pleasant duty to give you my best congratulations on the recent proceedings within and without your Halls of Congress. The vote on the

The Civil War and the Sumner Letters

amendment of the Constitution was a memorable and glorious event in your history. Another incident—that of your introduction of a coloured man to the Supreme Court—was hardly less interesting. In all these proceedings at Washington *you* ought to be allowed to indulge the feelings of a triumphant general. You served as a volunteer in the forlorn hope when the battle of emancipation seemed a hopeless struggle. *Your* position within the walls of Congress was very different from that of the agitators out of doors, meritorious as were their labours. I have served in both capacities, and know the difference between addressing an audience of partisans at a public meeting and a hostile Parliamentary assembly. The rapid progress of events and the sudden transformations of opinion must impart a constant excitement to your life; it must be something like the movements of the kaleidoscope! I heartily congratulate you, and wish I could shake hands and have a chat with you on all that is passing. Looking on from this distance, I cannot doubt that your *great* military operations are drawing to a close. The war is being driven into a corner. A few months must decide the fate of the armies in the field. If Lee is beaten, I see no other great army, and the Southern people are too intelligent to attempt to protract the struggle into a guerrilla warfare. But it is useless to offer speculations here on events which will be realized probably ere you receive this.

"I observe an attempt to alarm you with the prospect of European intervention. I need not tell you that this is the purest fiction. Nothing of the kind is now possible. You know that at first I was very apprehensive. And you know also that from the first the French Government has been courting the alliance of England in a scheme of intervention. 'Barkis is

Richard Cobden : The International Man

willing' has been the constant language of Napoleon to Madame Britannia. It is nothing but your great *power* that has kept the hands of Europe off you. When a deputation of free-traders applied to Minister Guizot in 1846 for authorization to hold meetings to agitate for Free Trade, they received permission, with the benediction 'Soyez fort, et nous vous protégerons.' This is about the amount of what your friends in Europe have been able to do for you. There is no denying the fact that your terrible struggle has demonstrated an amount of hostility on the part of the ruling class here, and the ruling powers of Europe generally, towards your democratic institutions, for which none of us were prepared. Still, it must not be forgotten that the common people of England were true to the cause of freedom. It has never been possible to call a public open meeting, *with notice*, to pass a resolution in favour of the rebellion. It would have been voted down by the working men. I know you are greatly and justly angered at the conduct of our upper classes —but do not forget the attitude of the workers.

"PS. I am more alarmed at the politico-economical delusions that prevail in your high places than at the arms of the rebels. Who is Mr. 'Maximum' Stephens, who thinks he can control the price of gold if he can only induce a majority of Congress to agree with him? The serious part of it is that he has so large a following.

"You have a most serious task before you, when the war ends, in clearing away the wreck and adjusting your pecuniary, political and social difficulties. The country is revelling in a Saturnalia of greenbacks and Government expenditure, and is under the delusion that it is a genuine prosperity. It is destined to a rude disenchantment, and this will test the statesmanship of the Republican Party."

CHAPTER XIII

COBDEN AND MODERN INTERNATIONALISM

In any attempt to appreciate Cobden's services to the cause of internationalism, and his position as an International Man, it is essential to clear away certain misunderstandings and misrepresentations which have gathered round his policy of non-intervention. Though primarily a peace policy, non-intervention is both less and more. It did not make Cobden a "peace at any price man"—an opponent of all war. Some war and some preparation for war he regarded as hateful necessities for a country living in a world where moral force had not everywhere and always got the upper hand. Nor does he advance the opinion that no war is ever justifiable except one undertaken for self-defence. He sometimes[1] admitted that a case might arise where a powerful nation was rightly called upon to take up arms for the protection of another weaker nation, or to assist the liberation of a subject and oppressed people. But he would have insisted that such a case must be extremely rare. For the right and obligation of such forcible interference must be justified first by considerations of our knowledge and our power. The Palmerstonian interventions had little regard to either. They were urged irrespective of reliable information as to the full facts and merits of the case, or of our capacity to intervene effectively in the interests of justice. But

[1] But compare p. 400.

Richard Cobden : The International Man

not only ought we to be sure of the equity and efficacy of our intervention, and that we are not secretly misled by some inherent pugnacity or some interested motives of our own ; we ought also to consider whether our forcible intervention may not involve the neglect of more sacred and more imperative duties at home. A naturally pugnacious people is likely to yield too easily to the temptation to undertake a spirited foreign enterprise under the direction of a statesman with an arbitrary domineering temper.

But non-intervention with Cobden meant more than abstinence from aggressive or other unnecessary wars. It meant a reduction of foreign policy, in its governmental, diplomatic sense, to the smallest possible dimensions. Sound internationalism could not be brought about by arrangements between governments. Such relations were governed by motives and conducted by methods positively detrimental to the free pacific intercourse of individuals. The classes of Government officials who conducted diplomacy, and the methods they employed, were poisoned by obsolete traditions of suspicion and hostility, the survivals of a world in which statecraft expressed the conflicting interests of rival dynasties and not the common benefits of peoples. The ignorance and the singular ineptitude for understanding the needs and interests of foreign nations which distinguish our governing classes made a very powerful impression upon Cobden, who took so much trouble to equip himself with the sort of knowledge which they lacked. He knew how perilous a foreign policy conducted by such men must be. So he concluded the less of it the better. If the peoples are to get into sane, amicable and mutually profitable relations with one another, that intercourse is best promoted by leaving it to them, with as little inter-

Cobden and Modern Internationalism

ference as possible either in the way of help or hindrance by their respective Governments.

Cobden's conviction of the essential rightness of this non-intervention policy was confirmed by the whole tenor of his public life. Growing up to manhood amid the poverty and degradation which were the sequel of the French War, he witnessed in his lifetime a constant recurrence of the peril. Now with France, now with Russia, now with the United States, we were embroiled at short intervals, in pursuance of that "filthy idol" (as Bright called it) the Balance of Power, or for the supposed furtherance of our colonial or commercial interests. With a single exception, we escaped the actual disaster of war with a great European Power. But the lesson of that war, its initiation, its conduct and its consequences, was such as to impress upon any sane-thinking man the enormity of the abuses to which a spirited foreign policy was prone. Cobden did not, indeed, live to hear a British Prime Minister confess that in the Crimean War "We had put all our money upon the wrong horse." But that war was to him the crucial experiment which proved the validity of his principle of non-intervention. It was reinforced by a whole array of lesser instances, the threats, the diplomatic bullying, the naval demonstrations, the punitive expeditions and minor wars with which the Victorian age, and especially the Palmerstonian section of it, was richly strewn.

Nor was it foreign policy alone that suffered from this vice. Our rule in India and in our colonies was rife with the same spirit of aggression and aggrandizement, in which trading interests commonly conspired with bureaucratic pride and rapacity. The terrible political and moral reactions of imperialism upon the subject peoples and upon the government and social life of our own nation were enforced by many instances. More

Richard Cobden : The International Man

clearly than any man in his time, Cobden detected the blighting influence of that unconscious hypocrisy which distinguishes the modern from the older imperialism—the parade of moral, religious and other laudable motives in which the secret lust of political and economic sway conceals itself. For he alone had acquired, from long persistent study, the actual knowledge enabling him to detect the intricate interplay of interests and motives which gives inner meaning to the processes of imperialism. The colonial policy of his time exhibited, indeed, one episode of supreme folly, not in the way of intervention but of non-intervention. It was the exception that proved the rule. Colonial self-government, extended in Cobden's time to our white colonies, was in itself a distinct movement towards non-intervention. But might it not have been accompanied by a stipulation that would have secured complete and lasting freedom of commerce among the peoples of the self-governing States ? Cobden felt that here a great opportunity had been lost for the promotion of actual internationalism (for our Dominions are nations) upon a sound footing. The same line of reasoning by which his negotiation of the French Treaty was defended is also applicable here. Such a provision, attached to the charters of self-government, though formally a limitation and restraint, would have operated to secure freedom of trade throughout our vast Empire, and to abate the jealousy with which other commercial nations have been disposed to regard our territorial possessions.

Non-intervention, thus interpreted in the light of the experience of Cobden's times, appeared to claim assent on grounds of reason, justice and utility.

The idea of a constructive foreign policy as an instrument of internationalism could not, he felt, seriously be entertained. For, wherever concerted action of a government was undertaken, it was always for the further coercion of some other government. Non-intervention was therefore, *ipso facto*, a double gain for amicable relations between nations, for by removing the active obstacles of diplomacy, war, and protective tariffs it enabled the mutual interests and good feelings of the peoples to operate freely.

It must not be forgotten, however, that the non-intervention policy of Cobden and his school was not merely a policy of external relations. It was the application of the same principle which led them to oppose all or most extensions of governmental powers for the regulation of the internal relations of citizens. Government was conceived as a bad thing in itself, always oppressive to individuals, frequently unjust, nearly always expensive and inefficient. A country had to bear government for its sins, as a provision against enemies outside and enemies within. Armaments and police were the essence of government. The more rigorous logic of this *laissez-faire* thought and policy dictated an opposition to the entire body of the factory laws and other State regulations of industry, and to all public provision or enforcement of sanitation and education. Their economic theory taught these thinkers to believe that unrestricted freedom of contract and of exchange would secure the greatest, surest, and most rapid growth of industrial prosperity, and that the natural play of competition under the pressure of self-interest would win for all classes their proper share. Their political Liberalism was thus directed almost wholly to the removal of the various impediments which law and custom offered to the free play of this enlightened self-interest. To Free Trade must be added removal of restrictions upon the transfer or the use of land, upon freedom of movement and settlement of labour, the repeal of "taxes upon knowledge," and the establishment of full religious liberty and equality, by the abolition of religious tests for Universities and public offices, by abolition of Church rates and the disestablishment of the State Church. This Liberalism on its constitutional side usually comprehended an extension of the franchise towards full self-government of the nation, and the absorption of all real governmental power in the hands of the representative House.

Cobden, like other thinkers, brought his personal variations into this creed. He did not, for instance, carry his opposition to all factory legislation so far as to oppose legislative restraints upon the hours of employment for children. Indeed, he was throughout his life a vigorous advocate of popular schools for working-class children, and supported in the House of Commons the education clauses in Sir James Graham's Factory Act of 1844. "In the case of children, Cobden fully perceived that freedom of contract is only another name for freedom of coercion, and he admitted the necessity of legislative protection."[1] As regards adult workers he recognized no such necessity. Familiar as he was with the terribly bad conditions of labouring life both in agriculture and in town industry, he persistently adhered to the conviction that governments could do nothing useful to remedy them, but that all effective remedies must come from individual energy and intelligence. He even accepted the ordinary position of the employing class, that trade unions were "founded upon principles of brutal tyranny and monopoly,"[2] and could do nothing effective to improve the general status of the labouring classes. Nor did he appear to recognize the inequality of permitting employers to combine for the regulation both of prices and of wages, while workmen were legally restricted. This view, how-

[1] Morley's "Life," i. 298.
[2] Letter to F. W. Cobden, August 16, 1842.

Cobden and Modern Internationalism

ever, was by no means due to any lack of enthusiasm for the improvement in the condition of labour, but to an unshakable conviction that individual bargaining was the only adequate method of obtaining it. In 1836 he summarized his view in the following language[1]: "I know it has been found easier to please the people by holding out flattering and delusive prospects of cheap benefits to be derived from Parliament rather than by urging them to a course of self-reliance; but while I will not be the sycophant of the great, I cannot become the parasite of the poor; and I have sufficient confidence in the growing intelligence of the working classes to be induced to believe that they will now be found to contain a great proportion of minds sufficiently enlightened by experience to concur with me in this opinion, that it is to themselves alone individually that they, as well as every other great section of the community, must trust for working out their own regeneration and happiness. Again I say to them, '*Look not to Parliament; look only to yourselves.*'"

It was partly this general disbelief in the virtue of government, and partly the conviction that effective reform in his time could best be achieved by the activities of the propertied middle class, that made Cobden somewhat tepid in his support of franchise extensions, and averse to placing any high value upon changes in political machinery. This sentiment was expressed in 1849 when, writing to Mr. Sturge in relation to Parliamentary Reform, he said: "I do not oppose the principle of giving men a control over their own affairs. I must confess, however, that I am less sanguine than I used to be about the effects of a wide extension of the franchise."[2] Elsewhere he gives this interesting commentary upon his change of view: "The citadel

[1] Letter to W. C. Hunt, October 21, 1836 (quoted, Morley).
[2] "Life," i. 37.

Richard Cobden : The International Man

of privilege in this country is so terribly strong, owing to the concentrated masses of property in the hands of the comparatively few, that we cannot hope to assail it with success unless with the help of the propertied classes in the middle ranks of society, and by raising up a portion of the working class to become members of a propertied order." [1]

His mind upon the matter is made even clearer by an interesting passage in a letter to Mr. Bright, written in 1859, when the latter was urging a comprehensive policy of financial reform and seeking to rally behind it a democratic sentiment. "You seem," he writes, "to take the working classes too exclusively under your protection. They are quite powerless as opposed to the middle and upper classes, which is a good reason why they should not be allowed to be made to appear to be in antagonism to both." [2]

In other words, Cobden, throughout the greater part of his career, believed that real political reforms, whether in legislation, foreign policy or finance, could only be accomplished in his time by the organized action of the intelligent middle classes, and that to bring in the uninstructed masses would alarm the substantial *bourgeoisie* and so strengthen the defences of the landed aristocracy, who were the real upholders of economic and political privilege.

This conviction of the desirable supremacy of the middle class, however, became sensibly modified in his later years, partly by disappointment with the warlike and imperialistic sentiments displayed by so many of his Free Trade adherents, partly by a growing recognition of the rightness and efficacy of the wider franchise to which his friend Bright devoted so much of his energy. It may, indeed, be fairly claimed that in his

[1] "Life," i. 53.   [2] Ibid., i. 347.

Cobden and Modern Internationalism

last years Cobden stood strongly for political democracy. Here are two passages from letters written in 1861:—

To Samuel Lucas.

"ALGIERS, *February* 23, 1861.

"There is more healthy Radicalism to be found scattered about our small towns and villages than in the larger boroughs. I mean that it is a more sturdy kind of democratic sentiment, for it goes directly against the feudal domination under which we really live, whereas in the great towns Radicalism often misses its mark and is assailing some insignificant grievance."

To William Hargreaves.

"ALGIERS, *March* 1, 1861.

"I wonder the working people are so quiet under the taunts and insults offered them. Have they no Spartacus among them to lead a revolt of the slave class against their political tormentors? I suppose it is the reaction from the follies of Chartism which keeps the present generation so quiet. However, it is certain that so long as five millions of men are silent under their disabilities it is quite impossible for a few middle-class members of Parliament to give them liberty, and this is the language I shall use when called on to speak to them. It is bad enough that we have a political machine that will not move till the people put their shoulders to the wheel. But we must face things as they are, and not live in a dreamland of our own making. The middle class have never gained a step in the political scale without long labour and agitation out of doors, and the working people may depend on it they can only rise by similar efforts, and the more plainly they are told so the better."

Richard Cobden : The International Man

From these letters, however, appear also the limitations of Cobden's democracy. He had little use for anything that could be called economic democracy, nor did he adequately recognize that an effective political democracy was impossible so long as the existing economic bondage survived. In some measure he was alive to this truth as it was illustrated in the rural feudalism. But he never saw its significance as a condemnation of the factory system and its town proletarianism.

As we look back upon that period, it is difficult for us to understand how a man of Cobden's keen intelligence and profound sympathy with injustice could fail to recognize the wrongs, the cruelty and oppression which underlay the normal methods by which the new middle-class prosperity was built up. On the one hand, the amazing growth of rich new families in Lancashire is for us quite discernibly due to causes in which the skill, intelligence and industry of the individuals who were said to have "made" this wealth played but a minor part. They contributed very little to the immense value of the new industrialism which machinery and steam-power brought into being. On the other hand, this growth of wealth was demonstrably conditioned by the use of masses of ill-paid, ill-clad, ill-housed, short-lived and degraded workers, whose overdriven toil was coined into these swollen profits.

If Cobden was blind to these truths, it was due to no lack of natural humanity, to no calculated selfishness. It was in the main a fault of intellectual and moral perspective, shared by most of the best men of his day, and aggravated by the too facile acceptance of a philosophy which, by the very stress it laid upon human liberty and equality, deceived its votaries into an excessive valuation of the powers of individual intelligence and will to achieve success and happiness.

Cobden and Modern Internationalism

Putting the matter on a more concrete basis, Cobden and his friends saw the power of landlords to impose oppressive and unjust conditions in substantially unfair bargains. They did not see that the entire system of industry and commerce was honeycombed with similar inequalities of bargaining power which stamp injustice and oppression in a hundred different ways upon society. Capitalism was to them the liberator of the people from the shackles of feudal landlordism. If its blessings were spread somewhat unevenly or were disguised, if some classes seemed to gain more than others, that was due partly to necessary friction in the play of the new economic forces, partly to the superior intelligence, industry, thought and other economic virtues which led some persons to avail themselves of opportunities which lay open to all alike, but which so many others neglected.

It was hardly to be expected that the beneficiaries of the new order should be keenly alive to the defects of that order. Engaged as were Cobden and his friends in fighting older evils that were real and deep-rooted, they were inevitably blinded to most of the evils in the new business world whose claims they championed. Though there existed even in the early decades of the nineteenth century powerful exponents of the claims of labour and of the co-operative as distinguished from the competitive system of society, the prosperous middle classes were incapable of recognizing the moral frailty of the fabric of their prosperity.[1] Schools of economists and social philosophers arose to furnish them with intellectual spiritual defences and to comfort them with the conviction that prosperity was the natural reward of virtue. Though not often openly avowed, the blunt verdict of Tennyson's Northern Farmer, that "the poor in the

[1] For valuable testimony to this truth see Mr. and Mrs. Hammond's "The Town Labourer," chaps. x. and xi.

Richard Cobden : The International Man

loomp is bad," was the self-flattering assumption of most of the respectable middle classes in mid-Victorian days.

This moral and intellectual atmosphere prevented Cobden from realizing adequately the fact that a middle-class Government was incapable of doing justice to the claims and needs of the masses. It also prevented him from recognizing that only if, as he would have admitted, liberty meant not only the absence of interference but the presence of opportunities, there was a great deal more work for governments to undertake than the mere task of keeping order in the competitive ring.

It was evident to him that children without access to education were not really free, and he was prepared for State interference to secure for them this liberty. We now recognize that, unless every human being has full opportunity of realizing all his healthy human needs and faculties, he is not really free, and that for the attainment of this freedom the operation of the collective as well as the individual will is necessary. This idea is everywhere transforming the conception of government, assigning to it a growing wealth of positive constructive functions in the furtherance of individual liberty. To take a single example: it is admitted that physical health is a prime condition of personal freedom. But individuals cannot secure this condition for themselves. There must also be public health, with restraints and aids which can only be applied by government. If these powers are wisely exercised, they cease to be resented as interference and come to be recognized as public benefits.

I have dwelt at some length upon the supersession of the principle of non-intervention or *laissez-faire* in internal affairs, because it has an important bearing upon international relations. If it seemed unreasonable to expect that government could make any positive con-

Cobden and Modern Internationalism

tribution to the liberty and happiness of individuals within a country, still less reasonable did it seem to expect that the governments of different countries could pursue any fruitful process of co-operation for the common benefit of the society of nations. Foreign policy was so deeply rooted in mischievous theories, so "enslaved by the black magic of dead words"[1] so poisoned with suspicion, jealousy, selfishness and all the separatist and antagonizing motives, that it should be kept at a minimum. In order to get the peoples to co-operate peacefully and effectively, keep their governments as much as possible apart. For the contacts of governments are normally hostile; even when governments get together in Alliances or Concerts, the underlying motives are the exercise of diplomatic or military force against other countries for the realization of their own separate or jointly selfish aims. This conception of foreign relations was not wholly justified. The Balance of Power, perilous as was the mechanical arrangement of force which underlay it, had some real regard to the peace of Europe, and the action of the Concert was in part directed to this object. But when foreign affairs were in the hands of such a man as Palmerston, it was difficult to realize safety and humanity in any other terms than those of non-intervention. Thus Cobden's early conviction was confirmed in every period of his political career by conspicuous examples of the perils and wrongs attending "a spirited foreign policy." If governments would keep their hands off and allow the mutual interests of free commercial intercourse to weave bonds of union between peoples, peace on earth and good-will among nations would be secured, the waste and provocation of armaments would disappear, and the material and moral resources of every nation would be

[1] Delisle Burns, "The Morality of Nations," p. 236.

Richard Cobden : The International Man

available for the improvement of the national life and for the enrichment of humanity.

The uncompromising attitude maintained by Cobden throughout his life upon the duty of non-intervention is perhaps best illustrated by the following passage from a private letter written in 1858 :[1] " You rightly interpret my views when you say I am opposed to any armed intervention in the affairs of other countries. I am against any interference by the government of one country in the affairs of another nation, even if it be confined to moral suasion. Nay, I go further, and disapprove of the formation of a society or organization of any kind in England for the purpose of interfering in the internal affairs of other countries. I have always declined to sanction anti-slavery organizations formed for the purpose of agitating the slavery question in the United States."

To most men of our time this doctrine of non-intervention seems no longer tenable, while, on the other hand, the economic intercourse between nations sometimes appears as a fomenter of conflicts in the business world which embroil governments and imperil pacific relations. Many men of Liberal upbringing and traditions have been tempted to belittle Cobden as a statesman because he relied overmuch upon the logic of Free Trade as destined to convince the intelligence and reform the fiscal and commercial policy of other States, and so to furnish a reliable cement of pacific internationalism. Things, they say, have turned out very differently. The governments of other nations have not seen their national interests in the light of Cobden's teaching, but quite otherwise. Overseas trade has become more and more not a mutually profitable interchange of goods, but a field of struggle between rival groups of traders supported by their governments. The foreign policy of every

[1] To Mrs. Schwabe, " Reminiscences," p. 299

Cobden and Modern Internationalism

Power has engaged itself continually more with pushing by diplomatic or forcible methods the commercial claims of its business classes. So far from foreign commerce bringing peace, it is maintained that "most modern wars are for markets," in the sense that the underlying motives and pressure, as distinguished from the immediate political precipitation, are of commercial origin. Most governments, instead of abolishing or lowering their tariffs, have raised them, and have put more restrictions upon free importation from foreign countries. Imperial and colonial aggrandizement has been largely inspired by a survival or a recrudescence of the very mercantilist superstitions which Cobden thought were disappearing from statecraft, the craving for exclusive or preferential markets and for territorial possessions to be developed for the peculiar benefit of the imperial or colonizing Power.

Now the element of truth in this criticism is for the most part attributable to economic developments, the character or the pace of which neither Cobden nor any other statesman of his time could have foreseen. Great Britain in his lifetime was in a very real sense "the workshop of the world." Though it was evident that other countries would copy the great factory system which she first erected, and would participate in the new world trade which railways and steamships were developing, neither economists, nor business men, nor statesmen foresaw the new conflicts to which this pressure for foreign markets was destined to give rise. If, as seemed only reasonable, it was as important to buy as to sell, the possibility of providing so many goods that they could not all find quick and profitable markets was an absurd supposition. Cobden, like most enlightened men of his time, looked forward to the time when France, Germany, Italy and other countries would be equipped

Richard Cobden : The International Man

with their own manufacturing plant and when the immense productive powers of the United States, in particular, would be organized for manufacture and commerce. But he saw no reason for alarm, quite the contrary, in this enlargement by each nation of its productive powers. Wealth could not be produced too fast, for the wants of man were illimitable. Each nation, by improving its own arts of industry and commerce, was also by a natural necessity adding to the wealth of every other nation with which, directly or indirectly, it was in contact.

Why should Cobden be blamed for not perceiving, what nobody of his time perceived, that, for some mysterious reasons which economists do not even now explain, the aggregate productive power of the industrial world, suddenly enhanced by the adoption of the new mechanical arts by a number of nations, would so largely outstrip the effective demand for the goods which they produced as to convert friendly competition into cut-throat hostility? When after 1870 all the Great Powers were advancing rapidly on the new industrial road, and most of them began to safeguard their home markets against importers in favour of their native goods, the backward countries of the world became areas of increasing solicitude to competing groups of traders and to the governments of their respective countries. The hustle for foreign markets, to take off the continually increasing surplus product which could not be marketed at home at profitable prices, then set in, and powerfully organized trades, especially in the textile and metal industries, began to strengthen their hold upon their governments, so as to secure tariffs for the protection of the home market and diplomatic aid for winning foreign markets.

Far more important and less predictable, however, was the later economic and political situation brought about by the rapid growth of foreign investments and the direct exploitation of the natural resources and the labour of foreign countries by members of the more developed Western nations. The stake which a trader has in the material prosperity and the good government of a foreign country to which he sells cotton, cloth, guns, gin, cooking stoves or furs, while he imports rubber, coffee, cotton, ivory or oil, is no doubt considerable, and if he can get his Chambers of Commerce to bring pressure on his government to support or to extend this trade by diplomatic or any other means, he will be disposed to do so. But, after all, his stake in the trade with a particular country is limited and fluctuating. If he finds his market falling off in one country, he can push for a market in another, and there are various countries willing and eager to supply the foodstuffs and materials he wants to buy. But when trade in the narrow sense has developed into " peaceful penetration " of an area in Africa or a South Sea island, trade begins to be supplemented by factories and collecting stations. You have now the more substantial stake of a trading settlement where white men live and sometimes keep their families, and from which they stretch out economic tentacles into the surrounding country, organizing the natives for production and transport of the natural produce, and setting up stores in the interior for the disposal of the manufactured goods which they import.

But this is only the initial stage in the more elaborate processes of development to which backward countries with rich natural resources, large submissive populations and weak or corrupt governments, are everywhere subjected. When money is lent to Eastern potentates for personal extravagance or to purchase warships; when canals, railways, docks and other solid foundations of civilization are supplied; when concessions to prospect for and work mines and to acquire land for plantations are obtained; when brand-new cities are built by Western enterprise and capital, the stake established in this foreign country is far bigger, more solid and more permanent.

Moreover, the business methods by which these schemes are financed and carried into operation involve the formation of powerful companies controlled by men of great influence, not only in the world of business but in that of politics. Foreign policy was thus destined more and more to come under the secret or open control of powerful financial groups, with great funds for investment at their disposal, whose success in making money depended to a large extent, directly or indirectly, upon governmental assistance. Obstructive governments must be bullied, competitors from other leading countries must be kept out, the rights of concessionaires must be enforced, foreign lives and property must be protected against mob violence or official injustice. The acquisition, protection and enlargement of these solid permanent stakes in backward countries have furnished the greater part of the inflammatory material in modern foreign policy, keeping alive all the time various issues between the Western Powers which at any moment might develop into dangerous conflicts. Some of this finance of foreign exploitation is sufficiently cosmopolitan in structure and methods to keep the Powers acting for a time in precarious Concert, as in the case of the six-, five-, or four-Power groups for Chinese loans. But for the most part competition runs along national lines, and each national group claims that its foreign and colonial policy shall be at its beck and call. The roots of this economic expansion of England run, of course, far back in our adventurous history, and have always played a prominent part in our colonial and foreign policy. But modern

Cobden and Modern Internationalism

conditions have made this political pressure of finance dominant as a directing agency. Cobden, as we have seen, encountered several notable examples of its activity, and the famous Don Pacifico case evoked a formal endorsement of the claim of private profiteers upon their government which inspired new confidence in adventurous business circles. But though the earlier loans to Turkey and Egypt came within Cobden's time, and he was quick to discern the new perils they brought into foreign policy, it was afterwards that the full flood of overseas investment with backward countries began to surge. The development of our own railway system, followed by that of the United States and our own Dominions, took off the great bulk of our surplus national savings during the middle of the nineteenth century. Not until the late seventies and the eighties, when machine industry and steam transport were developed by all the advanced nations of the West, did the immense expansion of overseas investment with backward countries transform the economics and the politics of the world. In every country there were strong financial and trading companies competing for overseas markets and financial properties. Foreign investments in this initial stage do not, of course, differ from ordinary export trade. For the money loaned to foreign governments or princes, or invested in their railways, harbours, plantations, mines and cities, means so much effective demand on the part of foreigners for British engines, machines, stores, or for goods obtained from other foreign countries, involving by roundabout trade a payment in terms of British exports. The difference comes later on, when the British capital is absorbed and fixed in irremovable concrete forms on a foreign soil, with its profitable use dependent upon the good government and social order of that country. The size, precarious-

Richard Cobden : The International Man

ness and influential manipulation of these large permanent stakes constitute the dominant factor in modern foreign policy.

Cobden could not forecast the full significance of this factor, and this disability more than anything else explains his too sanguine view of the spread of Free Trade and the healing and pacific influence of all economic intercourse between nations.

He could not foresee how with the ever-growing surplus of saving in the older countries over and above the demands for profitable home uses, and with the rapid expansion of credit institutions, the rush for lucrative investments overseas was destined to stimulate fierce conflicts between strong business groups, capable of being transferred, first into diplomatic, and afterwards, in extreme cases, into military and naval struggles.

Modern internationalists are no longer mere non-interventionalists, for the same reason that modern Radicals are no longer philosophic individualists. Experience has forced upon them the truth that governments are not essentially and of necessity the enemies of personal or national liberty, but that upon certain conditions they may become its creators, either by removing fetters or by furnishing the instruments of active co-operation by which both individuals and nations better realize themselves. These conditions for the liberative and creative service of the State are summed up in the term "democracy." They did not exist in this or any other European country in Cobden's time. He did not believe in the early practicability of popular self-government in any broad sense of the word. Governments, as he saw them, were necessarily controlled either by the aristocracy or by the new commercial middle classes, who were everywhere destined to displace the former rule. So far, therefore, as the

Cobden and Modern Internationalism

lives of the general population were concerned, all government must rank not as self-government but as interference. In the external policy of States it was still more obvious. For diplomacy and high politics were everywhere retained as the functions of a small privileged caste, working upon antiquated models which were neither understood nor influenced by representative bodies. Under such conditions it was entirely reasonable to look with jealous eyes upon every extension of governmental progress, whether at home or in foreign relations. Democracy alone can make the modern growth of the State compatible with individual liberty. What Cobden dreaded was "the servile State" which is actually upon us, and which can only be destroyed, not by cancelling the powers it has acquired, but by removing the servility. Extension of government has not been brought about, in this country at any rate, as the result of any accepted theory of State Socialism. Each new function has been taken on, either as a remedy for some concrete grievance which private enterprise seemed powerless to redress, or as an alternative to the oppressive power of some business monopoly, or, finally, as a means of securing such improvements in health, education and recreation as were in general demand and could not be profitably undertaken by private venture.

But only in proportion as national and local government become democratized do these new functions become really safe and salutary. In an oligarchy, or a sham-democratic State like ours, they continue to harbour interferences with liberty only less oppressive than the private tyrannies or the perilous neglects which they profess to remove.

In the domain of foreign policy the case for non-intervention, though, as we have seen, not absolutely

Richard Cobden : The International Man

practicable even in Cobden's lifetime, was substantially sound. For neither had the conditions ripened for a world intercourse which now makes constructive internationalism necessary, nor was it plausible to expect so radical a change in the heart and conduct of foreign policy as to make the organized, friendly co-operation of a Society of Nations seem a possibility. Non-intervention, in other words, was defensible and sound because genuine internationalism was impossible. It becomes possible so far and so fast as democracy gains ground within the several countries whose co-operation constitutes positive internationalism. For so long as the conduct and determination of foreign policy remain in the hands either of an aristocratic caste or a conspiracy of business interests, or a union of the two, the mediæval spirit of jealous statecraft will coalesce with modern business greed to keep alive and stimulate the combative separatist spirit in international relations. But, so far as the needs and interests of the peoples can find expression in foreign relations, the deep constant underlying identity of human interests will constantly react in efforts to mould international institutions that are favourable to co-operation. Much, perhaps most, of this co-operation will proceed, as it has begun, along other than political channels. The international government of the business world, its transport, trade, finance, may, after the political controls of war-time have passed, largely return to private management. The great internationalisms of religion, science, labour, hygiene and philanthropy, which have spread their elaborate network of associations and congresses, may remain for the most part outside politics. But in every one of these fields of free internationalism important occasions arise when inter-governmental aids and arrangements are necessary. In the business world it is exceedingly unlikely

Cobden and Modern Internationalism

that the inter-governmental control over trade, transport and finance which the war emergency has evoked will disappear for a considerable number of years. It may even extend its scope, taking in enemy and neutral countries which have lain outside, and establishing some sort of permanent inter-governmental control over the whole range of economic internationalism. The temporary necessity of rationing the world by means of inter-governmental agreement may furnish the first and most substantial basis for the constructive activity of that League of Nations in which, it is generally held, the sole hope for civilization resides.

Such swift transformations of half a century it was impossible for Cobden or for any other mid-Victorian statesman to forecast. Men born a generation later, in the closing decades of the nineteenth century, found themselves already hurried on in the eddying tide of the economic and political forces which, in their overhaste to remould the national States in terms of political and economic dominion, have plunged the whole world into disaster. As we look back, informed by the actual process of events, we can learn much from Cobden, both as the clearest-eyed and firmest principled interpreter of the visible tendencies of his time and as the statesman actuated more fully than any other by that practical enthusiasm of humanity which, recognizing as it does the rights and uses of nationality, finds expression in the ideas and the forms of internationalism.

APPENDIX

Letters from Cobden to Louis Kossuth and to Lord Dudley Stuart. From Midhurst, 27 September 1853.

Private. MY DEAR SIR, I found your esteemed letter here on coming from the sea-side yesterday.—Being always a day behind the news in this retired post, I have not heard of the intelligence of a rupture in the East which you say has reached you by electricity.—Are you quite sure that your correspondent has not misled you?—The electric telegraph is proverbially deceptive.—

You appear to be anxious that England should engage in hostilities in the East.—Pardon me, if I say, I believe, if you were, like myself, an Englishman, having, above all things an interest in the happiness of the mass of your countrymen, you would be of an opposite view.—With what object, looking to *their welfare*, are we to go to war with Russia or Austria? You allude to our commercial interests.—Now, I wholly repudiate the principle of going to war for a market.—The profits of our trade with Russia or Turkey would not in twenty years pay the cost of one year's hostilities.—Besides, I wholly differ from those who regard Russia as an anti-commercial country. . . .But let me not be understood as advocating Russian encroachments.—Here is the difficulty, I always have to encounter in discussing this question.—I am invited to go to war with Russia in defence of our trade with Turkey—and when in answer to this invitation I endeavour to prove that Russia is not less friendly to foreign trade than the Turks, I am instantly called upon to defend myself against the charge of advocating the aggressions of Russia—It is only when invited to go to war with her that I engage in the controversy about her commerce at all!

But, I do not conceal from myself that your object in wishing us to go to war is to promote the independence of your own Country.—This is a patriotic motive on your part, and I trust I have given proofs how much I honour Hungarian patriotism.—But on the other hand you will not refuse me the right—or, rather, exonerate me from the duty—of consulting English interests in this question.—I tell you candidly I do not consider that I am justified in plunging my Country into war to rectify the wrongs of other nations. The Almighty has not conferred upon me the right or the duty, or armed me with the power, as an Englishman, to execute his justice throughout the world.—But even if I were of an opposite opinion, —if I felt that I was bound to interfere by force of arms in your behalf— I would still oppose with all my might any warlike intervention on the part of *our government* in the affairs of the East;—for I am sure, whatever might be the pretended foreign policy of this country, it would not really be directed *to* the service of the *democracy* anywhere. I am sure I need not tell you, who have so well known how to appreciate the aristocratic regime under which we live in this Country, that our Foreign Office has very little sympathy for the cause of Hungary as represented by yourself or your fellow-patriots in exile.—We have had ministers who have *professed* great zeal in your behalf, and who have gained great popularity by their present efforts in your support, but you and I who have looked below the surface, know how hollow and insincere these professions have been.—There is one minister in particular, who is now called for by *shallow democrats*, on one side, and cunning Tories on the other, as the fit and proper man to resist the progress of despotism in the East; and oddly enough, that very statesman allowed Russia to pass over the body of Turkey to reach your heart in Hungary, without uttering even a protest in your favour;—and still more oddly, that same minister transferred to the Home Office, allows his myrmidons of the police to hunt you from house to house like a pickpocket, and yet a few fine phrases about Russian despotism/phrases which were never intended to be transferred into acts/at the close of the session are sufficient to set our cockney gobe-mouches in a phreensy of admiration for the champion of liberty—all over the world—*England excepted!*— Now what is a man of ordinary common sense or honesty to do, but to raise his protest against all intervention in foreign affairs, as the only means of protecting himself against such impostures?—You may say "no, take a part in foreign politics yourself, in order to prevent such deceptions."—I think I know sufficiently the force of the aristocratic principle in this country to comprehend what is possible and what is impracticable in the path of English politics.—In *home questions*, the people do from time to time carry a point, after long agitation.—Then, the aristocracy closes their ranks to recover from their disaster.—But in foreign politics the masses are too little informed to protect themselves against fraud; and depend on it we are, as a people, as yet too much addicted to an aristocratic organisation to tolerate, for the *personnel* of our government, any other class than that which at present composes our Executive Government.

To sum up then what I write to you:

I will not go to war for a market.

I will not trust our foreign minister to go to war for liberty.

Therefore, even if I could acknowledge that it is our duty as Englishmen to fight the battle of Freedom abroad/which I cannot/ I would still, under present circumstances, oppose to the utmost of my power all intervention on the part of our government, by force of arms in the quarrels of other countries.—I trust I need not add the assurance that it would be far more agreeable to me if I could write a note in harmony with the contents of your letter.—But I give you a honest expression of my views, which whatever they may be, is I know what alone you would wish to have—and believe me faithfully yours, R. COBDEN.

I must thank Dr Stephen Gál of Budapest for sending me a copy of this letter from Cobden to Louis Kossuth. The original is in the Private Letters of Richard Cobden to his Hungarian friends, preserved in the M.S.S. Collection of the Széchényi Library Budapest.

N.M.

Private. MY DEAR LD. D. STUART, You are the most scandalously ill-used gentleman of my acquaintance! Your good letter has been in my pocket many a day, whilst I was moving about at the sea-side, sometimes thinking of it when I had no check-book near, & then forgetting it when I had no such excuse. On my arrival here last night I found a letter from Kossuth in which he tells me that an electric telegraphic communication informs him that the first gun is fired in the East, & the purpose of his long letter seems to be to persuade me that we ought now to fire into Austria! I really cannot agree to a war for any pretence afforded by the present state of the "Orient". No good to us or any body else would come of our joining the Crescent against the Cross. Your friends the Turks are past all saving—I don't deny that they are nearly as good Christians as the Russians—but they are decaying under the influence of a religion the laws of which are opposed to the laws of nations, & therefore they cannot be preserved. If your young friend the Sultan were to turn Christian, and sweep out the Eunuchs and w—s who infest his palace, take a decent young woman from Germany for a wife & issue such a manifesto as would set Exeter Hall in a flame, he might preserve his European boundaries. But if not, not. You cannot preserve a Mahometan empire in Europe with a majority of Christian subjects. But I doubt whether Kossuth's information about a gun being fired is correct. I don't believe there will be any war. There is very likely to be an insurrection or a massacre of the Christians.

I enclose the £10—which you ought to have had long ago. Believe me truly yours, R. COBDEN

Communicated to me by Dr Thomas Kabdebo, from The Harrowby Archives
N.M.

SOME DATES IN THE CAREER OF RICHARD COBDEN

1804　　Born 3 June at Dunford in the hamlet of Heyshott near Midhurst, Sussex, the fourth child of a family of eleven.
1814–19　Sent to Bowes Hall School in Yorkshire.
1819　　Became clerk in his uncle's warehouse in Old Change.
1828　　Sets up business selling calico, Manchester.
1832　　Starts own factory, Sabden near Manchester.
1835　　First visit to the U.S.A. Publishes *England, Ireland, America by a Manchester man*.
1836–37　Visits Ottoman Empire, Egypt and Greece. Publishes *Russia*.
1837　　Stands as candidate for Stockport.
1838　　Helps to get Manchester incorporated. Becomes an alderman. Joins committee of Anti-Corn Law League. Till 1846 leading figure in Anti-Corn-Law agitation.
1840　　Marries Catherine Ann Williams from Wales.
1841　　Elected Member for Stockport. Persuades Bright on the death of his wife to dedicate himself to the Repeal of the Corn Laws.
1846　　Repeal of the Corn Laws. Cobden urges Peel in vain to lead the Radicals.
1846–47　Travels in France, Spain, Italy, Austria, Germany and Russia, interviewing, among others, Metternich and the Pope.
1847　　Becomes M.P. for the West Riding.
1849　　(12 June) Introduces motion in favour of international arbitration.
1849–53　Attends peace congresses at Paris 1849, Frankfurt 1850, London 1851, Manchester 1853, and Edinburgh 1853.
1850–51　Introduces motions (8 March 1850 and 12 June 1851) on international disarmament. Speaks against Palmerston's Don Pacifico. Royal Commissioner of Great Exhibition.
1851　　Meets Louis Kossuth at Winchester.
1853　　Publishes *How Wars are got up in India*

1854-55	Opposes Crimean War.
1855	Becomes adviser to peace paper *The Morning Star*
1856	6 April. Death of his only son.
	Publishes *What Next? and Next?*
	Helps to get arbitration clause in Peace of Paris.
1857	Introduces motion against Palmerston's support for Sir John Bowring's bombarding the Canton forts over the Arrow incident.
	Government defeated by 16.
	Cobden is defeated at Huddersfield in the general election.
1859	Second visit to the U.S.A.
	M.P. again for Rochdale. Refuses post of President of Board of Trade in Lord Palmerston's government.
1859-60	Negotiates Cobden—Chevalier Free Trade treaty with France.
1862	Publishes *The Three Panics*.
1861-65	Works to promote British neutrality during the American civil war.
1864	23 November. His last speech at Rochdale against Lord Palmerston's Schleswig-Holstein policy.
1865	Dies on 2 April.

INDEX

Aberdeen, Lord, 78, 121, 125, 128, 154, 167, 201, 284
Abolition and President Lincoln, 378-9; *see* Emancipation
Aborigines' Protection Society, 61, 240
Adams, Mr., American Minister, 309, 370-1
Advertiser, the, supports Palmerston, 203
Alabama, the, 295, 298, 309, 311, 327, 330, 372
Alcock, Sir R., 315
Algerian policy of France, 54
Algiers, holidays in, 260, 268, 278-9, 285
Alma, Battle of, 113
American Civil War, the, 281-2, 288-9, 331, 386
    arbitration, talk of, 360
    blockade during, 335, 352-3; *see* Blockade
    Cobden's sympathies concerning, 282
    Confederacy, Governmental attitude toward, 290
    cotton-spinners affected by, 366-8
    false prosperity during, 386
    international aspects of, 12, 13, 295
    intervention, Cobden opposed to, 300, 306-7; rumours of, 385-6
    Lancashire, effects of, in, 335
    Northern States, increasing sympathy with, 369
    smuggling during, 363
American Constitution, amendment of the, 384
American journalism, 176, 191, 214
    Cobden on, 310
American sympathizers hanged in Cuba, 77
Anglo-Saxon race, the, 171
Annexation of territory by Great Britain and Russia, 32
    fruits of, 338-9
Anonymity of the Press, 213-15
Anti-Corn Law agitation, 194
    League, 36; Cobden's speech at dissolution of, 38-9
    propaganda, 40-1
    repeal, Act of, 9

Arbitration, Bunsen on, 99
    Cobden's plan of, 55-6
    Committee for, 294
    Paris Peace Conference, at the, 56-7
    United States, and, 360
Arlès-Dufour, 7; letters to, 43-5, 246, 270-1, 296-8, 321
Armaments, limitation of, 76, 85, 91, 168
    Convention proposed by Cobden, 279
    cost of, 211, 263; general desire for, 336
    domestic order, to maintain, 337
    French and British memorial relating to, 282-4; possibilities of an understanding concerning, 287-8; discouragement concerning, 289, 291
Army, difficulty of recruiting the, 139-40
Arrow, seizure of the, 192-3, 195-6, 200
Athenæum, the, 79
Austria, alliance with, 177-8
    Cobden in, 50
    France, war with, 242
    German Confederation, heads the, 69
    Governmental murders in, 188-90
    revolution in, 54, 69

Balance of Power, the, 10, 26, 33, 177, 179, 301-2, 323, 330, 389, 399
Baronetcy, Cobden refuses a, 260
Barracks, Cobden on demoralizing influence of, 63, 76-7
Bastiat, 7, 41, 46, 273; his work on "Cobden and the League," 273
Baxter, Member for Dundee, 157-8
Belgium, fears for, 92
Berlin, Free Trade banquet at, 30-1
Blockade, effects of, 295, 299-300, 335, 349, 351-2, 354-5, 360
    enemy, a help to the, 356
    European politics, its effect upon, 362
    rights of, 280-2
    towns, of, 356
    War of Secession, in the, 282, 288; Cobden urges its abandonment, 292-3, 357; ineffective, 355
Bomba, King, *see* Naples
Borneo, massacre in, 58-62, 239-40
Bowring, Sir John, 192-3, 196, 199-200, 209, 217

415

Index

Bright, John, 7, 15, 22, 73, 115, 125, 207, 242, 295, 329, 330
  Anti-Slavery speech by, 346
  defeated at Manchester, 193
  faith in the Northern States, 364
  letters from, 200
  letters to, 60, 106, 108–9, 394
  speech at Coventry, 37–8
  talks with, 172–3
Brooke, Rajah, 59, 103 ; his diary, 60–1
Brougham, Lord, 271, 316
Brute force, the law of, 238
Bull's Run, 290
Bullfights, Cobden protests to the Pope concerning, 218
Bunsen, Chevalier, 99, 115
Burmese War, the, 86–9, 91–2, 95, 100–2, 144, 222
Business men, Cobden's belief in, 17

California, annexation of, 148
Cambridge, Duke of, 116
Canada, 162–3, 339–40, 383
Canton, trouble in, 209, 220–1
Capital and Labour, 16–17
Capitalism, Cobden's view of, 397
Capture at sea, right of, 11 ; see Private Property
Cecil, Lord Robert, 312
Central America, Great Britain i.., 148–60 ; see Crampton, Panama, Nicaragua, Walker
Charles Albert, King of Sardinia, Cobden interviews, 49
Chartism, 55, 395
Cheap food, 16
Cheapness and increase of trade, 35
Chevalier, M., 7, 242–5, 249, 250, 273, 274, 299–300
China, Free Trade in, 198–9
  revolution in, 198
  specie sent to, 221
  trade with, 197–8, 210, 221–2, 268, 328
China War, the (192–232)—
  Cobden moves vote of censure on, 193
  cost of, 209
  criticisms of, 210
  elections during, 238
  protest against, 305
Church, the, and the American Civil War, 133
Ciceroacchio, murder of, 188–9
Clarendon, Lord, 100, 152
Class cleavage, 22
Cobden, Richard—
  Austria, travels in, 50
  business sacrifices made by, 16
  calico printer, as, 23
  China War, his views on the, 193 ; see China, China War

Cobden, Richard (*continued*)—
  Correspondence, 11, 278–330 ; see Arlès-Dufour, Richard, etc.
  Crimean War, his opinions of the, 108–39
  Eastern Question, his knowledge of the, 24
  erroneous ideas concerning, 15–17
  European tour in promotion of Free Trade, 40–53
  Exposition, the Great, Cobden and the, 66
  financial troubles, 233
  Foreign policy, 6, 234, 327 ; see Foreign Office
  France, work for Free Trade in, 13, 43–6, 242–77 ; his love of, 272 ; appreciation of his work in, 274–7
  Free Trade, his belief in, 5, 15, 223
  French Commercial Treaty, his negotiation of, 242–77
  Germany, in, 50–1
  Huddersfield, candidate for, 205
  internationalism of, 13, 22, 23, 387–409
  Italy, in, 48–50
  Liberalism of, 22
  "Life of," by Lord Morley, 12
  Morning Star, chief adviser to, 141–2
  non-intervention, his belief in, 9, 20, 21, 26, 36 ; see Non-intervention
  Palmerston, his antagonism to, 54
  pamphleteer, as a, 26–39
  Peace Congress, at the, 56 ; on the, 80–1
  "Reminiscences of," by Mrs. Schwabe, 12, 46
  Rochdale, Member for, 234
  Rome, visit to, 48
  Russia, attitude towards, 29–36 ; travels in, 51–2
  son, death of his, 137
  Spain, tour in, 46–8
  travels abroad, 23–4, 36, 40–53
  United States, tour in the, 24–5
"Cob enism," 16
Co-operation, free, 21 ; international, 25
Colonial self-government, 390
Combe, Mr., 21 ; letter to, 55 ; 115
Commerce not furthered by force, 34–5
Competition, evils of, 402
Confederacy, see Southern Confederacy, the
Congress of Nations, proposed, 57
Constantinople, affairs in, 225–6
  anxiety concerning, 92
  preferably in Russian hands, 31, 34
Corn Laws, Repeal of the, 16, 36, 61, 248
Corruption in politics, 204
Cotton, 16, 365–8
  famine, 322

Index

Cowley, Lord, 244-5
Crampton, Mr., dismissal of, 151-60
Crimean War, the, 106-134, 306, 389
  Cobden speaks on, at Leeds, 117-19
  fruits of, 124
  general feeling as to, 114
  Leeds meeting on, opposed, 121-2
  peace proposals, 135, 143
  Press, the, responsible for, 167
  radical misconception of, 108
Czar of Russia, the, 109-10

Daily News, the, Cobden's criticism of, 70, 78 ; 120
Daily paper, need of an honest, 72
Dalhousie, Lord, 101, 230
Dallas, Mr., 153
Danish quarrel, the, 326-7
  intervention proposed, 324-5
D'Azeglio, Marchese, 188-9
Democracy, the limits of Cobden's, 396, 406-7
  sham, 407
Derby, Lord, 58, 135, 193, 307
Disarmament and Free Trade, 37
Disraeli, 201-2, 234, 325
Don Pacifico incident, the, 63-4
Duelling, Cobden on, 72

Economic expansion, 405-6
Economist, The, 218-19
Education, 164 ; Cobden's views on, 398
Egyptian fellahs as soldiers, 377
Election over the China War, 193-4, 238
Elgin, Lord, 261-2
Emancipation, the only justification of the American Civil War, 370, 374, 378-80
  Cobden on, 333
Employers' combinations, Cobden's attitude towards, 392
Enlistment affair, the, 155
"England, Ireland, and America," 26-8
England, suspicions of, abroad, 41
European policy, Cobden on, 140
  tour, Cobden's, 40-53
Evangelical missions in India, 236
Evarts, Mr., 373-4, 376
Examiner, The, 78

Factory system, Cobden's attitude towards the, 391-2, 401
Far Eastern policy, British, brutality of, 325-6, 328
Federation of the States of Europe, 140
Ferocity of public opinion, 217
Florence, Cobden at, 48-9
Food taxes, 17
Foreign Enlistments Act, 155, 311, 373-4, 376

Foreign Office, the, manners of, 313
  mischief done by, 53
  mismanagement of affairs by, 182-3
  Palmerston at the, 54
  Turkish tyranny, supports, 181-2
Foreign policy, the basis of Cobden's, 234, 327
Foreign trade, 403 ; as affecting policy and finance, 404-5
Fould, M., French Premier, opposes the Commercial Treaty, 250
France, Algerian policy of, 54
  alarms of war with, 358
  armaments, delusions regarding, 284
  Cobden's Free Trade tour in, 43-6
  Napoleonic wars with, 98
  Navy, her expenditure on the, 291
  war with Austria, 242
Franchise, extension of the, 208
  Cobden tepid concerning, 393-4
Free Soil Party, the, 332
Free Trade, 9, 16
  Austria, in, 50
  Germany, in, 50-1
  internationalism, an instrument of, 23, 26, 244
  Italy, in, 48-50
  Napoleon III converted to, 111, 243
  pacific influence of, 17, 36-7, 43
  propaganda in France undertaken by Cobden, 41-3
  proposed Prize Essay on, 37
  some results of, 400-1, 406
  Spain, in, 46-8
Freedom and Free Trade, Cobden's conception of, 350
Freedom of the seas, 135, 168, 280-1, 351
French Commercial Treaty, 9, 13
  Commission on, work of, 234-5
  Cobden's negotiation of, 242-77
  disarmament, hopes of, as a result, 259, 264
  Foreign Office delays signature of, 259
  importance of, 260
  opposition in House of Commons, 253
  signature of, 259
  vicissitudes of, 242-52
French invasion scare, 83-5, 93, 230, 263-4
  fostered by the Government and The Times, 205-6, 292-3
French Militia Law, the, 83
Friendly intercourse, international, 36
Friends, Society of, 37, 80

Garibaldi, 189, 323
General European War, talk of, 322
German Professors and Imperialism, 379
Germanic Confederation, the, 69
  desires a great war in order to become an Empire, 379-80

Index

"Germanism" of the Court, 181
Germany, in 1850, 69, 72
  British people veto war against, 324–5
  Cobden's reception in, 50–1
  France, idea of war with, 265
  war fever in, 320
Girardin, E. de, 9, 56, 76, 79
  his eulogy of Cobden, 274–5
Gladstone, 22, 126, 129, 163, 243, 244
  Cobden's opinion of, 201–2
  French Commercial Treaty, his high opinion of, 254, 267
  incredulous of power of Federal States to enforce the Union, 365
  Neapolitan prisons, his exposure of, 136
Godrich, Lord, 220
Guizot, 386
Governmental intervention, Cobden's disbelief in, 393
Grant, General, 381
Great Exposition, the, Cobden as Commissioner, 65–6, 73
Greece, trouble with, 64–7
Greeks, Cobden's opinion of the, 179–80
Gregson, letter to, 199
Grey, Lord, 126
Gurney, S., 61–2, 116

Haly, and the *Morning Star*, 141
Hamilton, succeeds Haly, 141, 163, 165, 190
Hansa Towns, 316
  blockades and the, 349
Hapsburgs, the, 190
Hardinge, Lord, 98
Hardy, G., 329
Hargreaves, W., letters to, 271–2
Herald of Peace, the, 57, 130, 144
Herald, the *New York*, 383
Hong-Kong, cost of, 196, 198–9, 269
Houston, General, 71
"How wars are got up in India," 144
Hugo, Victor, 56–7
Humboldt, 50
Hungary, revolution of 1848 in, 69, 80; further insurrection, 178–9

Illinois Central Railroad, Cobden's interest in, 233–4
Imperialism, birth of modern, 10
  Cobden on, 195
  hypocrisy of, 390
Imports, free, 20
India, abandonment of, foretold by Cobden, 224, 272
  aggression in, 389
  Cobden against British occupation of, 195
  defeat, Cobden's fear of, in, 235–6
  hatred of British in, 228

India (*continued*)—
  occupation, British, cost of, 319
  poor results of British government in, 228
  trouble in, 222–3
Indian Mutiny, the, 195–232
  Cobden's criticism of British policy, 236
Indian Reform Association, 102
Individual bargaining, Cobden's faith in, 393
Industrial system, evil results of, 402
Internationalism, Cobden and modern, 387, 409
  Cobden's, 13, 22, 23, 25
Ireland, Cobden on British treatment of, 27–8
Irish famine, the, 49, 54
  Church, the, 28
  question, interest in, abroad, 49
Iron, duty on, 247
Isturitz, Señor, on the executions in Havana, 77
Italy, Cobden's Free Trade tour in 48–50
  Cobden's opinion of, 180
  danger of empty encouragement of, 160–1
  Franco-Austrian intrigues against, 253

Japan, trouble with, 313–15, 319
Japanese, Cobden on the, 315, 319
Jingoism, Parliamentary, 323

Kaffir War of 1848–50, 73, 75, 86
Kagosima, destruction of, by Admiral Kuper, 311, 314, 317, 319, 321
Kincaid, Mr., 95, 100, 101
Kinnaird, Mr., 329
Kossuth's extradition from Turkey demanded, 74
  relations with Palmerston, 178
  visit to England, 73, 79, 81
Kuper, Admiral, 314, 319

Laird, Mr., and the *Alabama*, 326–7, 330
Laissez-faire Liberals, 391, 398–9
Lamartine, 56–7
  Asia Minor, his domain in, 69
  visits London, 67–8
Lancashire, effect of the Federal blockade upon, 335
  enthusiasm in, for French Commercial Treaty, 278
  feeling in, concerning the War of Secession, 289
  Radicalism in, 12, 193–4
Land, access to the, 17
Landlordism, 17
Landwehr, the Prussian, 72, 225
Law of Nations, the, 74–5
Leader, the, 174–5
League, the, and peace, 93–4, 105

Index

League of Brotherhood, Bazaar for, 71
of Nations, 409
Leeds Mercury, the, 142, 174, 231-2
Liberalism, Cobden's, 22
"Life of Cobden," by Morley, 12
Lincoln, President, 378
London, concentration of troops around, 75-7
Lucas, S., letter to, 395
Lyons and Free Trade, 44-5

Machinery, the power of, 18
Madrid, Cobden attends Free Trade banquet in, 47-8
Magne, M., 251-2
Manchester, Cobden speaks at, 206-7
decay of Liberalism in, 80, 194
political influence of, 180, 193-4
School, the, 16
Manin, 178
Maritime Law, reform of, 360, 363
Markets, wars for, 401
Mason and Slidell, 295, 309, 334, 343-4, 351, 359, 364
Maximilian of Mexico, 296
Mazzini, 173, 178
Mehemet Ali, 377
Memorial volume on Cobden published in France, 274-6
Metternich, Cobden's interview with, 50, 253
Meyendorff, Baron, 51-2
Mexican Civil War, 296
Mexico, Cobden on, 297
French, the, in, 301, 318, 321
Miall, Edward, on the Indian Mutiny, 228-30
Middle class, Cobden's faith in the, 17
views of social evils, 397-8
Milan, Cobden at Free Trade banquet at, 50
Militarism fatal to liberty, 163
German, 265
increase of, 243, 264-5
makes for war, 85
Militia, debate on the, 88
Minto, Lord, 54
Missionaries, Cobden's opinion of, 93, 100-1
Moniteur, Le, 173-4, 252
Monroe, D., 296
Morley, Lord, his "Life of Cobden," 12, 19, 22, 54, 245, 311
Morley, S., letter to, 282-3
Morning Star, the, Cobden's hopes of, 20
commences publication, 141, 144-5
policy controlled and criticized by Cobden, 63-8, 141-2, 146, 163, 171, 180, 195, 209, 214-17, 230-1, 288
Mosquito Coast, the, 147-9

Munitions of war, trade in, 371, 373
Mutual aid, Cobden on the principle of, 20

Napier, Sir Charles, 227, 291
Naples, the fleet sent to, 137
cry for intervention in, 145
King of, the, 145, 161, 170, 173-4
Cobden interviews, 49
Napoleon III, 83-4, 95, 128-9, 134, 142-3, 170, 226, 320-1
Cobden endeavours to convert him to Free Trade, 242, 246-8
Cobden's opinion of, 248
commercial treaty ratified by, 282
coup d'état effected by, 83
friendship for England, his, 348
general distrust of, 249-50
German ambitions, a check to, 380
hostility of British Government toward, 259
letter to Mr. C. Cobden from, 276
revolutions in France, on, 248
vacillations of, 251-2
Napoleon, Prince, 256
Napoleon, Jerome, 276
National vices, the British, 327
Nationalities, awakening spirit of, 338
liberation of oppressed, 177-8
Navy, built under false pretences, 355
large, useless if blockade abolished, 353
Negro apprenticeship, reform of, 316-17
Negroes in the Civil War, 376-7
Neuchâtel, insurrection in, 190
Neutrals, rights and duties of, 308
New Orleans and the cotton trade, 365-7
Newspapers, need of honest, 127; proposals for same, 129-30
Nicaraguan affair, the, 54, 136, 147-9
Non-intervention, Cobden's policy of, 9, 20-1, 26, 34, 54-72, 78-9, 113, 145, 171, 183, 387, 390-1, 398-9, 400
benefits of, 338-9
superseded, 406
Norton, Professor C. E., 12

O'Connor, Fergus, 55
Opium trade, the, 198, 211
War, the, 197
Oude, the case of, 230, 235
Owen, Robert, 18

Palmerston, 10, 52, 73-5, 77
Cobden sends letter of remonstrance to, 257-8; sends memorial to, 292
Cobden's criticisms of, 54, 123, 153-4, 157, 159, 175, 178, 186-8, 214, 226, 238, 287
Cobden's labours in Paris thwarted by, 311-12

Index

Palmerston (*continued*)—
  Don Pacifico affair, the, 64
  Greek coast, orders blockade of, 64
  intervention, his policy of, 387-8
  Schleswig, fails to involve England in war over, 310, 323-4, 326-7
  Turkish reforms, on, 104
" Palmerston fever," 205, 212
Panama, 148
Paris Conference, the, 137-8
  Congress, 304
  Declaration of, 135, 355
  Treaty of, 135, 288
Parke, Mr., action of, in Canton, 195
Parker, Admiral, ordered to blockade Greek coast, 64
Parliamentary procedure, modifications of, 224-5
  Reform, 73
Peace Conferences, 94-5, 102, 105
Peace Congress, in Paris, 56, 304; Brussels, 81, 97; Edinboro', 293
Peace Congress Committee, the, 81-2
Peace Movement, the, 11, 79, 166-7, 337
Peace Party, the, 66-7, 70, 80
Peace Society, the, 37, 80-2, 129, 211, 240, 303, 330, 338
  Borneo, and, 60-1
  Crimean War, and, 81
  the Liverpool, 77, 79
" Peaceful penetration," 403
Peel, 15, 248-9, 284
Penn, William, and government by moral force, 239
Persia, trouble in, 200
  war with, 137
Persigny, M. de, 250-1, 292
Polish insurrection of 1830, 33
  problem, Cobden on the, 32-3, 297
Pope, the, Cobden interviews, 48; 188
Portugal, fleet sent to, 54; 85
Press, the, 201
  corrupted by Government, 213-14
  gain to, in respect of railroads, telegraphs, etc., 184
Prince Consort, the, 66, 181, 295, 310
  attacks on, 185-7
Private property at sea, 280-2, 363
Privateering, abolition of, 135, 288, 308
Privy Councillorship refused by Cobden, 260
Prosperity, results of, 212
  the new, Cobden blind to unjust basis of, 396-7
Protectionism, 38; in France, 246, 254; in the United States, 384
Prussia, claims hegemony in 1850, 69
  internal troubles, danger of, 72
  King of, Cobden interviews, 50
  loan to, suggested, 71

Quakers in the Peace Society and Movement, 73, 80-1, 105

Radicalism, Cobden on, 395
Rationalism, Cobden's, 273
Rawson, Henry, 144, 146
Red Indians compared with Hindoos, 228
Reform Bill, proposed second, a, 208
Reform Club, the, 161-2
" Reminiscences of Richard Cobden," 46
Reprisals in India, cry for, 227
Revolution of 1848, 68-9
Richard, the Rev. Henry, 7, 11, 37-8, 59, 60-1
  Cobden's letters to, 58-65, 67-9, 75-93, 95-106, 109-17, 120-34, 141-91, 195-232, 261-9, 282-95, 300-9, 326-30, 383
  Morning Star, his position on the, 165
Richardson's murder in Japan, compensation demanded for, 310-11
  terrible reprisals for, 314, 317, 319
Rochdale, meeting at, 278
  speech at, on the Schleswig-Holstein question and war, 325
Roebuck, Mr., 183, 201, 310
Rome, Cobden in, 48, 188
Rothschild, Baron, 63
  Meyer, 249
Rouher, M., 7, 245, 250, 252
" Russia," 29-36
Russia, British relations with, 29-36
  Cobden's opinion of, 119-20; tour in, 51-2
  England defends Turkey against, 27
  peace with, unsatisfactory, 175
  protectionist policy of, and its results, 138-9
  war with, folly of, 33
  wood fuel a necessity to, 52
Russian invasion scare, 29
Russell, Lord John, 72, 155, 167, 187-8, 201, 314, 370
  Sumner's indictment of, 372-3
Russophobes, Cobden on, 30-4

Sarawak, bloodshed in, 59
Sayers, Tom, 271
Schleswig, 301, 310, 320, 339
  danger of war over, 310
Schwabe, Mrs., author of "Reminiscences of Richard Cobden," 12, 46
Schwann, J., letter to, 269-70
Scott, General, 71, 292-3, 350-1
Search, right of, 345-7, 351, 363
Sebastopol, 116
Self-interest as the basis of social harmony, 18
Servile State, the, 407
Seward, Mr., 341-4
  speaks on the annexation of Canada 349,

Index

Seymour, Admiral, seizes ports of Canton, 193
Sicilies, the Two, 36
Slave trade in Turkey, 31
Slavery problem in U.S.A., 169-70, 313, 343, 353; *see* Abolition, Emancipation
Smith, Adam, 21
— Goldwin, 381
Social evils, Cobden's peculiar attitude towards, 396-8
Southern Confederacy, the, British sympathy with, 333
— disbelief in the North's power of conquest over, 364-5, 381
— hasty action of, 342
— means of subduing, 357
— recognition of, urged, 310-11, 355, 369-70, 375
— ships built for, 370-6
— starvation of, impossible, 356
— union with England suggested, 169; *see* American Civil War, Blockade, Cotton, etc.
Spain, Cobden's Free Trade tour in, 46-8
Spanish Bonds, 63
Spanish Marriage, the, 54
Stamp duty, repeal of, 123
State Church, oppression of a, 72
Stratford de Redcliffe, Lord, 225-6
Sturge, J., Lord Brougham, and the negro apprentices, 316-17
Suffrage, suggested forms of, 208-9, 212
Sultan of Turkey gives domain to Lamartine, 69
Sumner, Charles, 7, 195, 282, 289, 292
— his career, 371-2
— indictment of Palmerston and Russell, his, 372-3; of France and England, 375-6
— letters to, 7, 12, 336-86
— Peace Conference, at the, 36-7
— physical assault upon, 159, 340

Tagus, the fleet sent to the, 54
Tariffs, French, 262
Thackeray, 225
"Three Letters, in 1792 and 1853," 93, 97
"Three Panics, The," 83, 279, 298, 311
Throat weakness, 211
Times, The, Cobden's criticisms of, 78-9, 126-7, 131-4, 142-3, 156, 162, 175-7, 181-2, 190, 227, 237, 240
— Cobden attacked by, 311
— Commercial Treaty, the, attacked by, 263, 265-7, 350

Times, The (continued)—
— inconsistencies of, 263
— Kossuth attacked by, 74
— pro-Southern sympathies of, 339
— reaction against, 360
Trade Unions, 166
— "brutal tyranny of," 392
Trafalgar, Battle of, 89
Treaty of Commerce; *see* French Commercial Treaty
Treaty Ports, the, 305
Trent, affair of the, 295, 334, 349
Trieste, Free Trade banquet at, 50
Tropical countries, defects of colonies in, 239
Turkey, Cobden on the folly of protecting, 27
— Cobden on the rotten condition of, 102-4
— Great Britain the protector of, 27
— slave trade in, the, 31
Tuscany, Free Trade in, 48-9

United States, the, Cobden's travels in, 24-5
— crisis in, Cobden on the, 169
— Democratic Party in, 309
— Great Britain's relations with, 28-9
— Ministers of, in England, 151-2
— place of, in the world, 34
— purchase of arms in England by, 309
— strained relations with, 54, 293; *see* American Civil War, Blockade, Emancipation, etc.
Universal Suffrage, 208
Urquhart, Mr., 26

Venezuela, debts of, 63
Victoria, Queen, 124, 167
— edits the "Queen's Speech" to avert war, 310
— Palmerston, her relations with, 187-8

Walker affair, the, 148-9
War fever, the futility of opposing, 342-3
Warren, Mr., at Berlin, 51
Wellington, Duke of, 75-6, 85
— his wars not defensive, but anti-democratic, 89, 96
"What next? And next?" 138
Wickoff, Mr., 214
Wilkes, Captain, 358
Wilks, Washington, 132-4
Williams, Mr., 161-2
Wilson, J., 218-19
Woolner, Thos., 7
Working classes, apathy of the, 395

www.ingramcontent.com/pod-product-compliance
Lightning Source LLC
Chambersburg PA
CBHW031324230426
43670CB00006B/231